—The— FINE PRINT OF SELF-PUBLISHING

FOURTH EDITION

Everything You Need to Know About the Costs, Contracts & Process of Self-Publishing

MARK LEVINE

Bascom Hill Publishing Group
212 3rd Avenue North, Suite 290
Minneapolis, MN 55401
612.455.2293
www.bascomhillpublishing.com

ISBN: 978-1-935098-55-3
LCCN: 2010915666

Cover Design and Typeset by Jenni Wheeler

Printed in the United States of America

DEDICATION

This book is dedicated to all the authors who know there is a book inside of them. One of the most amazing publishing experiences is holding a printed and bound copy of your own book for the first time. I hope *The Fine Print* helps you find the right publisher for your book.

CONTENTS

INTRODUCTION

The publishing world, as you probably know, is changing so rapidly it's hard to keep up. Amazon.com has eclipsed Barnes & Noble as the largest retailer of books in the U.S.[1] Borders, a onetime bookselling giant, laid off 878 employees between February and March 2009.[2] In January 2010, Borders announced that it was closing more than 185 WaldenBooks, Borders, and Express stores.[3] Also in January 2010, Barnes & Noble closed the remaining fifty B. Dalton bookstores.[4] By August 2010, B&N announced it was putting itself up for sale.[5] Toss in the brewing ebook turf war between Apple, Amazon, and Barnes & Noble, and *wow*—this industry is changing fast!

There are the headline-grabbing changes, and then there are the ones that affect those trying to get their books published. If you are reading this book, you probably already know that it's harder than ever to get published by a "traditional" publisher. In 2008, there were at least ten thousand fewer

---

1 "Amazon, Barnes&Noble and Borders Sales Numbers Annual Update," Foner Books website, accessed July 2010, http://www.fonerbooks.com/booksale.htm.

2 "Borders announces 742 layoffs," last modified March 5, 2009, accessed August 2010, http://www.mlive.com/business/ann-arbor/index.ssf/2009/03/borders_announces_742_layoffs.html; and "Borders lays off another 136 people, many at its Ann Arbor headquarters," last modified February 19, 2009, accessed August 2010, http://www.mlive.com/business/ann-arbor/index.ssf/2009/02/borders.html.

3 "Anticipated Waldenbooks Specialty Retail Store Closure List," Borders Group, accessed July 2010, http://media.bordersstores.com/content/mediarelations/BSRClosinglist.pdf.

4 Crosby, Jackie. "Closing the Book," *Minneapolis StarTribune*, January 6, 2010.

5 "Biggest U.S. Book Chain Up for Sale," the *New York Times* online, accessed August 2010, http://www.nytimes.com/2010/08/04/business/media/04barnes.html?_r=2.

traditionally published titles than there were in 2007.[6] This means that more authors are competing for fewer spots on a publisher's roster.

You should be looking at statistics like these as blessings in disguise. They force writers to abandon the notion that nabbing a contract from a traditional publisher is some kind of Holy Grail. For writers "lucky" enough to get such a contract, the reality is that many traditional publishers have small or even nonexistent marketing budgets for books by new authors. Many of these publishers make the expenses of book marketing the responsibility of the author, who gets a miniscule royalty from each sale. In these cases, if a title by a new author is successful, it is due to the author's efforts. Guess who has shelled out virtually all of the money in this scenario? The author. Guess who has spent all their time on the book? The author. Yes, there are exceptions to this, but the odds of being the exception are about as good as winning the Powerball.

While it's great to be a dreamer, in book publishing it's smarter to be a realist. In 2004, Nielsen Bookscan tracked the sales of 1,200,000 books through retail locations (including online retailers) in the United States. Of all books sold, 79 percent sold less than ninety-nine copies.[7] Another 200,000, or 16.67 percent, sold less than 1,000 copies.[8] Only 25,000 books, or 2.1 percent, sold more than 5,000 copies.[9] Fewer than 500 books, or 0.04 percent, sold more than 100,000 copies and only ten books, or 0.0008 percent, sold more than a million copies each.[10]

If you're serious about publishing your book, self-publishing (either on your own or through a good self-publishing company) might be your only option—and your best one, even if a traditional publisher were

6 "Bowker Reports U.S. Book Production Declines 3% in 2008, but 'On Demand' Publishing More than Doubles," Bowker, accessed June 2010, http://www.bowker.com/index.php/press-releases/563-bowker-reports-us-bookproduction-declines-3-in-2008-but-qon-demandq-publishing-more-than-doubles.

7 Chris Anderson, "A bookselling tail: why publishers should focus on the misses instead of the hits," *Publishers Weekly,* 2006, http://www.accessmylibrary.com/coms2/summary_0286-16030721_ITM.

8 Ibid.

9 Ibid.

10 Ibid.

interested. The biggest growth area in book publishing is in self-publishing (and short-run titles, which may or may not be self-published). The number of self-published titles has exploded since 2002, when there were only 32,639.[11] In 2008, for the first time, there were more self-published titles (285,232 POD and/or short run) than there were traditionally published ones.[12] In 2009, the number soared to 764,000.[13] Yes, the marketplace is more crowded than ever before. But the opportunities to distribute and market your book have also expanded like never before.

The internet has helped to level the playing field. It takes more than having a website and being on Facebook and Twitter to be successful online. There are many facets to successful online book marketing. The conclusion touches on a few of them but, believe me: online book marketing could fill a book by itself. If you want proof that online marketing works—you're reading it right now. Since the first edition of *The Fine Print of Self-Publishing* was released in 2004, I've marketed this book exclusively online. I've never purchased an ad in a magazine, on the radio, or on television. The website for this book is search engine optimized (SEO) and ranks high on search engines for terms that I know authors looking to self-publish are using when looking for information over the internet.. I also purchase pay-per-click ads on most major search engines, which help put my book in front of people who are already searching online for information about book publishing. These things really work.

Combining smart online marketing with an ebook can bring things to a whole new level. By cutting out the costs of a printed book, the postage fees, and the customer's wait for it to arrive, a nirvanic book

---

11 Ibid.

12 Ibid.

13 Kim Ode, "Authors rewrite the book on self-publishing," *Minneapolis Star Tribune*, January 30, 2011, http://www.startribune.com/lifestyle/114869199.html?elr=KArks UUUoDEy3LGDiO7aiU.

14 "Tracked July e-book sales at $16.2 million: 213.5 percent increase over same month last year," TeleRead, last modified September 23, 2009, accessed August 2010, http://www.teleread.com/ebooks/tracked-july-e-book-sales-at-16-2-million-213-5-percent-increase-over-last-year/.

15 "Kindle Milestone: Amazon Sold More Kindle Books Than Physical Books On Xmas," Business Insider website, last modified December 26, 2009, accessed July 2010, http://www.businessinsider.com/henry-blodget-kindle-milestone-amazon-sold-more-ebooks-than-physical-books-on-xmas-2009-12.

experience can be enjoyed (except by those who prefer the smell and feel of a physical book). This isn't to say that printed books are going away. They aren't. But, the advances in ebook reading technology (like Amazon's Kindle, the Sony eReader, B&N's Nook, and Apple's iPad) have made ebooks a very real and viable way for authors to sell and distribute their books. In July 2009, ebook sales rose 213.5 percent from July 2008.[14] On Christmas Day 2009, for the first time ever, Amazon.com customers purchased more Kindle ebooks than physical books.[15] At the time this book went to press the final numbers weren't available, but some experts predict that ebook revenue will top $500 million in 2010.[16]

While you still need potential readers to find your book in order to sell it to them in any form, having it available in every format readers want will help. As the e-reading devices move down in price and consumers become more comfortable with curling up with them instead of an actual book, ebook sales will grow even faster. In 2009, between one and two million e-readers were shipped worldwide.[17] Some industry experts predict that in the next four years, there may be as many as fifty million of these devices sold.[18] The Book Industry Study Group's January 2010 survey, *Consumer Attitudes Toward E-Book Reading*, revealed how and why American book-buying consumers are turning toward ebooks. The survey found that 30 percent of print book buyers would wait up to three months to purchase the ebook edition of a book by their favorite author.[19] The survey also found that the majority of print book buyers ranked "affordability" as the principal reason they would buy an ebook version, rather than the print version, of the same title.[20] In fact, almost 20 percent of the respondents said that

16 Sarah Rotman Epps, "Ten eReader And eBook Predictions For 2010," *Sarah Rotman Epps' Blog*, Forrester, December 1, 2009, accessed August 2010, http://blogs.forrester.com/sarah_rotman_epps/09-12-01-ten_ereader_and_ebook_predictions_2010.

17 Alexander, Steve. "Tech predictions you can (probably) count on." *Minneapolis StarTribune*, January 1, 2010.

18 Ibid.

19 "Consumer Attitudes Toward E-Book Reading," The Book Industry Study Group, January 15, 2010.

20 Ibid.

21 Ibid.

within the previous twelve months they stopped purchasing printed books in favor of buying ebooks. [21] If you haven't muttered "wow," go back and read the last few sentences. There is a revolution happening right before our eyes.

So, as the publishing world changes and evolves, authors like you and me have more opportunity than ever before to carve out our slice of the publishing pie without waiting for traditional publishers to open the door for us. What makes *The Fine Print* unique among books on self-publishing is that I've experienced the industry as an author, a book publisher, and a marketer. I know what it feels like to hold a copy of my own finished book for the first time. I also know what it takes to publish, print, and market that book. In addition to this book (and its three previous versions), I've published two of my own novels. I've made every mistake you can make in publishing and tried just about every type of marketing tool available.

Being a successful author can mean a lot of different things. For some, it's making enough money to write full time or to use the book as part of an ongoing business strategy. For others, it's having a book for your family and friends. For still others, it's the fulfillment of a dream. For me, it was a combination of all of these and has evolved over time. In August 1992, I decided I wanted to write a novel. Although my manuscript was finished by 1995, I had no idea what to do with it. In 1999, I started Click Industries, a company that does online business filings, including copyrights for authors. In putting together strategic partners for the company, I found a small book publisher who accepted my book. Sadly, the publisher went out of business in 2004.

In 2004, I published the first version of *The Fine Print.* Since almost everyone (well, those who read this book) asked me how I came up with the idea for *The Fine Print,* I'll tell you. I'm a gut-feel kind of businessman. One day I got a call from an author who had been published by the same publisher that released my first novel. He told me that he had signed a contract with a self-publishing company and wanted to get out of it. He knew that I had been a lawyer and asked if I could help. He sent me the contract. He had signed the contract despite the fact that it contained a clause that gave the self-publishing company the rights to the book for the term of the copyright. The term of a copyright is the life of the author plus seventy years. This author was a professor at the University of California-Berkley. I figured that if a professor from a top university would sign such a ridiculous contract just to be published, there must be thousands of other authors who might do the same thing.

That was my market research—one author. I started researching other self-publishing companies. Soon I had a book. In 2004 and 2005, it was only available as an ebook through my website, www.BookPublishersCompared.com. In early 2005, the president of one of the companies I covered in my book called me to complain about the way that I ranked his company. I was selling a lot of books from my site, but it never occurred to me that people in the industry would find out about the book. From that day on, I knew this book had some legs. I published the second edition in paperback in 2006. With each year and with each edition, I sell more and more copies. The more established this book becomes, the more people buy it and talk about it.

The same thing can happen to you. Don't plan on your book becoming an overnight sensation. Plan on spreading the word and telling others about you and your book. Create "buzz" about your book. As that happens, sales will follow.

There are a few important lessons from the story about how and why I published *The Fine Print*. They are true for most books. The first is that a book needs to fill a void or create a market that didn't exist before. So, if you don't have a first-class book (as judged by the public, not just by people you know), forget it. The second lesson is that you need to spend time and money marketing the book. The third lesson is that, above all, you need to get lucky—or the first two might not even matter.

This book was first published when the self-publishing industry as we know it was barely a blip on the radar. Also, no one had ever published a book that focused on the companies in the industry. *The Fine Print* filled the void. I was at the right place at the right time. Back in 2004 there were few industry leaders, and certainly no one was writing about the industry like I was. That got me noticed. I was invited to speak at writers' conferences all over the country. In 2008, I was invited to speak at the Erma Bombeck Writers' Workshop, one of the most prestigious in the industry. That really helped propel the book to greater heights. There I was, speaking at a conference with major authors like Garrison Keillor. You know why I received an invitation? A year or so earlier, the director of the conference bought a copy of my book online and found it very helpful in his self-publishing process. Every book needs lucky breaks to really make it. That was mine. It happened more than three years after the first edition of the book was published. Sometimes it can take awhile to become an overnight sensation. Keep that in mind. Remind yourself of it regularly.

After the 2006 edition of *The Fine Print* was released, I realized that there is an inherent flaw in the self-publishing company business model. It's a flaw that diminishes an author's chance to get retailers to take his book seriously. Print-on-demand (POD) technology, which allows a book to be printed in quantities as small as one copy, is probably the main factor in the explosion of self-published titles over the past seven years. It's also the thing that makes it even harder for self-published authors to be competitive in the marketplace. Printing in such small quantities is costly. When self-publishing companies mark up the printing costs significantly, the author has already lost the game—in most cases before it even started. Most companies reviewed in this book mark up printing from 50 to 100+ percent. Since most self-publishing companies use the same printer, it's easy to demonstrate the exact markup (more on this in chapter 5). This inflated printing "cost" (to the author) leads to an artificially inflated wholesale price, which of course leads to an even more inflated retail price. Because most self-publishing companies also take a piece of each sale, by the time they build some royalty in for the author, the retail price gets ridiculous. Retailers never overpay for books, so if the price point of a book doesn't work for retailers, they won't be buying. This topic is covered extensively in chapter 7.

With few exceptions, the inflated printing cost model severely damages an author's ability to sell his or her book to anyone other than family and friends, or at speaking engagements and other events. Once this became clear to me, I discussed it with the CEOs of several self-publishing companies. The response was a collective "Hey, that's the business."

One CEO told me, "If you think you're so smart, do it yourself. You can't make any money if you don't make it on printing."

Well, I did do it myself, and it turns out you *can* make money without marking up printing. In 2006, my company invested in a startup self-publishing company, Mill City Press (www.millcitypress.net), that charges authors wholesale printing costs and doesn't take any portion of the royalties. That business model made the investment attractive. Yes, Mill City Press makes less money than it would if it marked up printing, but this model makes Mill City authors better positioned to price their books at levels that give them a chance to sell copies. Over the years, I've become less and less of a fan of the POD model, and, while Mill City still offers it, 70 percent of Mill City's authors participate in more traditional book distribution channels instead.

I don't review Mill City in this book, not only because it would be completely unfair, but because Mill City's model is unlike almost all I review here. Charging the actual wholesale printing cost, dealing with traditional distributors, and not taking royalties are things that *should* be done by other self-publishing companies, but they simply aren't. However, those advantages alone aren't a guarantee that any author's book will sell better. They only guarantee that the author's book has a chance.

All of the publishers ranked highly in this book are excellent choices and you won't go wrong choosing one of them. Certainly, I'd like you to compare Mill City with any publisher in this book. Mill City is in a unique position because it approaches publishing with an author's mentality. (Or, at least, my mentality as an author who has needed publishing services.) The Mill City model has worked for my own books, and every product or service Mill City sells is always tested on my books first. Certainly, Mill City's publishing philosophy mirrors my own. If after reading this book you believe I know what I'm talking about, you should put Mill City on your list of companies to check out. Whether or not you choose Mill City, you will find a company in this book that is the right fit for you. Or, you may decide you want to handle the entire process on your own.

There are a lot of great companies to choose from. The right choice is more about not picking the wrong company or method than it is about selecting the right one for you. There can be a lot of right ones. Either way, this book will give you a greater understanding of the steps involved in self-publishing and the knowledge to make an informed decision.

The goal of *The Fine Print* has always been to give its readers straight talk about self-publishing by peeling back the layers and looking inside the industry and the major companies in it. This fourth edition delves into more topics than ever before, including book printing options, distribution options, ebook publishing, and online and traditional book marketing.

The most important thing to remember is that if you have a story to tell and you've actually completed a manuscript, you have accomplished a lot. You should be incredibly proud regardless of what happens to your book commercially. Most people want to write a book someday. Few of us really do it. So, if you've done it, congratulations. If you're still writing it, keep going. Finish it before you start worrying about publishing options. If you're just thinking about starting a book, write the first page soon. You'll be glad you did.

As you read through this book, know that publishing a book can be your reality. There will be highs and lows in this process—but the first time you get an email from someone you've never met who tells you how much they loved your book, you'll be glad you embarked on this journey.

CHAPTER 1

THE BASICS OF SELF-PUBLISHING

The Definition of Self-Publishing

Self-publishing can have several meanings depending on who you ask. People who work in traditional publishing say that if an author paid any money to publish his book, the book is self-published. But, the snooty world of traditional publishing uses that definition only when it suits its needs. Traditional publishers often make new, unknown authors pay most, if not all, marketing expenses associated with the author's book. So, to those in the hallowed (and increasingly empty) corridors of "Grey Poupon" publishers, a book is self-published if the author pays for editing, formatting, or cover design. But the book is not considered to be self-published if those expenses are covered by the publisher, even though the author is left with the marketing expenses. The hypocrisy is almost insulting.

In its purest form, self-publishing is when an author handles all of the book production processes, printing, distribution, and marketing (also called independent publishing). Under this definition, the author either has the skill set to carry out these processes (i.e., format a book) or hires out the various tasks to someone else. The author is essentially her own general contractor.

Authors who use self-publishing companies (sometimes called subsidy publishers) are obviously self-publishing, too. Under this definition, since the author is paying up front for services and/or publishing packages and is getting published because she is paying, the book is self-published. Even when the ISBN is in the name of a publisher, the book is still considered self-published because the author has paid a fee for publishing services.

The Difference between Self-Publishing and Vanity Publishing

The snooty folks inside the imploding walls of Grey Poupon publishing houses still insist that an author who pays a penny in publishing costs is engaged in "vanity" publishing. However, those same people have determined that authors paying for marketing costs are not considered to be vanity publishing. Depending on who you ask, you'll hear a variety of answers as to what the difference is between self-publishing and vanity publishing. If you are talked into purchasing ten thousand copies of your book even though you have no real marketing plan or dollars to spend, then, in addition to being a sucker, you've engaged in vanity publishing. If you are planning to publish a book just to tell people that you've published a book, you're vanity publishing. If you go into debt to publish a book because you "just know it will sell," you're crazy *and* engaged in vanity publishing. If you don't plan on spending any significant time or money to properly edit and design your book, you're engaged in vanity publishing. If you don't plan to spend any time or money to market your book but instead are waiting for sales to magically come pouring in once the book is released, you're definitely vanity publishing (and somewhat delusional to boot). Basically, the "vanity" part comes in if you believe that your book is so amazing that you can put out whatever you want and readers will flock to buy it, even though you've done little to promote it.

What makes self-publishing different from vanity publishing is that, in self-publishing, the author is publishing a book in a strategic, well-thought-out, and well-informed way. Strategic means that the author has the book professionally edited by a real book editor who is familiar with the appropriate style manuals (friends who teach high school English don't count), has the cover and interior professionally designed, has a realistic approach to the process, plans to spend hundreds of hours of his time spreading the word about his book, has a marketing plan and some kind of marketing budget (regardless of size), and intends to work hard to make sales. Those who sit around all day admiring themselves for having published a book are the vanity publishing crowd. Those who spend quality time marketing their book, and understand that sales opportunities down the road may be hatched by marketing ideas today, are what the spirit of self-publishing is all about.

The Difference between Self-Publishing and Traditional Publishing

A traditional book publisher (at least until recently) paid all of the expenses incurred in the publishing process: editing, cover design, formatting, printing, distribution, marketing, and so on. Under this traditional publishing model, authors didn't pay a dime toward any publishing or marketing cost. In exchange, they got their books published for "free." However, publishing is just like anything else—there is no such thing as a free lunch. Assume for the purpose of this section that the author being discussed is a typical first-time author getting a shot with a traditional publisher. This author gives away the rights to the book for some period of time (five to seven years) and receives a puny royalty (typically 5–8 percent of the retail price). In some cases, authors may receive advances against royalties. A typical advance given by a small publisher might be $2,000–$5,000.

Traditional publishing houses don't make it easy to get your work in front of them. So, the first step in getting a traditional publisher to even think about your book is to write a query letter that gets an agent or publisher to notice you. The "old guard" is still in place. In almost every case, you (the author) must write a query letter that explains who you are, what your book is about, who the intended audience is, and how you intend to market the book so that this audience will know that your book exists. Some helpful links about query letter writing can be found at http://www.charlottedillon.com/query.html.

As you probably know by now, sending query letters to agents and publishers often amounts to tossing these letters into a black hole in the middle of a remote galaxy. Sometimes an agent or publisher will contact you and ask for more material, which is a good sign. Sometimes they never write you back at all or send you a form rejection letter. Even if they ask for more material, it doesn't mean that you're getting a contract. It means that they are going to think about reading more of your submitted material whenever they feel like it—hence the black hole analogy. Remember, as the traditional publishing industry continues to contract, agents have fewer and fewer places they can go to pitch a new book. Similarly, getting your query letter to be read or acted upon by a traditional publisher (which is probably right now shedding mid-list authors and not taking on many newbies) is almost impossible.

Of course, every year a few authors break into this virtually locked-down universe. Let's assume for the sake of argument that you are one of them. Presumably, authors lucky enough to get a contract from a traditional publisher choose that route because the publisher brings years of design, marketing, PR contacts, and other important relationships to the table. How many of those relationships will be leveraged for the release of a book by a little-known author? Probably not many. More typically, the traditional publisher eventually breaks the bad news to the author that it doesn't have the budget for a marketing campaign or book tour. However, the publisher offers names of people to call who provide those services to the author for a fee, since the author is now under contract—enter the double-edged sword. The author got the contract she worked so hard to get only to learn that the chance of making significant book sales rests mostly on her shoulders (and wallet). If the author doesn't spend the marketing money required to help launch the book, the publisher's excitment will likely fade away and the book will inevitably lose traction as it becomes a blacklist title (the publishing world's purgatory). The author's own efforts—not the publisher's—have suddenly become the strongest indicator of the book's success.

Often, marketing is the most expensive part of the publishing process, so while not having to pay for up-front production expenses is attractive, that alone may not be a good enough reason to sign with a traditional publisher. The author will likely give away a lot (rights, control, subsidiary rights, most of the earnings) and end up paying for the marketing expenses, putting herself in the very financial position she may have been in had she self-published. If the book sells decently, and the advance was small, the publisher wins. Yes, the publisher spent some money up front, but it is taking little to no risk where it matters most—marketing the book. For such a minimal up-front risk, is the traditional publisher entitled to reap the rewards of the author's marketing efforts and money? The answer to this question will vary depending upon whom you ask. If you ask the publisher that put up money for an unknown writer to get his book out there, you'll hear one opinion. If you ask the author who had to pay a publicist $6,000 to run a PR campaign, you'll hear another.

The one way to avoid the question altogether is to self-publish your book. If you're going to spend money either way, you might as well control the process and the result.

CHAPTER 2

CHOOSING A SELF-PUBLISHING ROUTE

Once an author has come to accept that self-publishing is the route for his or her book, the author then needs to make a crucial decision—purchase all necessary publishing services á la carte, or work with a self-publishing company (where all of those services are contained under one roof). There are advantages and disadvantages to both. The first step in self-publishing your book is to decide whether you want to handle the entire process on your own, or employ a self-publishing company to assist you.

The advantage of handling the entire process on your own is that you can find exactly what you are looking for at every step of the way. However, the micromanagement of this process can be daunting and impractical. Instead of focusing your time and energy on a marketing strategy, you are learning the differences between paper weights and how they might affect the printing costs of your book. Unless you have the time to self-manage the entire publishing process, you'll probably be sorry once it starts. Like most people, I have a full-time job. I could never spend the amount of time it would take me to manage the publication of each new edition of this book. There are simply too many moving parts, and all of them need to be in sync with each other.

Managing your own publishing process is much like being your own general contractor. Unless you're already in the home-building business or know a lot about construction, being your own general contractor is tough because you don't even know the right questions to ask. It's the same thing in book publishing. I'm in the business and even I don't know the ins and outs of font choice or the nuances of cover design. If I used different professionals at every step, I'd be trudging along. (Just passing information back and forth can become hard to track.) When you hire separate designers, formatters, and so on, you often end up with territorial feuding between the various contractors. As a novice, you end up wondering whose advice is correct. This type of situation can stall the project and make authors second-guess everything.

When you choose a top-rate self-publishing company to provide all, or most, of your publishing and marketing services, you get cohesion and presumably collective good advice. Of course, if you pick the wrong company, that statement is false.

My number-one piece of advice to authors is to choose a company (or a person in the business) you trust, and let them guide you. Do not hire a yes-man. Authors with money often have a team of consultants who all tell them what they want to hear so the gravy train will keep chugging along. When you find an individual or company that you feel has your best interests at heart, hire them. As an author, I always want to convey my ideas about various aspects of the publishing process, but I also know when to stop talking and start listening. For example, I had three cover designs created for the cover of the book you're reading right now, by three different graphic artists. I had a favorite among the three, but I was not wedded to any of them. I sent the three designs to my distributor, my national sales reps (the ones who sell to the retailers), and other people I respect in the industry. All provided feedback and support for their positions. I chose the cover that the majority of those in the industry liked. I didn't get emotional about it. I didn't show it to friends and family. I elicited opinions from experts, then followed that advice. It's so smart and makes complete sense, yet I continue to be shocked at the number of authors I work with who do the exact opposite.

Before you choose the best self-publishing route for you, read through the following section and get a feel for the most essential elements of self-publishing. Whether you quarterback the project yourself or hire a company to handle it for you, you need to know the essentials.

CHAPTER 3

SELF-PUBLISHING ESSENTIALS—STUFF YOU NEED TO READ OVER AND OVER

Book publishing has a lot of moving parts. The longer I'm in the business, the more I understand how complicated it can be for a first-timer. The goal of this chapter is to educate you enough about the big-picture parts of the process so that you (a) know what to be looking out for, and (b) realize that you need to work with individuals or companies that know their stuff.

I am an expert in viewing book publishing in a healthy, realistic way. I am also an expert in giving people honest advice and feedback about the process that they need to hear (from someone). I am not an expert in editing, cover design, formatting, or the other technical aspects of the publishing process. I am, however, an expert in finding people who are and hiring them. Unless you have a wealth of experience in any of the steps in the publishing process, listen to people who do. I promise you, it's the smartest thing you will do as you publish your book. If an experienced cover designer tells you why the cover you want won't work or your editor tells you to cut out the parts of your novel that seem like a fifth grade history lesson—take the advice. You might think, "Well, everyone I've shown this to says…." Unless "everyone" is in the book publishing industry, listen to the experts. Certainly, targeting your book to the intended audience is important, but your family, friends, and acquaintances will always tell you what you want to hear, or water down the truth to the point where the only thing you'll hear is yourself being hoisted on your own pedestal.

The steps discussed in this chapter are meant to be introductory, providing a brief overview of a particular part of the publishing process. Each one of them could be a chapter itself. Neither of us wants that (well, at least I don't). With the exception of the first few, all parts of this process happen regardless of whether you're publishing on your own or using a self-publishing company.

If you ever speak with me on the phone, you are going to hear what I'm writing now. It's important. Really.

Your Credit Company Called—It Wants Its Limit Back

The most important step of the entire self-publishing process is one that you have complete knowledge of and control over—your budget. You've already read the statistics about book publishing success. Will your book be one of the 95 percent that sell less than one thousand copies, or one of the 5 percent that sell more than that? Your book's quality needs to be comparable to that top 5 percent, but your budget needs to be set based on being in the other ninety-five percent. This is the point in the process where you need to have a heart-to-heart with yourself, dig deep, and decide whether you're going to go for it (I'm talking Vegas-style), merely dip your toe into the publishing pool, or something in between. Any approach is fine, so long as your expectations are in line with your expenditure. Despite the widely held belief that if you put it on Amazon they will come, the publishing business doesn't work that way. You need time and money to market your book. Yes, there are always the "but what about…" authors who sold a million copies out of their car trunk. When you're setting a budget, assume you won't be one of them.

Your budget for the entire publishing process (including editing, printing, and marketing) should be a dollar amount that will not cause you to lose sleep at night. If you're lucky, you might make it back over a few years. There's a chance you may never see any of it again. You *must* budget in something for editing (see the next section). It's critical.

If you can spend $15,000–$20,000, your book will have a much better chance of getting noticed than if you spend $2,000. But, never spend more than you can comfortably afford. Don't sell anything to publish your book. Don't dip into your child's college fund. Don't mortgage your house. Don't take a cash advance on your credit card. Think with your wallet.

It's the Editing, Stupid

Just like Bill Clinton's 1992 presidential campaign had one basic message, so should the self-publishing industry: it's the editing, stupid. If you don't spend time and money with a good editor, everything else discussed in this book won't matter. A poorly edited book is a waste of time and money. Every dollar you spend promoting an error-prone book might as well be spent in Vegas. If you intend your book to be read by anyone other than your family and friends, you need to pay for the most extensive editing that you can afford, and you need to make sure that whoever edits your book is a professional book editor. Depending on the budget you've set, all or most of it could (and maybe should) be consumed by editing. Don't skimp on editing just so you can publish your book now. The world has waited this long for your book; it can wait until it's edited. If you can only afford one or the other, have your book edited, then save up money to have it published.

Every time I speak with an author, the first thing I ask is whether his or her book has been professionally edited. For some reason, many authors tell me what they think I want to hear and rationalize how certain individuals are just as good as a professional editor. The following are not professional editors or on par with them:

- Your friend, the high school English teacher
- Your friend, the English major
- Your friend who likes to read a lot
- The spell-checker on your computer
- Anyone who can count the number of books they've edited on one hand
- Your friend who edits a community newspaper (A manuscript edited for publication is subject to different standards and rules than a magazine or newspaper.)

If you can't afford to pay a professional editor, don't spend any money publishing your book; it won't be worth it. All books need editing. Even if you've had a professional editor edit your book, you still want some fresh eyes on it prior to publication, because between the time you submit the edited manuscript and the time that the final proof is sent to you, changes will likely have been made. If you have no one to edit those changes, all of the money you spent on editing in the first place is wasted.

Books put out by major publishers have many rounds of editing. In self-publishing, that is unrealistic (unless you have a huge budget), but you really need at least two rounds. (An additional polish-edit at the proofing stage is even better.) If you have just one round, who is going to edit the changes you made based on the editor's suggestions or comments during the initial edit?

Editing is the part of the publishing process that we authors hate the most. You have to pay someone to point out all of your errors, and all you get for your money is having to spend more time working on what you thought was a nearly finished book. If you want to be taken seriously as an author, you have to suck it up, get out the checkbook, and pay for great editing.

Finding a reliable, reputable editor can be tough. An association of editors is a great place to seek one. One group that I have worked with is the Professional Editors Network (www.pensite.org). A good Canadian group is the Editors' Association of Canada (www.editors.ca). Quality self-publishing companies also have solid pools of editors. There are many publishing and writers' associations that have lists of editors, too. Remember, you want to find an editor whose main editing focus is on books. Editing for a magazine and editing a book, while related in some ways, aren't the same. It's like tennis and racquetball. Both games use a racket, but everything else is different.

My book, the one you're reading right now, had at least four rounds of editing by two different editors. I only tell you this to stress the importance of good editing. Without it, your book is DOA.

Publishing is a tough business. It's doubtful that you'll get a second chance to make a first impression. Don't blow it. I'm not preachy about many things, but this is crucial.

My Book Is for Everybody

No…it's not. Knowing your audience is another critical step in the publishing process. Before you start writing a single word, you should be able to define the most likely reader of your book. If you haven't figured out just who your core audience is before you have the book edited, a good editor should be able to help you more clearly define your intended audience and shape your manuscript accordingly.

Inexperienced authors almost always assume that the potential audience for their book is much larger than it actually is. When I have consultations with authors, I always ask them who the market for the book actually is. The response that I get is typically, "Everybody." One woman writing an autobiography told me that her book was for "all women, ages fourteen to ninety." I'm not sure the last time you checked, but unless the fourteen-year-old and the ninety-year-old are both closely related to the author, they probably do not share the same interest in books.

A few years ago, I worked with a sixty-five-year-old male author who wrote about the perils of dating. As I started discussing marketing approaches and how we could target people within ten years of his age, he stopped me abruptly and said, "My book is for anyone who has had bad date experiences." I asked, "So, a twenty-eight-year-old woman could identify with a book chronicling the recent dating experiences of a sixty-five-year-old man?" His answer? "Yes." His approach made his book difficult to market. Retailers asked the same question that I did and didn't order the book. What a sixty-five-year-old man experiences in the dating world is completely different than what a twenty-eight-year-old woman experiences. By naïvely believing that anyone who'd ever been on a date would be part of his core audience, he cast the marketing net too wide and ended up with miniscule results.

Every part of the book publishing process depends on who the core audience is. When designing your book cover, you need to keep in mind who the reader will be. One test I use is to imagine my ideal reader reading my book on an airplane. If he or she would hide the cover because they were embarrassed by the title or cover art, there's a problem. A few years ago, we worked with an author who wrote a book about alpha males finding love. There are only a few potential audiences for this book: women who are in relationships with alpha males, women who plan to give this book to the alpha male in their lives, and the occasional alpha male who thinks the book may help him. The author was extremely credentialed and the book was well written. She insisted that her front cover depict six males from different walks of life (a shirtless construction worker, a doctor, a businessman, etc.), each with a scantily clad woman hanging off his arm. The only thing preventing it from looking like a Village People album cover was the lack of a uniformed cop and an Indian chief. No straight man would be caught walking around with that book cover. Not in a million years. We came up with a modern, sleek concept featuring the silhouette of a man in a business suit and let the title do the talking. It worked. You need to run the would-my-reader-be-embarrassed-to-buy-this-book-or-read-it-in-a-public-place test. Try it. It works.

Since so many new authors write self-help books and memoirs, there are a few things you need to know about that general audience. These kinds of books are purchased by people who find them relevant to their lives at the time. A great example is a book on how to keep your kids safe from predators. You'd think that every parent would want a copy of that book. Few will buy it, however, because it's not something they want to deal with unless they have to. As a consumer, if your family hasn't experienced that situation (e.g., your child or the child of someone you know has been abducted or almost abducted), you won't buy the book. We worked with an author who wrote about his child's life and subsequent death from cystic fibrosis. It is a beautifully written book, but the audience for it is limited. Outside of people who knew the actual family that it described, there weren't many people interested in buying it. The author assumed that parents with children struggling with the disease would buy the book. They didn't, because no parent wants to think about the potential death of their child.

With fiction, decide which genre (and subgenre) your book either fits in or is closest to. Adding a new twist to an old genre can help get people interested. There are plenty of blogs and websites that focus on various genres. Assuming you don't have a large promotional budget, you'll need to know who your core reader is and start marketing the book to them. As more and more people from your core audience read the book and spread the word, your audience may become broader.

Regardless of the type of book, *always* keep your core audience in mind. Write for them and market it to them first. If they don't love it, why would the casual reader?

He Who Designs His Own Cover or Interior Has a Fool for a Designer

We all judge books by their covers in many facets of life, however unfairly. This is especially true for actual books. A bad cover will kill your book. The book might be brilliant, but a cover that looks cheap and cheesy tells the world, "Hey, the rest of this thing is as crappy as the outside." People come up with crazy ideas for covers. Most are ridiculous. What you see in your head is not necessarily what the book-buying public wants to see. If you are creating the book just for your immediate circle of friends and family, do whatever you want. If you want someone who has never met you to buy the book, get professional help in this area. I beg you. For your own sake.

The interior design of a book is just as crucial as the cover. There are many important items to consider when formatting, like font choice. (Most books use a serif font for ease of reading, while a sans serif font is used for things like charts and graphs, some headings, and for online writing.) Other design elements to consider are the leading (the space between the lines of text) and kerning (the space between the letters).

Outside of the text itself, there are a number of style settings that need to be set in order to create a professional and clean interior. For example, the margins for a book with one hundred pages should be different from a book with four hundred pages to accommodate the gutter (the space between the pages when the book is opened). Page numberings throughout different sections of the book are treated differently. (For example, the front matter/introductory sections may use lowercase Roman numerals, and the actual content Arabic numerals.) Section and chapter headings are also an important part of the formatting process. Page headers and footers are another element of the design that need attention. Widows and orphans (partial or single words that dangle at the beginning of a page or the end of a paragraph) are sometimes overlooked, but like everything else mentioned above, they can't be forgotten.

There is a lot more to interior formatting than just slapping the text together and bolding a few things. To me, as is true for many readers, book interiors all look the same—but they're not. If you want your book to be taken seriously by the industry, it needs to be formatted in the standard ways that book retailers and wholesalers expect.

Many authors attempt to format their books themselves in Word or other programs. It's an art; and, while the public might not notice that you extended the margins to lower the page count and save on printing, the buyers for retailers and wholesalers will know the second they crack open your book.

Unless you are an actual book designer, leave this to the pros. You'll be glad you did. The cover and interior layout are just as important as editing. I beg you to listen to me on this one.

My Book Is the Most Important Thing Your Company Is Working On and I Can Be as Rude and Demanding as I Want

No, you can't. Most companies covered in this book are really trying hard to give you the best products and services they can. The publishing process has a lot of moving parts. Most authors never take the time to read the contracts that they sign, many of which spell out the process. For example, let's assume a publishing contract says that if an author has approved the final interior proof of the book, but then wants to make textual changes, there is a fee of $50 per hour. The author has signed this contract, has approved his final interior proof, and then decides he wants to make some changes to his text. The author emails the publisher and says, "Oh, I noticed these few things. Please change them." The publisher responds, "Sure, but we'll need to charge you $50 per hour to do this. We anticipate it will be about an hour's worth of work." The author then writes, "I am so sick of being nickel-and-dimed by you people. If someone would have told me about these extra fees, I would have reviewed the book more carefully!"

I've seen hundreds of variations of this. Whose fault is it? The author's—especially if everything is spelled out in the contract. Read the contract. Understand the fees before you sign. Don't go ballistic when you realize you legitimately owe a fee for additional work. Authors oftentimes forget that publishing companies are working with many authors, all at various stages of production, so something that you think should take "two seconds" may take a company a few days to schedule in.

If you're the kind of person who flies off the handle, screams at people who are trying to help you, and makes everything difficult, your publishing experience will not be a good one. Editors, formatters, designers—everyone makes mistakes. If you open your proof and your interior is in a different font than the one you expected, it can be fixed. The world is not ending.

Here's a great example of what I'm talking about: we had an author whose book was nationally distributed and sold to retailers, having a firm release date of August 2nd. This author decided in mid-July that he wanted to make little tweaks to his final interior. We kept telling him that he needed to let go or the book would never be on the shelves for the August 2nd release date—there is only so fast you can get a printer to move. The author didn't listen. We ended up rushing the print job, and by July 30th, his books were on the way to the retailers. Some retailers like Amazon.com didn't have the book listed by August 2nd (because they had probably just received inventory and hadn't had a chance to enter the book into their system). The author called and emailed nonstop, screaming about how his book wasn't available yet. He had a lawyer write an email explaining how we were in breach of contract and that his client had suffered emotional damage, knowing that his book wasn't listed as available on Amazon by August 2nd. Guess what happened the next day? He felt like an idiot for having a temper tantrum. Please don't behave like this. I'm begging you.

CHAPTER 4

WHY YOU NEED TO READ THIS BOOK

If you're thinking about hiring a self-publishing company, the rest of this book will be helpful. If you decided to buy a television or a car, you might read *Consumer Reports* to find the best price and highest quality. Just like when buying those products, comparing self-publishing companies isn't a pure apples-to-apples comparison. Whether one company's basic publishing package is $300 more than another's isn't something that can be rated very easily, as each company offers slightly different products and services. But, all companies can be compared in four major categories: printing markups, royalty splits, contract terms, and whether or not they return the original production files they create for your book. All four are easy to measure.

Spending hard-earned money to publish your book should be approached with the same care that you would give to any other major purchase. But, unlike buying a car, your book is an extension of you. If you choose any publisher ranked "Outstanding" or "Pretty Good" in this book, you won't be stuck with a lemon.

As you will read, most self-publishing companies use the same print-on-demand printer for most, if not all, of their on-demand printing. Since I know what that printer charges, it's easy to do the math and tell you exactly how big the printing markup is. Even if a company uses their own in-house printing, we can still use the same figure (except in those cases the markups will actually be more than I state here, since a company's internal costs for in-house printing will be less than what they would pay a third-party printer). As you'll read later, the printing markup is important because it not only causes you to pay more to print your books, but it also has a dramatic effect on the wholesale and final retail price of your book.

Royalties are also easy to measure. Because I know the actual printing costs, it's easy to calculate what the royalty split actually is. Some companies build in the inflated printing markup as the "actual" printing cost, and then do a royalty split. That causes a great royalty on paper to be not so great at all. Regardless of how the split is carried out, the math is easy to do.

Then there are the contract terms. Companies either have favorable terms, or they don't. For each company reviewed in this book, I point out any sections that I find problematic. You will learn some of the basics of self-publishing contracts in chapter 6. This will prepare you to spot negative sections of any company's self-publishing contract.

One contract term in particular is always an issue for me. If you pay a company to format your book, should you decide to leave, you should get those original production files back so you can publish and print with anyone else you desire. As you read about the specific companies, you'll see how this issue is treated. It's a biggie.

If you were signing a contract with Random House, you'd hire a lawyer, right? But when you sign with a self-publishing company, your legal fees could exceed all the money you hope to make from the sales of your book. That's why I wrote *The Fine Print of Self-Publishing*—to help writers understand self-publishing contracts and enable them to find the right publishing services for their particular goals and expectations.

CHAPTER 5

THE NINE QUALITIES OF A GOOD SELF-PUBLISHING COMPANY

Choosing the right self-publishing company comes down to finding one that offers the best mix of low printing markups, high royalties, and favorable contract terms, all at a reasonable price. Depending on your budget and expectations, not even every publisher rated "Outstanding" in this book will meet your needs. If you only have $500 to spend, then you need to compare the companies in that price range. As with many other products and services, in publishing you get what you pay for. Very few books published by a company that charges $500 will look as good as one where the cover designers and formatters are paid more. Some companies pay their formatters and cover designers more than what others charge for the entire process. When you make choices, price should be one of your considerations, but it can't be the only one.

The publishers rated "Outstanding" in this book come closest to possessing all of the must-have qualities listed on page twenty-two. If you're already considering a specific publisher, go through this list and make sure that your publisher matches up with it. If the publisher you're considering doesn't have most of these qualities, understand why and decide if it is a company you want to proceed with. That isn't to say that every "Outstanding" publisher is perfect. There are some that pay lower royalties than publishers ranked lower or that mark up printing more. But, all of the companies ranked "Outstanding" have one thing in common: they are author-friendly and continually take steps to make their contracts and services more favorable.

An excellent self-publishing company should have the following:

- A good reputation among writers
- Fair publishing fees
- Generous royalties without any fuzzy math
- Low printing costs and high production value
- Favorable contract terms
- Fair policy regarding the return of your book's original production files
- Fairly priced add-on services, such as marketing and copyright registration
- A standard offering of an ISBN, EAN bar code, and LCCN (Library of Congress Control Number) as part of any basic publishing package
- Availability through at least one wholesaler, and listings on major online retailers

A Good Reputation Among Writers

Every self-publishing company, including the good ones, has some disgruntled authors. Today, with message boards and blogs, even authors who have no legitimate right to complain about a company (but are nonetheless angry about something) use these forums to cloud a company's reputation. Yes, there are legitimate complaints that should be aired to warn others, but most of the complaints I've seen about good companies are just postings by whiners and brats who didn't read their contracts and would have posted the same type of thing about any publisher they had worked with.

I talk to a lot of authors, and some of the gripes that I hear are unfair to the publishers. If you spend a few hundred or even a few thousand dollars to publish your book, don't expect to be treated the way that Scholastic treats J.K. Rowling. Again, it's about living in the real world. So long as the publisher provides what its contract agrees to provide and does so within the time frame set forth in the contract, an author has no real complaint. If the publisher lied to an author to get him or her into the contract and the author can prove it (keep your emails), then complaints carry more weight. You don't have the right to expect that your email will be returned twenty minutes after you send it or to call your publisher fifteen times a day. When you start making the publisher millions of dollars, then you've earned those rights.

Remember, self-publishing companies are basically acting as general contractors with regard to publishing your book. When considering a publisher, talk to authors who've already published with the company. Most publishers' websites contain author pages or links to authors' websites, which provide contact information. Do not pay too much attention to authors who complain that a self-publishing company didn't help them sell books. Remember, some of these people have done nothing to promote their own books, and their disappointment in their sales may (unfairly) turn into disappointment in the publisher. This is still self-publishing, and the author is ultimately responsible for making his or her book sell.

When researching companies, you can also contact the Better Business Bureau in the state or city in which a publisher is located. Even if the publisher isn't a member, if people have made complaints the BBB will have a record of it. If you see dozens of unresolved complaints, that's a problem. If you see a few complaints and they have been resolved, don't be alarmed. Anyone can file any type of claim with the BBB, and these often get stuck on a publisher's record even if they are bogus. I know of a case where an author filed a BBB report accusing her publisher of stealing her books and selling them on the black market. (Trust me; it was a book that wouldn't have sold in any market.) The report was so outrageous that the BBB actually threw it out, but that's a rarity. All that aside, the BBB is a good first step in checking out a publisher that you're considering.

There are some websites that do the sleuthing for you and provide warnings about shady publishers. While these sites can be helpful, they don't often check out whether the information posted is true or not, allowing authors to complain about issues that either they caused themselves or that aren't accurate. And, even when publishers provide documentation to prove otherwise, some of these sites refuse to remove or modify the complaint. Thus, some good publishers get an unfair rap on these sites. So, relying on anything at these sites is like relying on an anonymous posting on a blog. Sites like *Writer Beware*, *Writers Weekly*

Warnings, and others simply can no longer be counted on to provide unbiased, credible information.

If a company has a solid BBB grade and you've talked to authors who've had a good experience, that's a good sign. Once you know these things, the next step is really an internal one for you. You need to choose a company whose personnel you feel comfortable with. Ultimately, it's all about that.

Fair Publishing Fees

Choosing a publisher involves more than price comparisons. You get what you pay for in self-publishing, just like with anything else. If all you have is $500 to spend, save up until you can afford a publishing package that includes a custom-designed book cover and interior, not just template-based design. Your book will scream "self-published" (or at least what people think a self-published or vanity press books looks like) if you don't pay for quality design work. If your goal is to be discovered as an author, pay to do it right. If your goal is to provide a book for friends and family only, then one of these cheap packages may work for you.

Don't be fooled by the "Publish for $299" offers. Like any other bait-and-switch offer, it's designed to get you in the door. Be wary of the "Free Self-Publishing" offers from sites like Lulu.com and CreateSpace .com. It might not cost you anything up front, but there is always a catch. Either the printing markups are astronomical, or the author is expected to handle much of the technical setup of the files prior to submission.

Once you get past the bait-and-switch packages, you'll find that most publishers offer a complete solution between $1,000 and $5,000. No matter what company you choose, a quality publishing package should include:

- A high-quality, custom-designed book cover (don't use any publisher's template—covers sell books)
- Professional layout of the book's interior
- Registration with Ingram or Baker & Taylor and listings on Amazon.com, BarnesandNoble.com, and other online retailers
- A page on the publisher's website or some other online venue (other than a third-party online retailer) where you can sell your book
- The ability to purchase your own books for a reasonable price

- A contract that you can cancel at any time
- The return of the original production files, or at least press-ready PDFs, of your interior and cover

When you find a company that meets these criteria, make sure to have your book professionally edited by either the company or an outside editor. Remember, this is one of the essentials. Don't skimp on editing. Yes, editing can be expensive, especially if you really do the amount necessary—but if your book is poorly edited, every dollar you spend on production and marketing is a complete waste.

Generous Royalties Without Any Fuzzy Math

Before getting into the mechanics of royalties, the most important thing to understand is that a publisher's offer to pay you a huge royalty (when they grossly inflate their printing costs) is meaningless. No one will buy an unreasonably priced book, so you'll never see that "huge" royalty check. You'll see moderately sized (250-page) paperbacks, from some of the largest self-publishing companies, for sale by online retailers at ridiculous prices like $22.95. No consumer will pay that price for a book by an unknown author. Such a retail price is the result of massive printing markups and allowing an author to choose his own royalty amount. Be wary of publishers that say you can make whatever you want on a book simply by increasing the retail price. Nothing from nothing is nothing.

Now that I've stepped off the soapbox, let's get back to royalties. One of the highly touted benefits of self-publishing is that the author's percentage of royalties is much greater than what a traditional publisher offers. Unless you're lucky or famous, many traditional publishers offer a royalty of 2.5–12 percent of the retail price. Self-publishing companies offer royalties from 20 to 80 percent (a few even offer 100 percent). The way the publisher calculates this percentage (and the built-in costs) is one of the most important aspects of self-publishing, and often the most deceptive.

Publishers calculate the author's royalty percentage in a few different ways. In many cases, 15 percent of the gross and 30 percent of the net may end up being the same amount. If the publisher you choose pays royalties based on the net sales price of your book, you must closely examine how it's calculated. Net sales figures can be manipulated by, for example, hiding inflated printing costs within the actual printing cost, which is backed out before a royalty is paid.

All publishers that pay a royalty on net sales prices subtract the cost of the book before calculating the royalty. Since you now know that most publishers pay the same cost to print a book, you can calculate the actual print cost on your own, then do the math based on figures the publishers provide on their websites. Publishers hate that I tell you this, but you need to know it. Look—they have the right to mark up the printing, and in fact it's necessary to cover expenses, but how much is too much? That's for you to decide.

When querying a publisher about its royalty calculation, the first thing you must ask is if it uses the actual print cost in that calculation, or a higher cost (generally based on the marked-up price the author pays for copies of his or her book). Always ask a publisher to give you, in writing, the cost to print a single copy of your book. If it's more than $0.015 per page and $0.90 for the cover (the cost to print a standard paperback), they are marking it up. So, then you'll know their "printing cost" versus the actual printing cost.

Most publishers covered in this book have two ways in which they sell your book: through their website, and through online retailers like Amazon.com and BarnesandNoble.com. What follows is a general overview of how royalties are calculated through these various sales channels. Each publisher review includes a breakdown and examples of how the publisher calculates royalties.

Low Printing Costs and High Production Value

This is where the rubber meets the road, where the men are separated from the boys, and where any other appropriate cliché could be inserted. Printing markups can kill your book before it's even been printed. Print-on-demand technology is the reason that self-publishing has exploded during the past decade. But, this one-off, short-run printing is much more expensive on a per-unit basis than printing in larger runs. So, the costs to print a book via POD technology are already high. When a self-publishing company marks up printing costs 50–100 percent, or even 170 percent (yes, one publisher does it), your book becomes priced out of the range that anyone other than your friends and family might spend.

With such a high printing cost, the chances of a retailer ever ordering your book are nil. That's because the wholesale price of your book will be so much higher than that of similar titles by traditional publishers. The price a retailer will pay for a typical book in your genre is set, and has been for a long time. They aren't going to change, and there isn't anything about your book that is going to make them rethink their buying strategies. Why expect casual readers to pay $19.95 for your paperback thriller when they can pay $7.95 for a Grisham thriller? The only way that your book is going to be priced in the "retail comfort zone" of the average reader or retailer who's willing to take a chance on an unknown author will be if the printing markups are relatively low.

Most self-publishing companies use Lightning Source to print and ship books. If you haven't already received your money's worth from this book, the payoff is here. As I have mentioned many times already, publishers typically pay about $0.015 per page and $0.90 per cover for each paperback with a standard trim size (e.g., 5.5" x 8.5" or 6" x 9") and black-and-white interior printed with a POD printer. A 200-page paperback costs the publisher approximately $3.90 per copy to print (in short runs, and less if they print more than one hundred copies). You've read this next line a dozen different ways in this book already, but it's important, so read it again: Any publisher that tells you the per-book production costs are higher than that isn't telling you the truth. They mark up the printing, and they certainly have a right to—but you have a right to know that the "actual printing costs" discussed on some publishers' sites are not accurate.

(While we're on the subject of Lightning Source, I don't cover this company in my book because it won't deal with authors unless you come to them with press-ready files. Lightning Source is a printer and distributor, not a self-publishing company.)

In most self-publishing company distribution programs, if your book is sold through an online retailer like Amazon, the order goes directly to Lightning Source, who prints and ships the book. When Amazon pays Lightning Source (or any other distributor for that matter), it takes its trade discount and then sends the remainder. Lightning Source keeps its $3.90 (in the case of our 200-page example) and sends the rest to the publisher, who then pays the author the agreed-upon royalty.

If you want to make any money from books that you resell yourself, don't sign with any publisher unless and until you know what the printing markup is and the publisher has justified it in some way. What you are charged for printing will directly affect your bottom line when it comes to sales.

Publishers have the right to mark up printing and make it a profit center of their business. I have the right to tell you what they are actually paying for printing. You then have the right, and now knowledge, to choose a publisher once you know what their printing markups really are. It's one of the few areas in self-publishing where you *can* do an apples-to-apples comparison. To me, anything more than a 15–20 percent markup on printing is simply not acceptable, unless you know what it is for and don't mind paying more than you should.

It's easy to figure out for yourself how much the printing markup is, if the quantity at issue is less than five hundred copies (books in quantities of more than five hundred copies are typically printed offset, and not print-on-demand). This formula is only set up to calculate markups for book with black-and-white interiors, standard trim sizes (e.g., 6" x 9" or 5.5" x 8.5"), and paperback covers. However, the markups you'll find here are probably going to be uniform with a particular publisher. So, you know the cost of these paperbacks is $0.015 per page and $0.90 per cover. Let's take a 200-page book, which we know costs $3.90 to print in very small runs ($0.015 x 200 pages + $0.90 for the cover). If a publisher says that it costs $7.80 to print that book, you figure out the markup by using this formula: (Publisher "Cost" – Actual Print Cost) / Actual Print Cost = Percent of Markup. In the above example, take ($7.80 – $3.90) / $3.90 = 100 percent markup.

Net vs. Gross Royalty Percentages from Book Sales Through the Publisher's Online Store

You want to find a publisher that pays a royalty based either on a fixed percentage of the retail sales price or on retail sales price less the printing cost. Period. Let's say your royalty is 50 percent of the retail price (less printing costs). If your book sells for $15.00 through your publisher's website and the cost of printing the book is $6.00, you should make $4.50 on each book sale.

Some publishers deduct the credit card processing charge incurred for each transaction (3–4 percent on average). If a customer purchases your book from the publisher's online store, the publisher is charged a credit card processing fee for running the transaction. If, with shipping, the cost of the book to the consumer is $20.00, and if the credit card processing fee is 3 percent, then the publisher pays $0.60 for credit card processing on that transaction. Often this amount is charged to the author. This is acceptable, because it's an actual cost incurred by the publisher when selling your book.

The "net sales price" approach can become muddied when publishers inflate the actual cost to print a book and then calculate a royalty based on that figure. For example, if the publisher is able to include its printing markup as part of the cost of printing, which is deducted from any net royalty amount calculation, they are double-dipping and not disclosing it.

Take a 200-page paperback that costs $3.90 to print ($0.015 per page and $0.90 per cover) and sells for $15.00 on your publisher's website. Assume a 50 percent royalty. If the publisher is using the actual print cost in determining the royalty amount, the breakdown looks like this:

$15.00 Retail price
-$3.90 Actual printing cost
$11.10 Profit to be split
x 0.50 Author royalty percentage
$5.55 Author royalty

The publisher also makes a $5.55 royalty.

If the publisher tells you the printing cost is $6.00, watch what happens:

$15.00 Retail price
–$6.00 Inflated printing cost
$9.00 Profit to be split
x 0.50 Author royalty percentage
$4.50 Author royalty

The publisher makes a $4.50 royalty, plus the printing markup of $2.10, bringing its total profit to $6.60. That's double-dipping. The publisher is making money on both ends of each sale. See how important it is to find out what the publisher includes in printing costs?

Publishers who pay based on a net price defined as something other than the retail price of the book with the cost of production and credit card processing fees backed out can be problematic. These companies often define "net price" however it best suits them. For example, some publishers give themselves a trade discount similar to that given to the third-party retailers that sell your book. This is very shady. Don't worry, I'll tell you about the ones that do this. A trade discount is usually 40–55 percent off the retail price. When the publisher builds the inflated printing charge into the equation and then subtracts an additional 40 percent for the trade discount it gives itself, the math looks like this:

$15.00 Retail price
–$6.00 Trade discount publisher takes for selling the book (40%)
–$6.00 Inflated print cost
$3.00 Profit to be split
x 0.50 Author royalty percentage
$1.50 Author royalty

The publisher makes a total of $12.60 from this sale (royalty + printing markup + trade discount).

Finally, stay away from any publisher that arrives at the "net sales price" by deducting vague items such as "administrative costs" and "marketing costs." That is a black hole that will suck up most, if not all, of your profits. There are a few self-publishing companies that operate like traditional publishers and have actual distributors that sell the books to wholesalers and retailers. In these cases, there will be a distributor fee and usually some shipping fees calculated into the costs. At this level, it becomes more like traditional publishing and less like self-publishing. The only difference is that in traditional publishing the publisher pays for the up-front costs, and in self-publishing, the author pays.

Royalties Paid by the Publisher for Sales by Third-Party Retailers

Most self-publishing companies state that your book has distribution through Ingram and is available through all major online retailers and twenty-five thousand other retailers. This statement means that if someone were to walk into a bookstore and specifically ask the store to order a copy, they could. It does not mean that a physical copy of your book is on the shelves of any bookstore.

When a publisher lists your book for sale on Amazon.com, BarnesandNoble.com, or any other third-party retailer, the money the retailer makes comes from the trade discount, which is typically 40 percent for brick-and-mortar retailers (i.e., bookstores) and 50 to 55 percent for online retailers like Amazon. Unless you have actual bookstore distribution, you only need to be concerned with the online retailers' trade discount. Whether your publisher pays you based on the retail price or on the net sales amount, when calculating the royalties for sales made by third-party retailers, the trade discount will almost always be taken off the top first (many publishers that base their royalties on the retail price, rather than net, will simply give the author a lower royalty percentage on sales via third-party retailers).

In order to compensate for the steep trade discount and for printing markups, self-publishing companies usually inflate the retail price of an author's book in order to create a situation where the author can see some kind of a royalty from sales on Amazon (or similar sites). The result is a book that should be retailing for $13–$15 selling for $20–$22. Why would a consumer pay that much for a paperback copy of your book, when a book by an author they know is sold for a retail price that the market supports? This is a huge problem in self-publishing, and it's the reason it is imperative that you find a publisher that pays the author the higher royalty percentage and doesn't mark up the printing costs ridiculously or set the retail price artificially high.

Assume you choose a self-publishing company that marks up the printing costs 40 percent (which is quite standard), gives a 50 percent trade discount to online retailers, and pays the author a 50 percent royalty based on the net retail price of $15.00. For the 200-page paperback example I've used throughout the book, here's how the math works:

$15.00	Retail price
–$7.50	Trade discount to third-party online retailer (50%)
–$6.00	Inflated print cost
$1.50	Profit to be split
x 0.50	Author royalty percentage
$0.75	Author royalty

The publisher makes a total of $2.85 on this sale (royalty + printing markup).

This should anger you. You pay a company a lot of money to publish your book, then every time someone purchases your book from Amazon—a sale the publisher is doing nothing to facilitate—the company makes 2.5 times what you do. Does the company deserve to make something? Sure. I don't know what the acceptable amount is (it can be subjective), but it's not more than two times what you're making on the same sale.

Unfortunately, this scenario is the rule; the exception is the company that doesn't inflate the printing costs. In that scenario, the numbers look like this:

$15.00	Retail price
–$7.50	Trade discount to third-party online retailer (50%)
–$3.90	Actual printing cost
$3.60	Profit to be split
x 0.50	Author royalty percentage
$1.80	Author royalty

The publisher also makes a $1.80 royalty.

This is a much more reasonable split. Should the publisher make as much as you for an Amazon.com sale? After you've paid fees to publish? I don't think so, unless the publisher is spending its own money to market your book. As long as you understand the process, the math, and how to calculate everything, you can discover what your potential publisher will make from sales of your book and decide if the amount works for you.

The Royalty Calculation Checklist

For each publisher covered in this book, I provide calculations similar to those in this chapter so that you can see if the author's royalty percentage is how the publisher describes it. Some of the royalties are just as good as the publishers represent them to be, but some border on blatant misrepresentation. One goal of this book is to make it harder for unscrupulous publishers to fool potential authors.

To determine whether a proposed royalty is acceptable, evaluate:

- Whether the publisher's method of royalty calculation is based on the retail price of the book or the net sales amount. If it's based on the net sales amount, the calculation should rely on hard numbers, such as production costs and credit card processing fees, and not on vague items such as administrative costs.
- Whether the publisher backs out the actual production cost of the book or an inflated printing cost.
- How much royalty is paid to the author. If an author receives less than 50 percent of the royalty amount, he should consider that a sign to pick another publisher.

Favorable Contract Terms

Before you sign any publishing contract, you need to make sure the contract contains the following provisions:

- A way for you to terminate the contract within thirty–ninety days without any penalty
- A clause that states that you own all the rights to your work and any derivatives of your work, such as movie rights

- A clause that requires the publisher, upon termination of the contract, to provide you with all original production files that contain the cover art, formatted version of your book, and any other material you paid to have created

A very detailed discussion of specific contract terms can be found in chapter 6.

Fair Policy Regarding the Return of Your Book's Original Production Files

You pay a lot of money to have a publisher create your book. A portion of that money goes into the creation of a cover design (assuming a custom cover, not a template-based one) and the formatting of the interior of your book. I believe you should own those original production (or source) files. Unless you have Adobe InDesign and Photoshop (the software most designers use to create the cover and interior files), you won't be able to do much with the files—but that isn't the point. You want these files because without them, should you terminate your contract and decide to publish the book on your own or with another self-publishing company (perhaps one that offers better royalties and smaller printing markups), you would have to pay for typesetting and cover design again. Now, if you have the source files, rather than redesigning the book, you can simply swap out the old copyright page, bar code, and publisher's logo and ISBN, which will cost much less money.

If all you can get are the press-ready PDF files, you may still be able to get a designer to tweak those parts of the book that need it. Cutting out the copyright page from the book and inserting a new one in a press-ready PDF is easy, but depending on the complexity of the cover design, covering up the bar code and replacing the publisher's logo could be trickier.

Many publishers will give you (or sell you) low-resolution PDFs of your cover and interior. Other than opening on your computer, there isn't much value to those. You can't use them to print from. If you are buying these files from your publisher, insist that they be high-resolution/ print-ready. Few publishers will give you the original production files, even though they are useless to the company if you leave. The only reason they make you pay for the PDFs (high or low-res) or the production files is to squeeze a few extra dollars out of you while you're walking out the door. It's wrong, and you should demand that a clause be inserted into any contract you sign that gives you these files for free upon termination.

The most egregious violator is iUniverse (and some of the other Author Solutions, Inc. companies): it makes you pay $750 for a press-ready PDF interior and *another* $750 for the press-ready PDF cover, should you terminate your contract within eighteen months.

Fairly Priced Add-on Services

When considering add-on services, this is one area where it's often hard to make apples-to-apples comparisons. Four add-on services that many publishers offer are cover design, editing services, copyright registration services, and marketing services.

Cover Design: A custom cover is essential, so figure its cost into your calculations. Some publishers include a custom cover design in their publishing packages. Avoid any cover template, which I define as any pre-designed cover into which you add a picture, photo, text, or graphic. Your book will look cheap and unprofessional.

Prices for a custom cover range from $200 to $2,000. This area is so subjective that I can't say that a $2,000 cover is always a rip-off or that a $200 cover is always a great deal. You need to examine sample covers created by the publisher's artists before you decide to purchase one (some companies now include a custom-designed cover in their packages).

When reviewing sample covers, remember that some covers may look bad because they were designed based on the author's input. Just because you can put whatever you want on a cover doesn't mean you should.

Editing Services: Different publishers may refer to the various levels of editing by different names. Here are descriptions of the most common levels of editing:

- Copyediting: correcting basic errors in spelling, grammar, punctuation, and syntax. You should be able to find a decent copyeditor for $0.015–$0.02 per word.
- Line Editing: copyediting on steroids—a detailed line-by-line process to correct errors in spelling, grammar, and punctuation. The editor will also make suggestions to improve syntax and word choice. A reasonable line edit costs between $0.03 and $0.04 per word.
- Content Editing: ensures the general accuracy and consistency of content and focuses on more extensive restructuring of sentences, as well as theme and character development. A fair price for a content edit is between $0.04 and $0.06 per word.

I've probably beaten this horse to death, but pay for as much editing as you can afford. One round isn't really sufficient, but it's better than nothing. Make sure you confirm that whoever is editing your book has had significant experience editing books. Also, watch out for "editors" posting on sites like Craigslist. While some of them might be legitimate, an editor who offers to do several rounds of editing for much less than the going rate should raise some questions.

Copyright Registration: Copyright registration is important, especially if you think you have a book that may really sell well, thus becoming a target for those who may want to misappropriate your work. By registering with the U.S. Copyright Office, you are eligible for statutory damages and attorney fees in the event that someone steals or otherwise uses your work without your express permission. Many publishers include copyright registration as part of their packages. You should never pay more than $150 for this service (which should include the Copyright Office filing fee of $35 for online filings and $50 for paper filings). The turnaround time by the Copyright Office is six months for electronic filings and up to twenty-two months for paper filings. Details can be found at http://www.copyright.gov/help/faq/faq-what.html#certificate. But the effective filing date of the registration is the date that it arrives at the U.S. Copyright Office, not when they process it. Also, under certain circumstances (like pending litigation), the U.S. Copyright Office will expedite the filing of a copyright. However, the fee for this is $760. For more details on the benefits of copyright registration, go to http://bookpublisherscompared.com/why_copyright.asp. If you want to file the copyright on your own, either online or with paper forms, you can start the process at http://www.copyright.gov/eco/.

Marketing Services: So many companies offer marketing and PR services that overlap with similar offerings by other companies that it's hard to do exact comparisons. You should be able to find a competent dedicated publicist for $2,000 to $2,500 per month. I've seen them as high as $4,000 or more per month. When it comes to marketing services, you really need to assess the offering and talk to the person who will actually be executing the service to determine if the person and the service make sense for you.

If you can't talk to the actual person who is going to provide you an expensive marketing service, take that as a red flag. For my $2,500 I want to speak to the actual publicist, not a salesperson.

Standard Offering of ISBN, Bar Code, and LCCN

These are explained below. The publisher should provide these three numbers as part of its basic publishing package. If you're required to obtain these items on your own, you might as well publish the book on your own. Some self-publishing companies provide these services à la carte, but be wary of the charges.

International Standard Book Number (ISBN): The ISBN is a thirteen-digit number that uniquely identifies a book regardless of format (hardcover, paperback, audio, ebook, etc). Books published before January 1, 2007 had ten-digit ISBNs. Since then, thirteen-digit ISBNs have become standard. An ISBN is needed to sell your book through online or offline booksellers. Each edition of a book, whether in paperback, hardcover, ebook, audio, or other such form, requires a separate ISBN. This number, which is also embedded in the bar code on the book, allows libraries and booksellers to find information about the author, the author's book, the book's price, ordering information, and other related information. The ISBN attached to the book lists the publisher as the party to contact for information.

Almost all publishers in this book purchase ISBNs in blocks (the smallest is a block of ten). The publisher, as purchaser/owner of the ISBN, assigns an ISBN to each edition of the book the author has licensed it to publish.

Most self-publishing companies won't allow authors to use an ISBN that the author purchases directly for the version of the book the company publishes. Some publishers allow authors to provide their own ISBNs, but that can be more hassle and cost than it's worth. The author is able to publish a version of the book either during or after the term of your contract with the publisher, using a directly purchased ISBN (assuming there is a contract that allows for that). The advantage: if you terminate your contract with the publisher, your ISBN is already in place and wouldn't have to be swapped out of the book's interior. The downside is that there will still be complications involved with the original publisher related to handling orders and royalty payments.

As said already, if you have different formats of your book (e.g., paperback, .mobi/Kindle, .epub, etc.) you will need different ISBNs for each. If you're buying ISBNs on your own, you can either buy a single one for $125 (be aware that industry professionals are able to tell by the number that the book is a single "self" publication rather than part of a standard publisher's block of numbers), or you can purchase a block of ten for $275 (which includes processing fees). You can assign them to any versions of any books you write (e.g., if you write three books and each has an ebook, paperback, and hardcover edition, you'd use nine of the ten ISBNs purchased). You can complete the entire process online at http://www.isbn.org/standards/home/isbn/us/secureapp.asp. A non-priority application takes about ten days to process.

Beware: Do not buy a single ISBN through any third party. Buy only through Bowker at https://www.myidentifiers.com. If you see an offer for a single ISBN that is less than $125 and is sold from a third party, don't buy it. The problem with those "single" ISBNs purchased from third parties is that they come from a "clearing house." Frequently those ISBN prefixes start with a 615, and when an author puts one of these third-party-purchased ISBNs in his or her book, the ISBN is not associated with the author (or the author's publishing company name), but rather is associated with the third-party company that sold them the ISBN initially. This can get messy.

Once the ISBN has been assigned to a book, it should be reported to R.R. Bowker, the database of record for the ISBN agency. Your book can be listed for free in R.R. Bowker's Books In Print database as long as you submit the information about your title at http://www.bowkerlink.com.

If a publisher wants to charge you for submitting your book's information to Books In Print, make sure the charge is reasonable, because there is no fee to register at Books In Print. Of course, it takes time for a publisher's employee to handle these things, and a fair fee is certainly reasonable.

Bar Codes: All books use the Bookland EAN bar code because it allows for the encoding of ISBNs. Almost all book retailers and wholesalers require the Bookland EAN bar code to appear somewhere on the back cover of a book, because this is what the retailer scans at the point of sale to identify the price and information from the bookseller's database. Like any other bar code, the computer then automatically reports the price to the cash register.

For mass-market books, which are sold in drugstores, department stores, and other non-bookstore retailers, a UPC bar code will likely be required, since these non-bookstore retailers are not properly equipped to scan the Bookland EAN symbols. (This isn't something you need to worry about if you're published by a self-publishing company that doesn't sell your book in such venues.)

Most self-publishing companies provide the bar code as part of their services. If you buy a single bar code directly from Bowker, the cost would be $25 (http://www.bowkerbarcode.com/barcode/).

Library of Congress Control Number (LCCN): The LCCN is a unique identification number that the Library of Congress assigns to titles that it is likely to acquire. This is not the same as a copyright registration. Librarians use the LCCN to access the associated bibliographic record in the Library of Congress's database or to obtain information on various book titles in other databases. The publisher prints the LCCN on the back of the title page in the following manner: Library of Congress Control Number: 2001012345.

Only U.S. book publishers are eligible to obtain an LCCN. To receive an LCCN, publishers must list a U.S. place of publication on the title page or copyright page and maintain an editorial office in the country capable of answering substantive bibliographic questions.

There is no charge for registering, but the publisher must send a copy of the "best edition" of the book for which the LCCN was pre-assigned (you apply for the LCCN prior to publication) immediately upon publication to the Library of Congress. If using the U.S. Postal Service, mail to: Library of Congress, US & Publisher Liaison Division, Cataloging in Publication Program, 101 Independence Ave. S.E., Washington, DC 20540-4320. If using a commercial shipper, send to: Library of Congress, USPL/CIP 20540-4283, 9140 East Hampton Drive, Capitol Heights, MD 20743. The "best edition" of a book is the retail paperback or hardcover version of the book.

Books published in electronic form are ineligible for an LCCN.

Should you wish to obtain an LCCN on your own, the first step is to complete the Application to Participate and obtain an account number and password, which takes one to two weeks. The application is found online at http://pcn.loc.gov/pcn007.html. Complete information about the LCCN process can be found at http://pcn.loc.gov/pcn006.html.

A publisher may try to tell you that there is a fee for an LCCN, or that it has to charge you a fee because it needs to obtain one for each edition of your book. Don't believe the publisher. Unlike an ISBN, the LCCN is assigned to the work itself and doesn't change with each new edition or version. Certainly, it takes time and effort to submit the application, and it is fair for a publisher to build this into its fee. It's not fair for a publisher to pretend that the Library of Congress charges a fee for the LCCN.

Availability Through at Least One Wholesaler and Listings On Major Online Retailers

Most self-publishing companies have a relationship with one of the major book wholesalers: Baker & Taylor or Ingram. If you want to make your book available in brick-and-mortar bookstores, it must be available through one of these wholesalers. This doesn't necessarily mean that your book will be carried in any bookstore. It means that your Aunt Mabel can walk into her local Barnes & Noble and "special order" a copy of your book.

In order to increase your sales opportunities, make sure your publisher lists your book on Amazon.com or BarnesandNoble.com (most do). Everyone knows Amazon.com; and, should someone hear about your book, chances are that person isn't going to know or remember the URL of the publisher's online store. The first instinct of many consumers when looking for a book online is to go to Amazon.com or BarnesandNoble .com. Making your book available through Amazon.com makes it appear more legitimate in the eyes of many consumers (and available for their online reviews). Anyone can put a book on Amazon.com but, to the general public, seeing a book there is a big deal. Another important reason to list your book on Amazon.com is that if you ever start to really sell books, a traditional publisher may consider Amazon.com sales rankings to be more accurate than sales figures from your publisher's website. The downside of selling only on Amazon.com is that because of the trade discount that Amazon.com takes, you will make considerably less in royalties per book than you would from sales through your publisher's website or your own.

There are about six million books on Amazon, so the "Amazon Sales Rank" number you see on a book's sales page means that out of the six million books on Amazon.com, that book is number [#]. So, if your book has a sales rank of fifty thousand, it means that it is the fifty thousandth best-selling item on Amazon on that day. A sales rank of one hundred thousand or less is very respectable. A helpful article on Amazon sales rank is at http://www.rampant-books.com/mgt_amazon_sales_rank.htm.

Other online retailers, such as Borders.com, Powells.com, and BooksAMillion.com, are also worthwhile venues for selling your book, but first make sure it's available on Amazon.com and/or BarnesandNoble.com.

Alexa.com ranks websites in terms of traffic. It isn't always the most accurate, but it's a good gauge of online retailers and can help determine where you should list your book. Like Amazon.com, the lower the number, the better. As of August 2010, Alexa.com ranked Amazon.com as the 18th most visited website in the world. BarnesandNoble.com was at 782, BooksAMillion.com was at 24,343, and Borders.com was at 2,710.

Any self-publishing company claiming to provide a complete publishing service will have your book listed with either Ingram or Baker & Taylor and will make it available for sale on Amazon.com and/or BarnesandNoble.com.

CHAPTER 6

THE FINE PRINT OF PUBLISHING CONTRACTS

Lawyers have often been accused of creating a language that only they can understand. This legalese forces the layperson to hire a lawyer who can decipher a document written in this funky little language. It took three years of law school and many years of drafting hundreds of contracts for me to approach these documents with ease.

The contract terms discussed in this chapter are common in most self-publishing contracts. Publishers all use slightly different verbiage in their contracts, so one termination clause may differ slightly from another, even though they mean essentially the same thing. The idea here is to help you recognize and understand the various terms when you read through the contract of any publisher whose services you consider.

I discuss the specific provisions and problems of each publisher's contract in their respective overviews. I also suggest ways to make the clauses more advantageous, either by persuading the publisher to omit or modify certain language, or by finding another publisher.

Surprises are fun, but not in publishing contracts. My number-one goal is to help you understand what you sign.

Read this carefully right now, and then read it again: if a publisher refuses to let you see a copy of a publishing contract before you provide them with a copy of your book, run away as fast as you can. If a publisher doesn't want you to see what it will ultimately ask you to sign, take that as the big fat clue that it is! The strategy behind this nondisclosure is that the company gets you all jazzed up about your book publishing adventure; then once you've "bought" into the program, they let you see the contract. By this time, you may not be thinking with your head.

Now that we have that out of the way, here are some general provisions found in most self-publishing contracts.

Parties to the Contract

This will always be you (the author) and the publisher. This introductory language identifies names that appear throughout the contract. The author will often be referred to as the "Author," and not by his or her name. The publisher will often be referred to as the "Publisher" or "Company," and not by its name. Your manuscript will usually be referred to as the "Book" or "Work," and not by its title.

License of Rights

This is one of the most important provisions in any publishing agreement because it states the precise rights the author licenses to the publisher during the term of the contract. In most self-publishing contracts, the author grants either an exclusive or a nonexclusive license during the contract term. An exclusive license prevents anyone who is not the license holder, including the author, from publishing the author's book in the format for which the right is being licensed. A nonexclusive license allows others, such as the author or other publishers, to sell, distribute, and publish the book during the contract term.

If you have your book published as an ebook, you will grant the publisher either an exclusive or nonexclusive right to publish and sell your book in an electronic format, which typically includes a downloadable ebook or another file type that can be read on an ebook reader, such as the Amazon Kindle.

If you publish your book as a paperback or hardcover, you will grant those specific rights. Granting paperback rights does not automatically include hardcover. Contract language that describes "all print rights" includes print and hardcover rights. Some publisher contracts are for "worldwide" rights. During the term of the agreement, the publisher can sell your book anywhere in the world in the format(s) you've agreed upon.

Some publishers ask only for rights to sell the book in the United States, Canada, and the United Kingdom. For example, if a publisher only has print rights in the United Kingdom, the author would still have the right to sell, distribute, and publish the book in print anywhere else in the world.

Print and electronic rights are the only rights that should ever be an issue in a contract you sign with any of the publishers covered in this book. Stay away from a contract that grants the publisher "all rights whatsoever," which would include subsidiary rights, such as movie, television, radio, or stage play rights.

There are companies listed in this book that take a percentage of any fees derived from an author's sale of subsidiary rights (e.g., movie rights). Still other companies build in a contractual right to sell the subsidiary rights and then keep a percentage of the sale. It won't be hard to find them—they're all in the chapter called "Publishers to Avoid."

Stay away from any publisher that demands an option or right of first refusal on any other books you may write. It's one thing if you sign a three-book deal with a major publisher and receive payment up front, but it's an entirely different matter in the self-publishing world.

Many self-publishing contracts specifically state that the publisher is not claiming an interest in any rights other than those directly related to the publication of your book (and then only those that allow them to print and distribute the book on your behalf). It's not required or necessary language to have in a contract, but it does make your rights indisputable. I prefer such language myself, and I include it in the contracts that I draft for publishing companies.

Term and Termination

The term and termination provisions are just as important as the license of rights. The term defines how long the contract will last. The termination provision describes what either party must do to cancel the contract, and when they must do so. The term and termination sections are often written together as one provision. It is important to read the license of rights and the term and termination provisions together to determine whether a contract is author-friendly. I always discuss these three provisions together when analyzing a particular publisher's contract.

Look for contracts that have terms that do not lock the author into a contract for a long period of time. The most author-friendly contracts will have one of these terms:

- exclusive, but only for one year;
- exclusive for [#] years, but the author can terminate at any time by giving [#] days written notice; or
- nonexclusive for [#] years, and the author can cancel at any time.

If a publishing contract you're considering doesn't have a term like one of these three terms, think long and hard before signing (you probably shouldn't sign at all). If you attempt to terminate a contract that doesn't have a term like one of these three, you're going to wish you'd followed my advice.

There are, of course, a few exceptions to the general rules. The goal is to always have the least number of restrictions on your rights, freeing you to search for a better publishing deal with a traditional publisher or other self-publishing company.

Avoid contracts that permit a publisher to retain nonexclusive rights after termination. Avoid any contract that grants the publisher a nonexclusive right to publish and sell your book after contract termination. I'm not talking about contracts that permit the publisher to sell its remaining inventory of your book after termination. There are few cases that I can imagine where a self-publishing company would even have more than a few copies of your book in stock. Here are two unacceptable situations:

- The publisher receives an exclusive term for one year, during which the author can cancel at any time. But if the author cancels the contract before the term is up, the publisher retains a nonexclusive right to sell the book through the original one-year term.
- The publisher receives a two-year, nonexclusive right, which allows the publisher to publish, distribute, and sell your book during that time period regardless of what you do.

The problem with both situations is that the author isn't in full control of his or her rights.

The ability to sell your book while someone else continues to sell it is not the same as having full control of your rights. Suppose a major publisher, such as Random House, wanted to purchase rights to your book and, before approaching Random House, you had signed a contract containing either of the aforementioned clauses. Although you'd have the right to sell to Random House the right to publish your book, your old publisher's nonexclusive rights would remain effective. Once Random House learned about this publisher's rights, it might lose interest. At best, Random House would first have to purchase your publisher's nonexclusive rights before it would purchase any licensing rights from you.

From your ex-publisher's perspective, the nonexclusive right is worthless unless a traditional publisher decides to publish your book. It's unlikely that your publisher will actively market or sell your book. When Random House enters the picture, your ex-publisher's rights to your book become valuable. Your ex-publisher may try to sell its nonexclusive rights to you or Random House, or it may print as many books as it can sell. You want to avoid a situation where your current publisher is suddenly a factor in your negotiations with a traditional publisher.

You must address these nonexclusive contract provisions, which are present in many self-publishing contracts, in one of these ways:

- Remove the language that gives the publisher nonexclusive rights after termination.
- Modify the language to permit the publisher to sell any remaining inventory it has as of the termination date, but prohibit the publisher from printing and selling additional copies after the termination date.
- Modify the language to give the author the right to purchase the publisher's nonexclusive rights upon termination for an amount equal to the publisher's net profit from sales it would have made during the nonexclusive period. The net profit should be based on the net profit during the previous [#] months (equal to the remaining term of the nonexclusive period after termination). For example, if the publisher had a nonexclusive right to sell

> the book for a year after termination, then the buy-out price should be based on the net profit during the year that preceded the termination date. Define the net profit as the retail price of the book less the production costs, author royalties, and trade discounts.

If I terminated the agreement in order to sign with a bigger publisher, I'd attempt to buy out my current publisher's nonexclusive rights (without telling them why) before signing the new contract with the bigger publisher.

Avoid contracts whose terms extend for the length of the copyright. If you learn only one lesson from this book, remember this: never, ever, under any circumstances, enter into a contract containing a term that equals the length of the copyright. A copyright term lasts for the life of the author plus another seventy years. This term allows your heirs to receive your copyright's benefit after you're gone. Once you sign a contract that has a term that extends for the life of your book's copyright, you've lost control over your work forever.

Pay special attention to terms that renew automatically. Some publishing contracts have an initial term of [#] years that automatically renews on a year-to-year basis until terminated. Oftentimes, termination requires the author to give notice at least [#] days before the expiration of the initial or renewal term. In theory, there's nothing wrong with this requirement.

In practice, it may prove tricky. Let's say you signed a one-year agreement on January 1, 2011, which renews automatically on a yearly basis unless terminated ninety days before the expiration of the initial or renewal term. If you want to terminate the agreement after the first year you must give notice at least ninety days before December 31, 2011, or by September 29, 2011. If you gave notice on November 15, 2011, the publisher could require you to honor the automatic renewal term through the end of 2012.

Automatic renewal clauses exist for your convenience as much as for the publisher's. Without the clause, the publisher must stop selling your book and remove it from its website at the end of the initial or renewal term. To resume sales and earn more royalties, you would have to notify them of your desire to extend the contract. Most self-publishing companies include renewal clauses. The best way to avoid a problem is to schedule a reminder on Outlook or a similar calendar system before the deadline passes.

Author Warranties

Author warranties are promises the author makes about the submitted work. These warranties are usually the most intimidating provisions of any self-publishing contract because of their lawyerly sounding language. Author warranties can be summed up like this: don't break the law or violate anyone else's rights with your book and you'll be okay.

Below are eight author warranties commonly found in self-publishing contracts. Not all publishing contracts contain all eight warranties, nor will the language match exactly, but the information below should give you the gist of what each means:

1. *Author is the sole author and proprietor of the work.* You cannot make this representation if another writer has any interest in the book, unless you have a written agreement with the other writer in which he or she has agreed that you are the sole author and owner of the work. (The exception would be a writer paid to provide certain services, such as ghostwriting.) Examples of individuals who may have an interest in your book are coauthors and illustrators, unless you have work-for-hire or other similar agreements with them.

2. *Author owns all rights in the work free of any liens and encumbrances and has full authority to enter this agreement.* This clause expands on the first and confirms that no one else has made or can make a claim to any of the rights. For example, let's say that someone sued you for

copyright infringement and the case was ongoing at the time you signed the publishing contract. The lawsuit would be an encumbrance, because you would not have the ability to sell your work in its present condition until the lawsuit was favorably resolved.

3. *The work is original and has not been previously published.* This one is self-explanatory. The work is your own and not created by another person, and the work hasn't been published anywhere else. If you have published the work previously, make sure you inform the publisher so that this clause can be amended.

4. *For work not in the public domain, legally effective written licenses have been secured.* This section means that you are warranting that you've obtained legal permission to use any work not in the public domain (something you can use because the copyright protection has expired).

5. *No part of the work, including the title, contains any matter which is defamatory, unlawful, or which in any way infringes, invades, or violates any right, including privacy, copyright, trademark, or trade secret of any person.*

It's easier to break this one down by giving examples.

- If your book claims that your neighbor, John Smith, is a child molester, that would be defamation—unless the claim is true. Truth is always a defense to defamation. (However, truth may not prevent someone from suing you, requiring you to incur legal expenses for your defense—even if you ultimately win. More about this later.)
- If your book instructs people how to blow up government buildings, most publishers consider this instruction to be unlawful, regardless of your First Amendment rights.
- If you put your girlfriend's private diary in your book without her permission, you are violating her right to privacy and infringing on her copyright of her diary.
- If you take a portion of this book and use it in your book without obtaining my permission, you've infringed on my copyright.

- If your book has Harry Potter as a character, you've infringed on J.K. Rowling's copyright and trademarks. However, stating that a character drank Coke or appeared on CNN isn't considered infringement.
- If you print Coke's secret recipe in your book, you've infringed on Coke's trade secret (its recipe).

6. *The publication doesn't breach any oral or written agreement the author has made with anyone else.* You are confirming that you don't have any other agreement with any publisher or third party that would preclude you from publishing your book with the publisher whose contract you're about to sign.

7. *The representations and warranties are in full force and effect on the date of publication.* You are promising that all representations and warranties you made will be as true on the publication date as they are on the day you sign the contract.

8. *The warranties survive the term of the Agreement.* This means that if you defamed someone in your book, and that person sues the publisher several years after your publishing agreement has expired, you will still be liable for the representations and warranties you made.

Publisher Indemnification Warranties

When you indemnify a publisher, you are saying that if any warranties you made turn out to be false, you will cover all of the publisher's legal expenses if it gets sued. Here are three typical indemnity clauses you may see in publisher contracts:

1. *The author indemnifies and holds the publisher harmless from any losses, expenses, or damages arising out of or for the purpose of resolving or avoiding any suit, demand, etc., as a result of the author's breach of the representations and warranties.* If you used someone else's copyrighted material in your book, all legal expenses incurred by the publisher in defending a copyright infringement lawsuit, any damage awarded by a court, and any settlement

amount the publisher makes to avoid a lawsuit will ultimately be paid by you. It's simple. Make sure your representations and warranties are true, or prepare for a legal mess should a third party sue.

2. *The publisher can extend the benefit of the author's representations and warranties and indemnities to any party affected by the author's breach.* If the publisher sells your book through Amazon.com and the person defamed in your book sues Amazon.com, the representations, warranties, and indemnifications you made to your publisher will also cover Amazon .com. You'll be responsible for Amazon.com's costs, attorney's fees, losses, damages, and more.

3. *Author has to pay legal fees, costs, etc., to defend any suit brought against the publisher as a result of the author's breach of any representation or warranty.* This language is usually included in the first indemnification clause mentioned earlier. The publisher may choose to set it apart so that it's crystal clear that the author is responsible for the publisher's legal fees and expenses if the author breaches representations and warranties.

Permission and Releases

Provided there is a legal review of the final, complete manuscript of the work, the author, at the author's own expense, agrees to obtain from any person or entity from whom, in the publisher's opinion, permissions, releases, or licenses shall be required in order to exercise the rights granted hereunder... If your characters work at XYZ Café, and XYZ Café happens to be a real restaurant in the city in which the story takes place, the publisher may require you to secure written permission to use the cafe's name from the establishment's owner. However, this is sort of a gray area because, unless there is something happening in your book at XYZ Café that puts the real XYZ Café in a bad (and false) light, you may not need to obtain permission. If you have questions about whether or not parts of your work may require you to obtain permissions, I suggest contacting an intellectual property lawyer.

Use of Author's Name and Likeness

The author grants the publisher and its licensees the right to use the author's name and likeness in the sale, promotion, and advertising of the work... Granting a publisher the right to publish your book doesn't automatically give it the right to use your picture or name on its website or a third party's website (like Amazon.com), or in retail stores where your book is for sale. This clause gives the publisher permission to use your name and picture in the marketing and promotion of your book.

Publisher Bankruptcy

If the publisher commences bankruptcy proceedings, all rights to the work shall immediately revert to the author. This clause protects the author. All assets of a publisher that files for bankruptcy become the property of the bankruptcy trustee. Without this clause, the license you gave to the publisher under the publishing agreement also becomes the bankruptcy trustee's property. This would create problems for the author because the author must then deal with the court-appointed person handling the publisher's affairs.

In some bankruptcy situations, the publisher reorganizes and continues to run the company. Bankruptcy clauses in publishing contracts, however, don't differentiate between the various types of bankruptcy.

In theory, the second the publisher files for bankruptcy protection, all of the author's rights immediately revert to the author. In reality, the clause may not be enforceable. The automatic stay provision of the bankruptcy section of the U.S. Code (11 U.S.C. §362[3]) controls what would happen in a situation like this. The provision states that upon filing for bankruptcy, a stay applies to any act to obtain possession of property of the estate or to exercise control over property of the estate. Of course, a creditor can always apply for relief from the stay, but for an unsecured creditor like an author—good luck. When a publisher files for bankruptcy, most bankruptcy trustees return the rights to the author in exchange for the author's agreement to drop any claims for all unpaid royalties or other monies due.

Notices

Notice provisions explain how the author and publisher must provide notice of events or situations requiring notice, such as termination of the contract. Some termination clauses permit notice by fax, email, or regular mail. Others require notice by certified mail only.

If a contract requires delivery of notice in a specific manner, you must follow that manner for the notice to be effective. For example, if a contract requires notice to be sent using certified mail and you fax the notice, your notice is not legally effective.

Governing Law, Venue, Attorneys' Fees

These individual clauses are sometimes combined under one clause. If your contract lacks a separate clause, look for relevant language in the "General Provisions" or "Miscellaneous" contract clauses.

In the example below, I use Minnesota and Hennepin County (Minneapolis and surrounding suburbs) as the venue. The counties and states will be different depending on the location of the publisher. The clause may read like this:

This Agreement will be construed and controlled by the laws of the State of Minnesota, and each party consents to the exclusive jurisdiction and venue by the state or federal courts sitting in the State of Minnesota, County of Hennepin. If either the publisher or author employs an attorney to enforce any rights arising out of or relating to this Agreement, the prevailing party will be entitled to recover reasonable attorneys' fees and costs.

Let's break it up to review each point.

Governing Law: This Agreement will be construed and controlled by the laws of the State of Minnesota...

Should a legal dispute arise, the court will use Minnesota's case law and statutes to interpret the provisions of the contract. Usually the laws of the state where the publisher or its lawyers are located will be used to interpret contract terms. Why? Because the publisher's lawyers are familiar with the laws of the state in which they already practice. The publisher won't be billed extra fees while its lawyers learn the nuances of another state's laws.

There are times when a publisher may choose to have the contract governed by the laws of another state because a particular state may have a statute or law more favorable to the publisher. Note that the publishing contract clauses discussed in this book cover basic contract law principles and are not particular to any state.

Venue: ...and each party consents to the exclusive jurisdiction and venue by the state or federal courts sitting in the State of Minnesota, County of Hennepin...

This provision specifies that if one party sues the other party for a contractual breach, the lawsuit will be brought in the state or federal court located in the state identified in the agreement—in this case, a state court in Minnesota or federal court in Hennepin County, Minnesota.

Without the author's consent to a specific venue in the state of the publisher's choosing, the publisher could have a difficult time suing the author in that state. By agreeing to sue and be sued in the state of the publisher's choosing, the author cannot sue the publisher in the author's own state (unless it's the same state) because, once the publisher's lawyers move to dismiss the author's action and present the contract to the court, the author's case will be dismissed, assuming the contract is valid and enforceable (e.g., not signed under duress, fraud, etc.).

Attorneys' Fees: If either the publisher or the author employs attorneys to enforce any rights arising out of or relating to this Agreement, the prevailing party will be entitled to recover reasonable attorneys' fees and costs.

I call this provision the "keep-it-honest" clause because it makes a party think twice before filing a lawsuit. If you bring a weak case and lose, you will likely pay 100 percent of the publisher's attorneys' fees. The reverse is also true. These "prevailing party" clauses are fair. Some publishers try to sneak in language that says (1) the author pays the publisher's attorneys' fees regardless of the case's outcome, or (2) if the publisher prevails in a lawsuit it can recover its attorneys' fees, but the same does not apply to the author. Many publishers get away with this tactic because people don't bother to read these clauses before signing the agreement. The party who drafted the contract banks on the other party overlooking it.

Most self-publishing contracts don't have such unfavorable language as the two examples I've just given, but I've seen these exact clauses in other commercial contracts. If you run into an unfavorable attorneys' fees clause, ask that this clause be removed. Some publishers may agree to remove it, as litigation under these contracts is not common. If the publisher refuses, then it's time to find another publisher. Reluctance to change this clause indicates that the company will use it as a way to prevent even legitimate author claims from being brought. If you have to pay the publisher's legal fees regardless of the outcome, you lose either way. An inequitable attorneys' fees clause makes it financially difficult, if not impossible, for you to pursue legitimate claims against a publisher. To me, that is unacceptable.

Entire Agreement

This Agreement constitutes the entire agreement between the publisher and the author with respect to the subject matter hereof and supersedes all prior written or oral agreements made by the parties. This agreement may not be modified or amended except in writing and signed by both parties.

Virtually every commercial contract I've seen includes this standard clause, and I've never drafted a contract without including it. Look for this clause as a separate section entitled "Entire Agreement" or as part of the "General Provisions" clause. These clauses mean that only terms included in the contract count. Nothing said or written prior to the execution of the contract is valid or enforceable.

If you received an email from the publisher telling you that the royalty is 50 percent of the retail price of your book, and the contract you later sign states a royalty of 30 percent of the net, the prior written communication by the publisher is meaningless. If you could show that the email was an inducement to get you to sign the contract and that it was fraudulent, you might be able to get out of the contract—maybe. But how far are you willing to go and how much money are you willing to spend to compensate for not reading and understanding the contract?

Read the following language continually until it is branded in your brain: Carefully read the contract and make sure it is complete. It must include every promise and representation by the publisher, whether oral or written, based on your review of the publisher's website and any other relevant information.

If you believe that the written contract is incomplete or different than what you understood it to be, *do not sign the contract until you are absolutely satisfied with the written terms!*

General Provisions/Miscellaneous

Often, the governing law, venue, attorneys' fees, and entire agreement clauses may all be part of the "General Provisions" or "Miscellaneous" provisions. Here are three additional clauses typically found in these contract provisions:

1. *Author may not assign this Agreement or any rights or obligations hereunder, by operation of law or any other manner, without the publisher's prior written consent, such consent which will not be unreasonably withheld.*

This language prevents you from transferring your rights under the contract without the publisher's permission. However, the publisher can't unreasonably refuse permission if you request to assign your rights. For example, if you're assigning your rights to the new corporation you formed, or to your spouse, the publisher should agree to your request. If you assign your rights to another publisher, you'll probably encounter resistance.

2. *If any term or provision of this Agreement is illegal or unenforceable, this Agreement shall remain in full force and effect and such term or provision shall be deemed deleted or curtailed only to such extent as is necessary to make it legal or enforceable.*

If a court finds a portion of the contract illegal and unenforceable, the rest of the contract remains valid. The problematic term will need to be deleted or rewritten to make it comply with the law.

3. *No modification, amendment, or waiver shall be valid or binding unless made in writing and signed by all parties hereto.*

I've already covered this, but it bears repeating. If you and the publisher orally agree to change your royalty percentage, the agreement will carry no weight and remain meaningless until it is put in writing and made an addendum (addition) to the original publishing contract. Both you and the publisher must sign the new agreement.

A few final thoughts on these publishing contracts: Don't expect much flexibility from publishers when it comes to changing minor provisions of the contract. If there are one or two major points you want revised, suggest it. If your issues are mostly semantic, skip it. Even the best publishers aren't going to rewrite a contract just to accommodate you. Having a lawyer review the contract before you sign it is always a good idea. Having that same attorney start negotiating with the publisher is not. In many cases, the lawyer is nitpicking unimportant language just to justify his or her legal fees. Authors who get bogged down in meaningless contract semantics are people publishers want to avoid. If you get a lawyer involved and the process becomes adversarial before you even start, you'll get off on the wrong foot with your publisher. So remember, for major issues (like subsidiary rights), it may be worth making suggestions if you really like everything else about a publisher. For minor issues, if the contract terms bother you, find another publisher.

CHAPTER 7

ANALYZING EACH PUBLISHER'S CONTRACT AND SERVICE

All of the publishers reviewed are given an author-friendly ranking and placed into one of five categories. The categories are:

- Outstanding Self-Publishers
- Pretty Good Self-Publishers
- Publishers Who Are Just Okay
- Publishers to Avoid
- The Worst of the Worst

The factors used to determine a publisher's ranking have evolved. As in previous editions, my assistant and I posed as ordinary authors and contacted each publisher to inquire about the publisher's services. The difference between us (me and my research assistant) and you is that we asked the questions you may not know to ask until after you've read this book. What we found was shocking, especially when we started asking the tough questions about excessive printing markups and demanding justification for the publishers' policies regarding the production files for the author's book.

Some publishers treated us with respect, provided thoughtful answers, and offered professional customer service. Other publishers lied to us about the costs of printing, chastised us for asking the questions we did, and instructed us that we should find another publisher if we wanted the original production files returned to us. Some publishers took weeks to respond to initial inquiries; others didn't respond at all. As you read through the reviews of each publisher, you'll read about our experiences as a prospective author with that publisher.

All of the publishers were asked the same basic questions (which comprise the categories below). Obviously, based on the answers, we veered off onto different lines of questioning.

How is the Retail Price of an Author's Book Determined?

The average reader who peruses Amazon.com and finds a novel by an unfamiliar author will probably not spend $22.00 for it. People who argue otherwise live in a fantasy world. Who is going to spend $22.00 on your book (other than your friends or family) when Patricia Cornwall's latest thriller costs only $7.99? The reason so many books published by self-publishing companies have retail prices that are out of line with the market is that those prices include steep printing markups and fat publisher royalties. It's my goal to uncover these ploys.

What Does the Author Pay for Copies of His Book?

The price the author pays for printed copies of his own book is another biggie. Aggressive marketing of your book is essential to its overall success. You will need sales avenues besides any provided by your publisher. In order to actually make money selling your book on your own, you need to be able to purchase it at a reasonable price. Companies that allow you to purchase books at no more than a 15 percent markup of the actual print cost score high in this book (although there aren't many). Some publishers double or triple the printing costs, one reason so many authors fail to make any money self-publishing. Few things irk me more than a publisher who charges a ton of money up front and then gouges the author again when she purchases copies of her book. Since almost all publishers pay about the same amount of money to print books digitally, you will be amazed at how some charge so much more than others for copies.

Do You Allow Bookstore Returns?

Authors can successfully sell books through personal appearances, their websites, and Amazon.com and other online retailers. Most self-publishing companies critiqued in this book don't have distribution that will ever result in a bookstore actually ordering books, except in situations where the author arranges for it or where someone asks the store to order them a copy. However, you have even less of a chance of getting into bookstores if your publisher won't accept bookstore returns. You must find a publisher that accepts returns from bookstores. Some publishers include bookstore returns as part of their packages and others charge for returnability. Somewhere between $200 and $400 is reasonable for this service. Anything more than that is not reasonable.

What Is the Level of Author Support?

You, as the author, are a customer of the publisher. You pay them money for a service—to publish your work—and, as a customer, you should be able to call them with questions. Your book is a personal and important achievement. You're entitled to talk to the people you've entrusted it to, not a customer service rep in the Philippines who knows little about your book.

Is the Contract Author-Friendly?

Author-friendly publishing agreements contain most (or all) of these provisions:

- Authors grant only print and electronic rights, on a nonexclusive basis, which are terminable at any time or for an exclusive term that is terminable at any time or extends for less than one year.
- The publisher doesn't retain a right of first refusal or other such option on any future books, and the publisher doesn't require payment from the author in the event the author signs with a bigger publisher or sells television or movie rights.
- Authors can terminate the contract easily and with no further obligation.

- Upon termination by the author, the publisher only maintains a limited nonexclusive right to sell any of the author's remaining books the publisher has already printed.
- Upon termination, the author receives original production files containing the book's cover art, layout, design, and more—all of the products the author has paid for.
- Calculation of royalty amounts is based on a percentage of the retail price of the author's book, or if based on a percentage of the net price, the calculation is clear and not subject to padding.
- The author's book is priced competitively.
- The author is allowed to purchase his or her books for no more than 15 percent more than the actual printing costs.
- There is no requirement that the author pay the publisher's attorneys' fees in the event of a dispute, except for defamation or the author's misrepresentation as to ownership of rights. Clauses that require the non-prevailing party in a lawsuit to pay the prevailing party's legal fees are equitable.

Based on these factors and a few intangibles, such as how fast the publishers responded to our emails, their sales techniques (some are pure shakedown artists), and the overall truthfulness of their websites and sales materials, I grouped the publishers into one of five categories. For easy reference, I've listed publishers alphabetically within each category. The order is not a ranking within that particular section.

One important thing to note while reading through the publisher descriptions in chapters 8–12 is that the publishing packages and services change periodically and, depending on when you are reading this book, may not be exactly as described here. Some of the URLs noted in the sections may also have changed. The contract terms, price authors pay for books, and royalty amounts often remain the same despite changes in services and pricing. These three things are more important than any price increase or alteration of publishing packages and services.

Remember, the offerings of each publisher may have changed since this review. These reviews are a snapshot in time (spring/summer 2010), in terms of the publishing packages and services. Contact any publisher for updated information on any products or services they sell.

CHAPTER 8

OUTSTANDING SELF-PUBLISHERS

The publishers in this category are simply the best in the business. These companies are the most dedicated to providing the author with a great publishing experience. Not every publisher here possesses every ideal quality; some mark up printing costs more than I think is reasonable, but then they provide a lower-priced publishing package. Overall, you won't go wrong with any publisher listed in this category. My ranking of these companies does not guarantee that your experience with them will be wonderful, as every publisher has authors who are disgruntled for one reason or another. But, my ranking does guarantee that you will get a fair deal at a fair price, that you will retain all of your rights, and that you won't sign a contract that contains questionable clauses.

Understand that not every publisher in this section is right for every writer, but there is a publisher here for just about everyone. Both the most expensive and one of the least expensive self-publishing companies made this list. All these companies share a proven commitment to author-friendly policies. Five of the "Outstanding" publishers, after speaking with me, modified their contracts to make them more author-friendly. They all get it. It's about understanding writers.

AVENTINE PRESS

http://www.aventinepress.com

FORMAT OF BOOKS: Paperback and hardcover

GENRES ACCEPTED: All

PUBLISHING FEES: Aventine's $399 Basic Service Package, found at http://www.aventinepress.com/services.html, includes:

- Choice of covers:
  - Author supplies design
  - For an extra $175, a template-based cover, for which the author supplies art or images
  - For an extra $295, a custom cover, which includes consultation with the designer and choice of two designs (after you approve, any changes will cost $50 per hour)
- Choice of interior style templates
- ISBN
- Author's bio, photo, and cover photos or graphics; supplied by author
- Indexing, up to twenty-five words
- Electronic galley proof: Includes only minor changes that do not affect the layout (substantive changes are billed at $50 an hour)
- UPC bar code
- Two copies of the book
- Listing with online booksellers, including Amazon.com and BarnesandNoble.com
- Book and cover art production files on a CD
- Submission to Ingram's ipage database

OTHER SERVICES OF INTEREST: Custom cover design, image scanning, editing, and other services can be viewed at http://www.aventinepress.com/services.html.

Aventine Press Marketing Program: This service, which costs $995 and is detailed at http://www.aventinepress.com/market.html, includes:

- Website: Six pages, non-template design, domain name, and a year of hosting (after which hosting is $50 per year and any updates are $75 per hour). The website can be purchased on its own for $800. See a sample at http://www.notamachine.org/.

- Ingram Advance Catalog listing
- Professionally drafted press release
- Library of Congress Control Number (LCCN)
- U.S. Copyright Office registration

RETURN OF DIGITAL COVER AND INTERIOR FILES: Authors are given a copy of the digital cover and interior production files as part of their package.

RETAIL PRICE OF AUTHOR'S BOOK:

Page Count	Retail Price
108–200	$10.95–$12.95
204–300	$13.95–$16.95
304–400	$17.95–$20.95
404–500	$21.95–$23.95

PRICE AUTHOR PAYS FOR BOOKS: The author's price is based on the cost to produce the book ($0.015 per page plus $0.90 per paperback cover or $7.55 per hardcover) plus 10 percent. So, a 200-page paperback would cost:

$0.015	Per-page production cost
x 200	Page count
+$0.90	Cover fee
+$0.39	Aventine markup (10%)
$4.29	Author price per book

ROYALTIES PAID TO AUTHOR: All of Aventine's books are sold through a third-party source, such as Amazon.com. The publisher pays authors 80 percent of the "net amount"—the retail price of the book less the trade discount and actual cost to print a single copy—received from each book sale. A sale on a 200-page book will look like this:

$12.95 Retail price
–$7.12 Amazon.com discount (50%)
–$3.90 Printing cost
$1.93 Net profit
x 0.80 Author royalty percentage
$1.54 Author royalty

Although this isn't much of a royalty, Aventine isn't getting rich taking what's left over (thirty-nine cents). A royalty ratio that favors the author is highly unusual in self-publishing.

NOTABLE PROVISIONS OF THE PUBLISHING AGREEMENT: The contract, which is straightforward, is available at http://www.aventinepress.com/pub_agree.html.

The "Warranties" section is standard and reasonable.

"The Rights to Your Work" makes it clear that the publisher claims no right to the author's work. The author also acknowledges that the publisher has no responsibility to correct or review the work prior to publication.

"Indemnities" says that, if warranties made by the author are false, the author is financially liable for any losses sustained by the publisher as a result of a lawsuit, including legal fees. This is fair. If an author lies about ownership of the work or even assumes she can use some material without checking to see if it's copyrighted, and the publisher is sued by the actual owner because of it, the author should have to pay the publisher's legal fees.

"Terms and Exclusivity" is as author-friendly as it gets: the agreement is nonexclusive, so the author can enter into other publishing agreements. This section also describes the publishing fee portion, which will be refunded to the author under specific circumstances.

"Complete Agreement" voids any and all promises made prior to the signing of the contract that fail to appear in the contract.

The "Law and Venue" section of the contract requires arbitration for any issues that arise under the contract (e.g., all monetary disputes). However, the clause doesn't preclude a court action instead of arbitration when the issue involves intellectual property (e.g., unauthorized use of an author's material by the publisher). The arbitration clause doesn't require that the arbitration be held in California. This evens the playing field when a dispute arises, since an author won't have to travel to California to arbitrate. When a contract doesn't state where arbitration must occur, it can be done either by phone or somewhere convenient to both parties.

AUTHOR-FRIENDLY RATING: Aventine is one of the few self-publishing companies that doesn't gouge authors on printing fees and royalties. In fact, the 10 percent markup on print costs is one of the lowest in the industry. The only downside to Aventine is that it doesn't have an online method for authors who wish to make direct-to-customer sales (either through Aventine or some kind of link from the author's website to any site other than an online retailer, who takes a large trade discount). An author could only sell books directly if he purchased copies of his own book and sold it himself. So, while the 80 percent royalty is great, by the time the trade discount and printing costs come out, there isn't much left. However, this deficiency *isn't* enough to keep Aventine from being a great company. If you choose Aventine, make sure you have a way to sell books directly.

The $995 marketing package is good, but it's not really a marketing program. A six-page website isn't robust enough to ever get a lot of traffic on its own. But, the sites the company creates are nice—not worth $1,000, but nice. A press release without anywhere to send it isn't worth much. Overall, the marketing package won't even get you close to where you need to be marketing-wise, but you'll get a nice site out of it.

Aventine is doing things the right way and is worth your consideration.

BOOKLOCKER

http://publishing.booklocker.com

FORMAT OF BOOKS: Ebook, paperback, and hardcover

GENRES ACCEPTED: BookLocker accepts all genres of nonfiction and fiction. The publisher does not select all submissions for publication, because the bulk of its money comes from selling books.

PUBLISHING FEES: BookLocker offers two publishing packages, one for black-and-white (http://publishing.booklocker.com/glance.html), and another for color. The latter will not be discussed here, but can be found at http://publishing.booklocker.com/booklocker-color-pod-program/.

Black-and-White Interior: This package is priced at $317 ($299 setup fee, plus $18 first annual print-on-demand file hosting fee). Authors must provide their own cover or purchase cover art from BookLocker, either custom-designed or template-based. For a paperback book, a template-based cover design costs $150, and a custom cover $200. BookLocker graphic artists work with authors to come up with cover ideas, if the author is paying for a custom design. Authors may provide images but are not required to do so. Minor changes are included in the price (i.e., font, color, copy), but if an author requires a full redesign of the cover, he or she will have to repay the cover fee. This package also includes:

- Interior formatting, including graphics, charts, and photos
- Choice of trim size:
  5.5" x 8.5"
  6" x 9"
  8.25" x 11"
- Distribution through Ingram
- Listing with online booksellers: BarnesandNoble.com, Amazon.com, and others
- Free ebook version
- Printed physical proof: There are additional charges if you make changes ($99.50 after the electronic proof has been finalized, and $149 after the finalized PDF has been sent to the printer)
- ISBN (You can use your own, if you wish)
- Bar code
- Author blog (For an example, see http://travel.booklocker.com)
- Option to print in hardcover for an additional $300 with a custom cover or $250 with a template-based cover
- Option to list in the Ingram catalog, a one-time group print ad, for a $70 fee

RETURN OF DIGITAL COVER AND INTERIOR FILES: BookLocker says on its website that departing authors will be given copies of their digital interior and cover production files at no charge—a rarity in the self-publishing business. When I asked whether the returned cover file would be a flat PDF or a layered PDF, the publisher's representative replied: "If the designer uses an image from a firm that prohibits us from distributing the artwork as an individual item, we can only provide the author with a flat cover file. If the author provides us with the artwork and/or the artwork comes from a place that allows us to redistribute it individually, we can provide the author with the layered file."

This makes sense.

RETAIL PRICE OF AUTHOR'S BOOK: Authors have the option to set the retail price of their books, provided they are at or above BookLocker's minimum price, based on the length of the book.

Page Count	**Retail Price**
Up to 108	$11.95
109–150	$12.95
151–200	$13.95
201–250	$14.95
251–300	$15.95
301–350	$16.95
351–400	$17.95

PRICE AUTHOR PAYS FOR BOOKS: BookLocker's author discount is 35 percent off the list price for purchases of up to twenty-four books; larger quantities garner higher discounts, determined by the size of the book. An example of the author discount can be found at https://secure.booklocker.com/booklocker/book/AuthorDiscounts010108.pdf.

For a 200-page paperback at the minimum list price, the numbers would run like this:

Quantity	Discount	Author Price	Markup
1–24	35%	$9.07	133%
25–49	35%	$8.82	126%
50–74	40%	$8.57	120%
75–99	45%	$8.17	110%
100–149	50%	$7.27	86%
150–499	55%	$7.07	81%
500–999	60%	$6.82	76%
1,000+	65%	$6.42	157%*

For large print runs, I am assuming BookLocker prints the books offset, which is much cheaper than print-on-demand—hence the asterisk (*). If you went to any online book printer you could get one thousand copies of the mythical 6" x 9", 200-page paperback for around $2.50 per copy; however, offset pricing can vary a lot. So again, the printing markups for the big runs are estimates only.

These markups are huge. But, the reasons BookLocker remains one of the best companies are (1) it tells you that it is not the company for you if you're planning on selling in stores due to the fact that printing costs are greater in print-on-demand (http://publishing.booklocker.com/reasons-not-to-use-us/), and (2) its initial setup fees are so low.

ROYALTIES PAID TO AUTHOR: BookLocker's royalties are paid on the book's retail price. For ebooks, royalties are 70 percent for those that retail for $8.95 or higher and 50 percent for those that retail for less than $8.95. For paperback or hardcover, royalties are 35 percent for those sold through BookLocker's online bookstore and 15 percent for those sold through Amazon.com or another third party. Details can be found at http://publishing.booklocker.com/pod-and-ebook-faq/questions-about-print-on-demand-publishing/.

If a 200-page paperback book retails for $13.95, your royalties on a book sold through Amazon.com would look like this:

$13.95 Retail price
x 0.15 Author royalty percentage
$2.09 Author royalty

On that same sale, BookLocker takes:

$13.95 Retail price
–$4.19 Amazon.com discount (30%)
–$3.90 Printing cost
–$2.09 Author royalty
$3.77 BookLocker profit

For sales on BookLocker's website for that same book, the breakdown is as follows:

$13.95 Retail price
x 0.35 Author royalty percentage
$4.88 Author royalty

BookLocker makes $5.17 (after printing costs) on each sale of this book through its site.

NOTABLE PROVISIONS OF THE PUBLISHING AGREEMENT: BookLocker's author agreement can be found at http://publishing.booklocker.com/contract.txt.

Section 1 makes it clear that the contract is nonexclusive.

Section 2 states that the author can terminate, via email, his or her relationship with BookLocker at any time, for any reason, effective immediately. It also requires the author to terminate the contract with BookLocker prior to entering into another contract (fifth paragraph). Later, the contract states that there will be a 25 percent cancellation fee after files have been transferred.

Section 4 states that the publisher will review book sales annually, and if the author's book is not selling at a rate of at least five copies per month, the company reserves the right to remove the work and terminate the contract.

Section 6 sets forth publishing fee information. Section 6 details a 25 percent cancellation fee if an author cancels after signup, but before any formatting has been done. This is reasonable. Publishing companies do a lot of work on the front end. Paragraph 6 states that only the author has final approval of the work. If publisher mistakes are discovered after the author has approved the work, the author will be charged a $199 change fee. If the author is at fault for the mistakes, the publisher will charge a new setup fee ($299) for corrections. Either way you are going to get charged, so make sure you review the proof carefully before approving it.

Section 7 provides pricing guide information for hardcover and paperback books. The last paragraph in Section 7 confirms that the author is free to sell the book on his own. However, as long as you are under contract with BookLocker you agree to not sell the ebook for a lower price than BookLocker.

Section 8 discusses royalty payments and states that the author can monitor sales and royalties online. Authors receive monthly royalty payments, provided that they are owed at least $20. (Royalties of less than $20 will be rolled over to the following month until the total amount owed reaches $20.)

Section 11 discusses promotional activity of the authors, stating that authors who use spam messages—defined primarily as an unsolicited email sent en masse—to promote their books will no longer be eligible to sell books through BookLocker and will lose their contracts.

Section 18 states that any lawsuit against BookLocker must be brought in Bangor, Maine, and the forum will be binding arbitration.

AUTHOR-FRIENDLY RATING: What makes BookLocker a great company is that it tells you right up front exactly what you will and will not get. The printing markups are really high and the royalties a bit low. If you believe you will sell thousands of books each year, BookLocker's model won't be profitable. But, if you think you have something to say and want a small financial commitment up front, then BookLocker is perfect for you. I love BookLocker because it is an honest and genuine company. It even tells you the reasons not to use it.

The contract details what will happen and what you can expect from the company. The contract is simple, straightforward, and honest.

BookLocker is a no-frills publisher. It's all POD, all titles are only listed with one wholesaler, and available trim sizes are limited. For many first-timers, this is perfect. One downside to the no-frills approach is that BookLocker only communicates with authors via email. New authors have tons of questions, and the process can be confusing. Not being able to talk to someone would be hard for me as a newbie. But, to its credit, BookLocker tells you up front that if you can't handle only email communication, you need to find another publisher.

The publishing agreement is easily terminated at any time, and you can take the bulk of your production files with you, without charge.

I know that this publisher is selective, but I'm not sure that matters so much these days unless the publisher has wider distribution or is spending its own money to promote books, neither of which BookLocker has or does. It's nice for authors to feel that their books were accepted on grounds more selective than their checks clearing; but at the same time, don't let the exclusiveness lull you into thinking you'll have a leg up. You won't. The book-buying public has no idea who BookLocker is or that it publishes selectively.

However, BookLocker remains a solid choice, especially for the author who wants to dip a toe into the publishing pond. You'll get fair treatment, and the prices are reasonable (except for the printing markups). The policy of only communicating with authors through email could be problematic for first-time authors, as this is a business that sometimes requires more than just email communication. But, you have to accept that going in. It's the one downside to their model. If your book starts selling well, you may want to seek out other publishing alternatives that offer higher royalties and smaller printing markups. There are always tradeoffs. In this case you trade a larger royalty percentage and better printing prices for working with a company that is over-the-top ethical and cares about its authors.

BOOKPROS
http://www.bookpros.com

FORMAT OF BOOKS: Paperback and hardcover

GENRES ACCEPTED: BookPros states that it only accepts a certain percentage of submitted manuscripts, although it receives hundreds of inquiries a month. The low acceptance percentage, BookPros says, is due to the nature of their publishing program, the cornerstone of which is traditional book PR campaigns and distribution. Most submissions aren't accepted because their PR hooks aren't strong enough. The company accepts all genres of books, with the exception of poetry and romance. In order to help determine a book's PR potential, BookPros conducts a free analysis of each title submitted for consideration (http://www.bookpros.com/bp2006/divbp/free_book_analysis.php).

PUBLISHING FEES: BookPros has three publishing imprints: Bridgeway Books, Synergy Books, and Ovation Books. The fees range from around $13,000 to publish under the Bridgeway Books imprint, to as much as $35,000 for the top-tier Ovation Books imprint. BookPros does not offer set package prices; instead, the previously mentioned "media analysis" is conducted to determine what level of services an author's book would require based on its media and distribution potential. These individual services are charged as line items and presented to the author as a custom package. Services are not available on an à la carte basis.

Bridgeway Books: The base price for this package (http://www.bookpros.com/bridgeway) is $4,950, plus mandatory additional fees; the total price typically ranges from $13,000 to $16,000, plus the cost of printing a minimum of five hundred books. The base package includes, but is not limited to, the following services:

- U.S. Copyright Office registration in the author's name
- ISBN
- Bookland EAN bar code
- Library of Congress Control Number (LCCN)

- R.R. Bowker's Books In Print registration
- National direct wholesale distribution through Ingram Book Group and Baker & Taylor, including listing in catalogs
- Listing in BookPros' catalog, distributed at BookExpo America and mailed to bookstores around the U.S.
- Listing and monitoring of your book with online booksellers (Amazon.com and BarnesAndNoble.com)
- Submission of book to Amazon Search Inside! and Google Books
- BookPros' management of stock and inventory of book, which includes management of the author's book at a third-party warehouse and transfers to author, company, and distributor (author pays fees associated with shipping and handling)
- Monthly sales and activity reporting via emailed reports to authors
- Guidelines for successful book signings and a list of the best bookstores for events
- Sell sheet: An illustrative sheet designed to sell an author's book, for use by the author in scheduling book events. (For Synergy Books and Ovation Books titles, the sell sheets will also be used by the distributor's sales force when pitching the book to buyers.)

In addition to the base fee, there are additional fees an author must pay to publish under the Bridgeway imprint. As indicated previously, the total package costs between $13,000 and $16,000, not including printing. The following services, subject to additional fees, may be required:

- Editing: At minimum for Bridgeway titles, a professional copyedit is required, and includes correcting grammar, syntax, spelling, and content. Additionally, BookPros offers professional full edits that include a copyedit as well as critical analysis of plot development, character, flow, and consistency. Copyediting is priced on a sliding scale from $0.034 to $0.021 per word based on the total number of words (higher word count decreases the cost per word). Full edits are priced on a sliding scale from $0.056 to $0.035 per word, also depending on word count.

- Layout: Includes manual formatting of the book, with up to one chapter and three sections per every ten pages, as well as title page, dedications, table of contents, drop caps, and so on.
- Cover design: Pricing includes custom design of the book's front, rear, and spine; drafting back cover text and author bio; two reviews of the design; one optional stock photo; and the development of up to two additional design files for special cover enhancements. Cover design price for Bridgeway titles is $1,995. (For Synergy titles the price is $2,495; for Ovation titles the price is $2,895.)
- Print method: Digital or offset, depending on the quantity—inventory will be stocked in a third-party warehouse.
- Custom website: A website is created that mirrors the aesthetic design of your book. This website consists of seven unique pages: a home page with embedded blog, about the author/about the book, book excerpt, purchase page with shopping cart, media, events, and contact information.
- Personalized marketing services: Includes a copy of BookPros' Literary Marketing Guide, pre-release contact of targeted bookstores, a list of local bookstores (in author's area) with full contact information for the author's use, marketing training via webinar, and a marketing strategy created by BookPros with input from Phenix & Phenix.
- Professional book publicity campaign: BookPros uses Phenix & Phenix Literary Publicists (http://www.phenixpublicity.com), its corporate partner. Services vary depending on book and campaign length but basically include strategic planning; a media campaign including television, daily newspapers, radio, print and online; creation of press materials; and detailed reporting. Bridgeway Books offers a six-week local and online media campaign for $3,495 (plus any associated postage).

Synergy Books: The base price for this package (http://www.bookpros.com/synergy) is $6,950; the total price typically ranges from $19,000 to $24,000, plus the cost of printing a minimum of

1,500 books. This package includes everything in the Bridgeway Books package, plus:

- Cataloging-in-Publication (CIP) registration
- Direct distribution in the U.S. and Canada through Midpoint Trade Books
- Publicity and marketing updates to distributor
- Print method: Offset—requires minimum run of 1,500
- Publicity campaign: Includes media training and pre-publication mail-outs when applicable; minimum of nine weeks for $6,950 (plus any associated postage, galley book fees, etc.)

Ovation Books: The base price for this package (http://www.bookpros.com/ovation) is $7,950; the total price typically ranges from $25,000 to $35,000, plus the cost of printing a minimum of 2,500 books. According to the literature, BookPros only offers this imprint to five to ten titles per year and is extremely selective in determining the titles that qualify for it. The package includes everything in the Synergy Books imprint (but with a different distribution program), plus:

- National distribution through National Book Network, Inc.
- International distribution opportunities in Canada, Australia, and New Zealand through National Book Network, Inc.
- Print method: Offset—requires minimum run of 2,500
- Publicity campaign: Minimum of three to four months; fees range from $3,000 to $3,500 per month (plus any associated postage, galley book fees, etc.)

RETURN OF DIGITAL COVER AND INTERIOR FILES: Per BookPros' contract, should an author decide to leave BookPros, he or she will be entitled to take all of the book's artwork and production files without further fee.

RETAIL PRICE OF AUTHOR'S BOOK: BookPros works with authors to set a retail price. For example, a visit to the Bridgeway Books website found books between 215 and 228 pages ranging from $13.95 to $16.95.

PRICE AUTHOR PAYS FOR BOOKS: BookPros manages the printing process for each author. Although book printing prices are not listed on the website, BookPros requires printing larger runs of books, from 500 to 2,500 copies. BookPros does not print the books; they act as a "print broker" and take competitive bids from a wide range of printers both in the U.S. and abroad.

Since you are paying all of the setup fees and printing costs, BookPros does not require you to work with one of its printers; however, if you choose your own printer, the publisher will require you to present it with three samples of the printer's work, and reserves the right to reject the printer's services. If they approve your printer, you will have to manage the printing process yourself, from start to finish, including shipping and customs clearance if your printer is outside the U.S. Whether you print small digital runs or offset through BookPros, the printing markup is harder to quantify, as pricing for larger print runs can vary. However, Bookpros provided a cost of $3.50 per unit for 1,500 books of a 200-page, 6" x 9", standard paperback. Average pricing for this type of print run directly from a printer is about $2.30 per unit. Based on this single example, the printing markup is 52 percent.

ROYALTIES PAID TO AUTHOR: BookPros does not take a royalty. Authors receive 100 percent of the amount paid by the distributor. Unless the author is selling the book through his own website or directly to the consumer, author payments from the distributor are as follows: a Bridgeway Books author will make 45 percent of the retail price, a Synergy Books author will make 40 percent of the retail price, and an Ovation Books author will make roughly 38 percent of the retail price, depending on the wholesale discount offered by the distributor. It's harder with this company to figure out exactly how much the author's profit will be on each book because there is no way to know exactly what the author paid for printing. The book printing cost of $0.015 per page and $0.90 per cover, which is often quoted in this book, does not apply here. The majority of books published by BookPros are printed offset and are therefore individually cheaper to print.

Let's say you publish under Bridgeway Books, and your publishing package total is $14,000 (the cost to edit, design, publish, and publicize your book). Assume also that the book will retail for $15.95, and the cost to print 1,500 copies of your book offset turns out to be $3.50 per book. So your total cost for printing is $5,250.

Your royalty per book is 45 percent of the retail price, which comes to $7.18. If you subtract the printing cost ($3.50) from this royalty, you have a net of $3.68 per book.

If you were to sell all 1,500 books through retailers, you would receive:

1,500 Books
x $3.68 Net author royalty per book
$5,520 Net profit

You invested $14,000 for the initial package. If you sell all 1,500 books you recoup $5,520, but *you still have another $8,480 to go before you've paid off your investment.* Obviously, retail sales are not the best way to make your money back. So let's look at a different scenario that includes direct selling in addition to retail sales. To recoup your investment faster, you will need to figure out a way to engage in direct selling. When you sell the book directly (i.e., "back of the room" sales at an event or through your website), you make the full margin between what you sell it for and what it costs to print, because there is no retailer or distributor to take a cut. So, in this case:

$15.95 Retail price
–$3.50 Printing cost
$12.45 Net author royalty

Let's say you plan to sell 40 percent of your inventory through retail outlets and 60 percent direct. Of your 1,500 books, that's 600 for retail and 900 for direct.

For the retail sales, you would make:

600	Books
x $3.68	Net author royalty per book
$2,208	Total net author royalty for retail sales

For direct sales, you would make:

900	Books
x $12.45	Net author royalty per book
$11,205	Net author royalty for direct sales

Your total net sales would be:

$2,208	Net royalty for retail sales
+$11,205	Net royalty for direct sales
$13,413	Total net sales

This gets you closer to recouping your initial $14,000 investment, but you are still $587 in the hole—and keep in mind that these scenarios do not take into account miscellaneous shipping or storage fees. Also, you can't just assume that you'll sell 1,500 books quickly. It could take you months or even years to sell your entire inventory—or you may never sell it. On the other hand, if your book takes off through publicity and marketing, you may sell your entire inventory within a matter of weeks. There's no way to predict whether or not a book will be successful.

NOTABLE PROVISIONS OF THE PUBLISHING AGREEMENT: The contract isn't available online; you'll only receive one if your book is accepted. I do not like that you cannot see a contract prior to submitting your book. However, because I have worked with the publisher in the past, it sent a contract to me.

The contracts for the imprints are similar, but there are some differences, mostly in the media sections. This review only covers the company's Bridgeway contract.

The biggest problem with the contract is that it contains no timelines for any part of the publishing process. There is no time period set forth as to how long it takes to edit your book, format the interior layout, design the cover, create your website, and so on. BookPros certainly provides the services it says it will, but when you have a contract with no deadlines, you are at a slight disadvantage when it comes to knowing when aspects of your book's production and publication will be completed.

The first five sections spell out the services BookPros provides and the prices of each service. If you are unclear about any of the services or prices, you should request clarification.

Subsection 5.11.10 states that the author is responsible for all shipping and postage fees incurred during the publicity campaign up to a cap of $500, after which the publisher must seek permission from the author before spending more. The author will be invoiced for fees and has fifteen days from the invoice date to pay the invoice.

Section 6.1 states the minimum number of books the author must print. Subsections of 6.1 state that the author is not required to use the publisher's printer, but any other printer they use must provide three sample books and is subject to the publisher's approval. Further, the publisher will not manage print jobs if the author uses his own printer — so you'll be on your own.

Printer payments are also outlined in Subsection 6.1.1, which states that the author will receive a price quote (including printing costs and shipping and handling fees), and that the author must pay 50 percent of the quoted price within fifteen days of receipt. The rest of the payment is due ten days from the author's notification that the book is ready to print.

Sections 6.2 and 6.3 cover off-site storage (not to exceed $100 per month per every 2,500 books) and annual service fees ($250).

Section 7 addresses expenses associated with additional services requested by the author that are not outlined in the contract—such as last-minute additions of images or indexing—stating that the publisher must inform the client of expenses associated with these services.

Section 8 deals with accounting and payments to the author. Since each imprint has a different distribution arrangement, the amount that you make for retail sales varies, but the Bridgeway Books contract we looked at offered 45 percent of the retail price of the book.

Subsection 8.1.1 also states that the author will be subject to various fees charged by the distributor, which are here undefined, and that the author may ask the publisher to provide definition and documentation of the fees. Payments come from the distributors, and the method of payment is very different from other self-publishing companies. Typically, the distributor pays BookPros about 120 days after the reporting period. Then BookPros pays the authors about fifteen days after that. So, for sales made in January 2011, an author would be paid on or about May 15, 2011.

Section 8.2 deals with accounting and payments.

Subsection 8.2.1 says that returns will be charged against the author's royalty payments and clarifies the payment schedule. Half of the net amount (meaning sales, less any of those undefined fees) will be paid 120 days after the close of each accounting month, with a thirty-day grace period; the remaining half will be paid thirty days later, with the same grace period.

Subsection 8.2.2 says that if the author doesn't make enough money to cover distributor fees, the publisher will carry the negative balance forward, but also has the right to demand payment of the author (due within thirty days of author's receipt of an invoice).

Subsection 8.2.5 says that all returns are charged against the author's royalties, and the distributor will withhold a percentage of royalties as reserve payment for returns. If no returns are made or the reserve is unspent, the money will be returned to the author a year from the date it was pulled for the reserve. The specific percentage isn't stated, but the company tells me it's approximately 15 percent.

Subsection 8.2.7 indicates that the author will be paid monthly, if his or her royalties equal fifty dollars or more; otherwise, payments roll over until the next period.

Section 11 clarifies that you not only own the book's content, but also the layout, the design, and the cover art, which is important. BookPros allows you to take all of the production files with you, so you won't have to recreate the cover art or reformat the interior of the book should you determine to print the book on your own or with another publisher.

Section 12 says that the publisher will provide the author proofs to review changes made in preliminary revisions of the book. The publisher will also provide one opportunity to review the finished layout and edits. After these proofs, there will be a final proof; any changes the author makes after the final proof may be subject to undefined fees. Authors will have five days to review the proof. This is reasonable if you want to keep production of the book moving.

Section 13 says that the author indemnifies the publisher against any claims should the book, allegedly or otherwise, violate someone else's copyright or intellectual property. This is reasonable—you plagiarize, you pay.

Section 15 says that either party can cancel with sixty days' written notice. If BookPros cancels, they will refund all of the monies you paid that have not been spent in the production of the book. If you cancel, you will be refunded *up to* 15 percent of the monies you have paid at the time of cancellation. BookPros says this is because when you sign its contract, the publisher makes "commitments to different vendors and provides a lot of information and expertise to the author that can't really be quantified." Nevertheless, 85 percent of a $25,000 contract is quantifiable: you'll lose at least $21,250 if you cancel your contract after paying the full fees associated with your project. BookPros says that it will consider special cases for terminating the agreement (death, illness, etc.), but this is not included in the agreement, so if you sign up with them be prepared to follow through or pay anyway.

Section 17 states that any arbitration over the agreement is subject to the laws of and must occur in Travis County, Texas. Such a clause is standard.

Section 19 says neither the publisher nor the author is responsible for acts of nature that may hinder the publishing of the author's book (such as a flood, fires, strikes, etc.). Basically, if the printer's offices collapse in an earthquake, the publisher is not responsible for the fact that your book cannot be printed on schedule.

Section 20 states that the entire agreement is contained in the contract and that any amendments must be made in writing and signed by all parties.

AUTHOR FRIENDLY RATING: BookPros is one of the publishers that does not provide a contract or fee schedule to querying authors until it has accepted their book, which is generally a bad sign. In fact, at the beginning of the book, I say that this will often land a publisher in the "Avoid" section of *The Fine Print*. However, because I have worked with BookPros in the past and they were willing to send me a contract to review, I have more information about the company than I would if I were simply an author querying the publisher for information.

BookPros provides a high-quality service with a dedicated staff of people who know the publishing business. Is the BookPros model worth the money? That is something you'll have to decide for yourself. As with any business venture (or investment of any kind, really), if you can't afford to lose the investment, then don't make it. That's true whether you're paying a few thousand dollars or $13,000–$35,000 with BookPros.

Whether you use BookPros or anyone else, the odds are that you will not recoup your publishing investment. You have to get out there and sell a lot of books to make your money back under the BookPros model. Unless you already have a following of some kind, are on the speaking circuit, or have other ways to sell large quantities of books, you have to be prepared to personally get out there and work hard at selling your books. That's not to say you won't have sales through BookPros' distributors, but book sales are not automatic. No matter how good BookPros is, if you're an unknown author, you still have an uphill battle.

The success of any book, especially those from new authors, comes down to the participation of the author. So, you need to be sure that the BookPros model will work for you. If you have second thoughts after you sign the contract and pay, it may be too late. BookPros makes it clear that once you pay and they start working, you are not getting your money back for services they've provided—and that isn't just the stuff you see, like editing and design. Publishing a book requires a lot of background work with distributors and registrations, too. So keep that in mind, and don't sign up with them unless you're serious about seeing the project through to completion.

The BookPros model relies on book distribution and traditional book publicity to make a book sell. Can a $3,000-a-month publicist make your book sell? Every book is different, and even the greatest publicist can't guarantee results. While BookPros' corporate partner, Phenix & Phenix, is a highly respected publicity firm—the company handles publicity for some major publishing houses—whether that experience will pay off for your book is not something you'll be able to measure until you've completed a publicity campaign.

Will BookPros provide a service that is $20,000 better than anyone else in this book? If your book takes off, then yes. However, if your book isn't very successful, you may not think so.

I know the people at BookPros well. They are a professional group of individuals, and the company will provide a publishing experience similar to what you might encounter at a traditional publishing house, with large distribution opportunities and experienced publicists. If you can afford to make the investment, and if you have realistic expectations, you will have a solid publishing experience.

DOG EAR PUBLISHING

http://www.dogearpublishing.net

FORMAT OF BOOKS: Paperback or hardcover

GENRES ACCEPTED: All

PUBLISHING FEES: Dog Ear offers four publishing packages.

Basic Package: Priced at $1,099, this package (http://dogearpublishing.net/pricingbasic.aspx) includes:

- Custom interior and cover design with up to thirty interior images or five tables
- Up to five free paperback books or five hardcover (dependent upon format and page count)
- Book and author webpage in the Dog Ear website that links to a sales page at Amazon.com or author's website

- Book fulfillment
- Registration with all major online booksellers, Ingram, and Baker & Taylor
- R.R. Bowker's Books In Print registration
- ISBN and bar code
- Library of Congress Control Number (LCCN)
- Listing in the Google Books program and other internet search programs

Professional Package: Priced at $1,699, this package (http://dogearpublishing.net/pricingpro.aspx) includes everything in the Basic Package, with the following upgrades and additions:

- Up to thirty interior graphics and ten tables (supplied by the author)
- Marketing and promotional support including:
  - Personalized domain name
  - Custom search-engine-optimized (SEO) website: Dog Ear will manage the site for one year; renewal is $83 each year following. Buyers follow a link to Dog Ear's bookstore, which is managed by Lightning Source, and profits are calculated the same as for Amazon sales. A few examples are http://www.nurturingjourneys.com/, http://www.leighmartinauthor.com/, and http://www.humansolitaire.com/.
  - Email marketing campaign to your database of up to 500 addresses
  - Press release writing and distribution to 250 targeted media outlets
  - Ten posters, 100 postcards and 1,000 business cards

I wouldn't call these five-page websites search engine optimized. An SEO website would have many more pages built around specific terms related to the subject matter of the book and would use much cleaner code. Putting an author's name in the meta tag of the site might make it optimized for that author's name (maybe), but do not believe these sites are optimized. They are not. For what they are, these websites are a good value. However, understand that, at best, this is a "starter" website that on its own won't get you a lot of traffic. You do get your own domain name, and for an additional $175, the publisher will add a shopping cart, so you can sell books and avoid the huge discount taken by Amazon.com. For each sale you make through this fulfillment service, you will pay a 5 percent credit card processing fee (e.g., if a customer buys your book for twenty dollars, including shipping costs, the credit card processing fee is one dollar). Dog Ear also charges the author a two dollar handling fee per order, which is reasonable. This is a good deal for the author and is worth the $175.

The email marketing campaign portion is just sending an email to your existing list of contacts. The press release program is a nice feature, but don't expect big results. (This is not Dog Ear's fault—it's just that media outlets are inundated with press releases for many products daily.)

Professional Plus Package: Priced at $2,199, this package (http://dogearpublishing.net/pricingproplus.aspx) includes everything in the Professional Package, plus:

- Up to fifty interior graphics and ten tables (supplied by the author)
- Submission to Amazon's Search Inside! program, allowing shoppers to look at pages of your book
- Marketing and promotional support, including:
  - Email marketing campaign to your database of up to one thousand addresses
  - Press release writing and distribution to five hundred targeted media outlets
  - Author SEO website: Includes an "Open for Business" shopping cart link, which processes payments directly to the author's bank account. If you can get people to your website and make sales through it, then your profitability will increase. Still, there is a 5 percent credit card processing fee and a two dollar handling fee assessed by Dog Ear. Both are expected and reasonable.

Masterpiece Package: Priced at $3,499, this package (http://dogearpublishing.net/pricingprem.aspx) includes everything in the Professional Package, with the following upgrades and additions:

- Total design customization, including up to one hundred interior graphics and twenty tables (supplied by the author)
- Professional copyediting before the book is formatted for printing (up to 53,000 words)
- Submission for availability on Amazon's Kindle
- A marketing campaign that includes:
  - The same SEO website as in the Professional Plus package
  - Professionally-drafted press release distributed to 1,000 targeted media outlets
  - Ten posters, 250 postcards, and 2,000 business cards
  - A search marketing campaign: Includes up to 250 search terms that promote the book to search engine visitors and directs them to the author's storefront or a specific page on the author's website. This is a nice feature. However, pay-per-click (PPC) campaigns are not very effective for fiction. They can be effective for certain types of nonfiction, especially how-to and reference books. If you plan on having a PPC strategy, you'll have a nice launching pad, but it's something you'll need to learn about and spend time tweaking to achieve any real results.
  - Support materials free to stores that order your book

OTHER SERVICES OF INTEREST:

Expedited Service: For $500, this service, under the Basic or Professional publishing packages, guarantees that your books are delivered to press in thirty business days or less (color books in sixty days or less) from the time that you deliver all materials to Dog Ear. The package only includes one proof, so find a good editor and make sure your manuscript is clean, clean, clean.

Bookstore Returns Service: For $200, this program marks the author's book "returnable" in the Ingram Title Database. This is important because it reduces the risk brick-and-mortar bookstores take by stocking your book and makes them more likely to do so. The administrative fee for this service must be paid annually, and Dog Ear will deduct the cost of returns from your outstanding author net profit balance.

Editing Services (http://dogearpublishing.net/serviceseditorial.aspx): As is now true of many self-publishing companies, Dog Ear offers a soup-to-nuts array of reasonably priced editing services, from a simple proofread to a ghostwriter taking your project from notes to novel.

- **Proofreading:** For $0.015 per word, an editor will address potential issues with grammar, spelling, punctuation, and syntax.
- **Copyediting:** For $0.020 per word, an editor will perform the services provided at the proofreading level, and will also address style, word choice, consistency, and other readability concerns.
- **Literary Editing:** For $0.022 per word, an editor will provide you copyediting services, and will also include an in-depth analysis of your book's development and feedback on character, plot, development, and structure.
- **Literary Critique:** A senior editor gives your manuscript a thorough read and provides constructive criticism, recommendations, and an outline looking at various aspects of your writing style, all with an eye towards getting your book ready for publication. The $250 flat fee is a fair price for this kind of feedback, which you will never get from your best friend or Aunt Sarah.
- **Developmental Editing:** This service, for $0.040 per word, takes your project from outline to manuscript. Dog Ear's website describes its developmental editors as "writing coaches," closely assisting the author with organization and development of the complete manuscript.
- **Ghostwriting:** For a flat fee, determined on a case-by-case basis, a writer will take your rough draft or notes and craft them, with your input, into a manuscript. The fee for an initial writing sample is $199, which can be applied to the fee for the service, if purchased.
- **Proofreading (post-production):** This service, for $0.009 per word, searches the text after it has been put into book form for any editorial or formatting errors. A previous edit is required.
- **Indexing:** An index will make your nonfiction work that much more useful to the reader and is priced at $0.015 per word.

Book Cover Copy: A Dog Ear marketing person will write your back cover copy, author biography, and extended website versions of each for a $99 flat fee.

RETURN OF DIGITAL COVER AND INTERIOR FILES: If you terminate your book contract with Dog Ear, the publisher will return your digital cover and interior files upon request without a fee.

RETAIL PRICE OF AUTHOR'S BOOK: Dog Ear allows authors to set the retail prices for their books, but they recommend that the price is set at least 2.5 times higher than the single-copy print price to allow for bookseller discounts and a reasonable royalty.

As explained in detail in the next section, a 200-page, paperback book costs the author $5.28. Per Dog Ear's suggestion, you should a retail price of at least $13.20.

PRICE AUTHOR PAYS FOR BOOKS: Dog Ear marks up its printing costs, but less than most companies do. For a standard paperback with a full-color cover and black-and-white interior, Dog Ear charges $0.02 per page plus $1.28 per cover for each book it prints, while the actual costs are $0.015 per page plus $0.90 per cover.

When I had my research assistant email to ask about their printing markup, she was scolded: "Our mark-up on printing is proprietary. This is like asking McDonald's how much their Happy Meal really costs." The question was only posed to see their response—I already knew the answer. Since Dog Ear prints through Lightning Source, we know that for the 200-page paperback that Dog Ear charges an author $5.28 to print, the actual cost of printing is $3.90. Even though a 35 percent markup may seem high, it's still one of the lowest printing markups in the industry.

ROYALTIES PAID TO AUTHOR: As noted in the previous section, you make 100 percent of the retail price of the book less printing fees and bookstore discount. If you sell the book on your website, you pay Dog Ear $5.28 to print the book, which means that if you sell it for $13.95, you make $8.67. If you want Dog Ear to handle all book fulfillment, credit card processing, and so on, a $2-per-order fee is added, but you still come out ahead.

If you sell the same book on Amazon, the math looks like this:

$13.95 Retail price
–$7.67 Trade discount
–$5.28 Printing charges
$1.00 Author royalty

On Amazon and most other retail sales, Dog Ear earns $1.38 (the amount of the printing markup) and the author earns $1.00. This isn't a true 100 percent royalty because there is a printing markup built in.

NOTABLE PROVISIONS OF THE PUBLISHING AGREEMENT: Unlike many publishers, Dog Ear's publishing agreement is easily located on its website at http://www.dogearpublishing.net/resourcesauthoragree.aspx.

The contract is simple and straightforward. The simplicity, however, can also be a curse of sorts because important details, such as production schedule, revision rounds, and other issues, are not addressed. If an issue not covered in the contract becomes a problem, it makes resolving that issue a lot trickier. For example, in some of the packages, you get a website and domain name. If you terminate the contract, who owns those? Dog Ear assured me in an email that the author does, but that's not stated in the contract or on the website. I'm a fan of a more robust contract that sets out everything in the publishing process. There are a lot of moving parts, and if you and Dog Ear (or any publisher) disagree on something, you'll wish the contract had addressed the issue.

AUTHOR-FRIENDLY RATING: Dog Ear continues to be one of the best self-publishing companies around. Even though I'm not a fan of marking up printing at all, Dog Ear's markup is still far less than almost everyone else. While the royalties are not totally 100 percent (because the printing markup is included in the "actual" print cost), they are better than most other self-publishing companies.

The company's owners are all book industry veterans. Together, they have a true understanding of the book business and have created a company with an affinity for writers—the website is easy to navigate and informative, and when we emailed the company, we received a personal reply within two business days—without having to fill out a request form or send in a manuscript.

Dog Ear has a solid business model, one that benefits both the company and the author. Dog Ear should be on your list of companies to consider.

INFINITY PUBLISHING

http://www.infinitypublishing.com

FORMAT OF BOOKS: Paperback

GENRES ACCEPTED: All

PUBLISHING FEES: The $499 publishing package (http://www.infinitypublishing.com/book-publishing-services/book-publishing-services.html) includes:

- ISBN
- Bar code
- Custom cover and template-based interior: Includes royalty-free or author-provided artwork and placement of all interior graphs, photos, and illustrations. The graphic artist will design only one cover, and the author has one chance to respond with "reasonable adjustments." After that, the author must pay $50 an hour for further adjustments.
- R.R. Bowker's Books In Print registration
- Listing with online booksellers such as Amazon.com and BarnesandNoble.com
- Book and author webpage on Infinity's online bookstore (http://www.buybooksontheweb.com)
- Three galley proofs—one for the author, one for corrections, and one for the U.S. Copyright Office for copyrighting: Includes up to thirty corrections. Subsequent errors can be corrected for a fee of $50 an hour (this pertains to all typos, including those made by the publisher).

- Choice of trim size:
  5.5" x 8.5"
  8.5" x 11"
  8" x 8"

OTHER SERVICES OF INTEREST: Infinity offers fewer additional services than some publishers, which include:

Photo Scanning: $7 per scan

Copyediting: Includes correction of syntax, grammar, and spelling at $0.013 per word. For more extensive editing, Infinity refers authors to outside editors.

Advanced Reading Copies: For $275, you receive twenty-four advance copies of the book with mailers, labels, and announcement cards.

Marketing Packages (http://www.infinitypublishing.com/additional-book-publishing-services/book-marketing-services.html): Each marketing package (there are four, ranging in price from $125 to $470) includes copies of your book (2–25, depending on package), bookmarks (25–250, depending on package), business cards (100–1000, depending on package), and—with the exception of the $125 package—posters (5–50, depending on package). These packages are best suited for the author who can and is willing to handle all marketing on his own. The marketing packages include two books that contain many book promotion ideas and techniques. This publisher also owns a commercial printing operation, and the pricing on the printed materials seems reasonable, but do you need them? Bookmarks and business cards for your book are fun extras, but I'd spend my money on marketing tools designed to have readers actually find my book.

Extended Distribution Package: For $149, Infinity will distribute your book through Ingram. Books distributed through Ingram will be printed using Lightning Source instead of Infinity's own in-house printing facilities.

RETURN OF DIGITAL COVER AND INTERIOR FILES: The publishing guide I was sent states that Infinity Publishing will provide authors with a print-ready cover file after publication (for a fee of $100). Interior files (if not too large and if in Word format) are emailed upon request at no charge. However, Infinity does not use a standard interior formatting program, most likely all formatting would be lost, putting the author back at square one. When I inquired about this, a representative assured me that for $125 they would send a PDF of the interior; as long as the copyright page is removed, the author is free to do what he wishes with this print-ready file.

RETAIL PRICE OF AUTHOR'S BOOK: Infinity allows authors to set the retail price for nonfiction books as long as it meets or exceeds the publisher's minimum retail price, based on the size of the book. I couldn't find a minimum retail pricing chart on the website, but according to the Infinity representative, the minimum price for a 200-page, 5.5" x 8.5" paperback book is $13.95. On the website, Infinity says: "Please note that these are the suggested prices for books based solely on page count. You may elect to price your book higher and in turn earn a much higher royalty percentage on sales. However, we strongly recommend that you stay within marketplace standards for books similar to yours."

Now, that's good advice. Authors may choose any "value-added" price for their nonfiction book, and any amount over the minimum retail price will receive a royalty of 75 percent of the additional value. Fiction books may not be value-added. For details on how that royalty works, see the section below.

PRICE AUTHOR PAYS FOR BOOKS: Infinity bases the author's discount on the book's minimum retail price; they offer authors a 50 percent discount on their initial order and a 40 percent discount on every order thereafter. To figure out how much the printing markup is, first go to http://www.infinitypublishing.com/book-publishing-services/suggested-book-pricing.html and determine the retail price. For a 200-page, nonfiction paperback with a retail price of $13.95, the math on your first order of books from Infinity looks like this:

$13.95 Minimum retail price
x 0.50 Author discount percentage
$6.98 Author price per book

This is an 80 percent markup. On all subsequent orders for this same book, an author will pay $8.38 per book, which is a 115 percent markup. Infinity prints most of its books in-house, so I'm guessing that its cost is less than the $3.90 per book, as the printing is not subbed out. It's okay for a publisher to mark up printing. Most publishers do it. You have to decide if you can live with 80–114 percent markups.

ROYALTIES PAID TO AUTHOR: Royalties are based on both the minimum retail and the value-added price, which is initially a bit confusing. Here's how it works:

Direct Sales: Infinity pays a 30 percent royalty on retail sales through its online bookstore, http://www.buybooksontheweb.com. So, let's say we have a 200-page book selling for $13.95. The royalty would look like this:

$13.95 Minimum retail price
x 0.30 Author royalty percentage
$4.19 Author royalty without a value-added markup

From this sale, Infinity makes:

$13.95 Minimum retail price
–$4.19 Author royalty
–$3.90 Printing cost
$5.86 Infinity profit

Now, let's say we mark up our 200-page book to $16.95. Infinity pays an additional royalty of 75 percent on the $3 value-added markup:

$3.00 Value-added markup
x 0.75 Author royalty percentage
$2.25 Author royalty on value-added markup
+$4.19 Author royalty on minimum retail price
$6.44 Total author royalty

That's 37 percent of the value-added price of your book, but Infinity makes:

$16.95 Value-added retail price
–$6.44 Total author royalty
–$3.90 Printing cost
$6.61 Total Infinity profit on a value-added book

Indirect Sales: These are sales through wholesalers (like Ingram) or retailers (like Amazon.com). Infinity offers a 15 percent royalty on wholesale sales, less the 40 percent trade discount (55 percent for Ingram and Amazon.com), plus 45 percent of the value-added markup. So for the same book, sold on Amazon.com, the royalty would look like this:

$13.95 Minimum retail price
–$7.67 Trade discount (55%)
x 0.15 Author royalty percentage
$0.94 Author royalty without a value-added markup

On that same sale, Infinity makes:

$13.95 Minimum retail price of book
–$7.67 Wholesale discount (55%)
–$0.94 Author royalty
–$3.90 Printing cost
$1.44 Infinity profit

Again, if we mark up the book to $16.95, the author gets an additional 45 percent:

$3.00	Value-added markup
x 0.45	Author royalty percentage
$1.35	Author royalty on value-added markup
+$0.94	Author royalty on minimum retail price
$2.29	Total author royalty

Meanwhile, Infinity makes:

$16.95	Marked-up retail price of book
–$7.67	Wholesale discount (55%)
–$2.29	Total author royalty
–$3.90	Printing cost
$3.09	Infinity profit on value-added sale

For a complete explanation of the royalty structure, see: http://www.infinitypublishing.com/book-publishing-services/self-publishing-author-royalties .html.

NOTABLE PROVISIONS OF THE PUBLISHING AGREEMENT: The contract can be found at http://www.infinitypublishing.com/book-publishing-agreements/book-publishing-agreements.html.

Paragraphs 7–8a under "Infinity Publishing" state that the publisher agrees to pay the royalty percentages as described in the royalty section of this review. Section 8a of the contract is rather confusing, but basically states that the publisher will base its wholesale royalties on the discounted price (retail price less a 40–55 percent discount) of the book.

Paragraph 6 under "The Author" clearly states that the publisher has no ownership in the work, and that "the author is free to pursue any and all publishing ventures…." You can publish and sell your book anywhere else during the term of the agreement.

Paragraph 10 under "The Author" allows the author to terminate the agreement at any time.

The "General Provisions" paragraph states that the agreement is governed by the Commonwealth of Pennsylvania, USA, which is common. Oddly, the publisher does not state that all arbitration must take place in Pennsylvania, which is uncommon but works in favor of the author. This section also contains the following language: "This written Agreement contains all and is the only Agreement, and supersedes any other agreement, oral, written, or otherwise construed as a prior agreement between the author and IP. This Agreement cannot be appended, changed, modified, word or words added or deleted except by the mutual written agreement of the author and IP; and further, is binding upon the heirs, executors, administrators, and assigns of the author and IP." This provision is standard in almost any business contract. When it comes to getting the original production files back, this clause becomes important. It means that, even if the Infinity representative told you that you could get your original digital files back upon termination, if that promise is not in the contract it doesn't count (and Infinity is under no obligation to give them to you).

AUTHOR-FRIENDLY RATING: The printing markups are high and the royalties low, so why is this company "Outstanding"? While both of these deficiencies are enough to cause most publishers in this book to drop in rank, Infinity stays at the top because its publishing package is one of the lowest-priced at $499, yet still comprehensive. (Even though, if you want the standard distribution that every other self-publishing company offers, you'll have to pay an additional $149.) You are getting a very basic package, but the quality is still high. That's why Infinity is great.

The website could be easier to navigate. The royalty section in particular is very confusing. However, upon request, Infinity mails out a short paperback, *Become a Published Author*. Not only will you benefit from reviewing a sample book, but you will also benefit greatly by having answers and explanations about the publishing process at your fingertips.

Also, Infinity is not an author mill, and its staff is attentive and helpful. As with every publisher in the book, my research assistant or I contacted Infinity just as any other author would. Our emails were all answered the very next day by a friendly and helpful representative. We dealt with the same person most of the time. She either provided us with the answers we needed or pointed us to the relevant page in the paperback publishing guide, every time.

Infinity's pricing structure and royalty model is best suited for writers who don't expect to sell a lot of books, at least initially. The low package price allows you to get into the publishing game with little risk. But, if you sell more than a few hundred books, Infinity's royalty structure is detrimental. Because of the high printing markups and low royalty, if the author sells a lot of books Infinity comes out much further ahead than the author. If sales of your book take off, you'll want to find a better publishing situation—one with lower printing costs and higher royalties. For the author with little money to spend up front, Infinity is a fantastic option.

TATE PUBLISHING

http://www.tatepublishing.com/

FORMAT OF BOOKS: Ebook, audio book, paperback, and hardcover

GENRES ACCEPTED: Tate is a Christian publishing company, but it does not specify that its books need be on Christian topics. Tate accepts most genres, but will not accept books that contain any: obscene or explicit material, unnecessary profanity, vulgarity, or inappropriate or graphic love scenes. Tate does have an extensive "Statement of Belief" that all authors must acknowledge. The Statement is provided along with the publishing contract.

PUBLISHING FEES: Tate is a hybrid of self-publishing and a more traditional publishing model. It doesn't offer publishing packages, but rather asks the author to participate in a partnership. In this partnership between Tate and the author, both parties contribute funds toward the process of getting the book designed, marketed, and distributed.

In most cases, the author is asked to contribute $3,985.50 to the publishing process. Tate promises to contribute $15,700 to $19,700 of its own resources to the book, saying, "We pay for the production, printing and distribution and marketing of the books we publish." Tate's contract provides that if an author sells five thousand copies of her book (or purchases five thousand of her own books), not only will her investment be returned, but her next book will be published for free. However, the author is not required to publish any additional book with Tate.

As part of its publishing services, Tate provides:

- A choice of an audio book, book trailer, website, or social networking site setup (one option is included in the publishing package). The author can pay for any of the others; prices denoted below.
- Audio book ($999, if purchased separately)
- Copyright, LCCN, bar code, and UPC code
- Distribution through Ingram, Spring Arbor, Appalachian, and smaller distributors
- Book sales and availability through 25,000 stores and libraries, including Amazon, Barnes and Noble, Borders, Walmart, and Tate Publishing
- Marketing: A representative told me that the bulk of Tate's $20,000 investment in each author goes toward marketing, which would initially focus on local bookstores and media. A Tate informational email says that the publisher promotes the book through catalogs, online promotion, publicity, and the annual CBA (Christian Booksellers Association) conferences.
- Ten copies of your book
- Editing: copyediting, technical editing, and conceptual editing
- Custom cover design
- Custom interior
- Ebook creation and distribution (through Amazon.com and Tate's website)
- Website design and hosting ($399 if purchased separately): The website is part of the Tate website and not an individual domain and author site.
- Video book trailers ($299 if purchased separately)
- Dedicated marketing representative
- Publicity: Every event and book is promoted to local and national media for the life of the work.
- Distribution: Tate Publishing's books are all 100 percent returnable and warehoused, not simply made available for order or on a list.

RETURN OF DIGITAL COVER AND INTERIOR FILES: A Tate representative told me that, if the author should determine to leave Tate and publish elsewhere, the book's design files would remain with Tate. When I asked if it would be possible to pay a fee for the files, the representative said that I would have to discuss that with the acquisitions editor and that, if it were possible, a clause stating the specific terms and price would have to be added to the contract.

RETAIL PRICE OF AUTHOR'S BOOK: Although pricing seems to vary, while scanning the Tate bookstore, I found a 208-page fiction paperback for $13.95 and a 200-page nonfiction paperback for $15.95. These prices seem in line with the rest of the industry.

PRICE AUTHOR PAYS FOR BOOKS: Authors receive at least a 60 percent discount off the book's retail price. Assume that the author of the 200-page book that retails for $13.95 wants to buy copies. Here is the breakdown:

Quantity	Discount	Author Price	Markup
0–99	60%	$5.58	43%
100–249	70%	$4.19	7%
250–999	75%	$3.49	?
1000–2499	80%	$2.79	86%*

The 48 percent markup is based on 2,000 books at $1.50 per book (a reasonable wholesale cost). Again, on orders this size it's hard to calculate an exact markup given that pricing at different printers can vary widely. As for the price per book for 250–999 copies, $3.49 is quite low. Tate has its own printing facilities for short runs of under 5,000 books per order, so their cost is most likely less than companies who go through Lightning Source—and when an author prints larger quantities, the savings are quite good. Good job, Tate! These prices are good.

ROYALTIES PAID TO AUTHOR: Tate's royalties are based on the retail price of the book. If the book is sold on Tate's website, the author earns 40 percent of the retail price; for third-party and wholesale (e.g., sales on Amazon.com) the author earns 15 percent of the retail price.

So, for a 200-page paperback book sold on Tate's website, the royalty would break down as follows:

$15.95 Retail price of author's book
x 0.40 Author royalty percentage
$6.38 Author royalty

On that same sale, Tate makes $5.70 after printing expenses. For a sale on Amazon.com, that same book would earn you:

$15.95 Retail price of author's book
x 0.15 Author royalty percentage
$2.39 Author royalty

On the Amazon.com sale, Tate makes $1.68. ($15.95 – $7.98 (Amazon .com 50 percent discount) – $3.90 (actual cost to print) – $2.39 (author royalty) = $1.68.)

When you look at Tate's royalty structure, keep in mind that they are providing many extra services for the author's initial investment. These royalties are low if you only consider the up-front fee paid to Tate relative to the up-front fees of other self-publishing companies. But, when you factor in the included editing services, warehousing, marketing, and related services, these royalties are quite good.

NOTABLE PROVISIONS OF THE PUBLISHING AGREEMENT: The publisher does not provide sample copies of its publishing agreement until it has accepted a book for publication. This is not a practice I'm a fan of, but they did send me a contract for review.

There is a publishing agreement, which covers the actual book publishing process, and a multimedia agreement, which covers the creation of the audio book, book trailer, website, or social networking setup.

Publishing Agreement

The contract is good, and quite straightforward. Section 1 (2) details that once the author sells five thousand books (even if he buys them himself), Tate will publish his next book at no cost to him. This is optional, obviously.

Section 2 (5) makes clear that, at the publisher's discretion, the author will get an audio book, website, book trailer, or social media setup.

Section 2 (9) indicates that the author owns and controls all rights to his work, such as serialization, motion picture, and so on.

It's important to note that Section 3 stipulates that the publisher gets the final word with regard to things like trim size, retail price, and type of paper stock. Normally, this would be an issue considering that you are paying almost $4,000 to publish. However, given that Tate is assuming a lot of the risk and has to sell books in order to recoup its investment in an author's project, Tate's ability to make final decisions regarding the presentation of the book is fair and reasonable.

Section 4 (8) is worth noting. If the author wants to create items related to the marketing of his book, (e.g., bookmarks or T-shirts), Tate must approve them.

Section 5 sets forth the responsibilities of the author during the publishing process.

Section 6 details how disputes are resolved, which is by arbitration held in Oklahoma City, Oklahoma. It is quite standard for publishers to require that disputes be resolved in their city of operation.

Per Section 6 (1), an author can terminate the contract at any time, but the author will not get any money back, regardless of the stage of the publishing process. Section 6 (7) indicates that authors have ninety days from the date of termination to purchase all remaining inventory of their book. If not purchased within that time, it becomes property of the publisher and the publisher may sell the remaining inventory.

Multimedia Agreement

This agreement covers the creation of an audio book, book trailer, website, and social networking website setup. As the publishing agreement states, the author and publisher will jointly decide which service will be provided as part of the publishing package. The author will then have the option to pay for any of the other three if he or she so chooses.

AUTHOR-FRIENDLY RATING: I trashed Tate in earlier versions of this book. While I don't apologize for it based on what I knew then (Tate wasn't very forthcoming with information and wouldn't provide me with a contract to look at), my opinion is now completely different.

Tate's biggest problem is that it does a terrible job of demonstrating that it really does put in substantial money above what the author contributes to the publishing process. However, I wouldn't have believed it unless I saw it with my own eyes. Ryan Tate called me after reading this book and said, "You've got it all wrong. Come see what we're doing down here." I took him up on his offer. What I saw was an energetic staff of at least sixty people, including ten full-time editors, fifteen illustrators, and fifteen graphic designers.

When you start adding up items included in every publishing package, like complete editing and unlimited cover and interior changes, Tate really is investing money in an author's book.

Also, if you accept Tate's assertion that they take 4–6 percent of ten thousand submissions received per year, it comes to about five hundred books. If each author is paying $4,000, that is only $2,000,000. That amount of money can't even cover the payroll. So, Tate has to make money from sales of authors' books to the public. It needs the portion of royalties and printing revenues to pay for its existence. The only way to get sales is to invest time and money to promote books. Is Tate putting in $20,000 toward every author's book? Probably not. For some it might be more, and for others it's probably less. Regardless, Tate is definitely investing money and resources to promote its authors' books. It's making a nice profit on the printing and taking a healthy royalty, but that's not unlike any traditional publisher. Because the author is investing money up front, the royalty taken by Tate is substantially less than a totally traditional publisher would demand.

Tate is a solid choice with great management, staff, and continuing vision. Tate doesn't need to sell the sizzle. The facts are good enough.

WASTELAND PRESS
http://www.wastelandpress.net

FORMAT OF BOOKS: Hardcover and paperback

GENRES ACCEPTED: Wasteland Press's submission guidelines do not address content, so one can assume they will accept any genre.

PUBLISHING FEES: This publisher offers six black-and-white packages and three color packages. Only black-and-white packages are covered in this review. A comparison chart of the black-and-white packages is available at http://www.wastelandpress.net/Compare.html.

Wasteland's base prices refer to books that range from 40 to125 pages after production. If your book is longer than that, there is an additional charge of $30 to $400 per fifty-page increase. (It's unclear from the website how the price jump is determined, because there is so much variance.) Note that I have included the price for a 200-page book in parentheses next to the base price.

Basic Plan: At $195 ($195 for a 200-page book), this package is for authors who simply want to get their book in print for personal use. It includes:

- Five paperback books, shipping included
- Custom cover, designed in-house with input from the author: The designer creates one cover and then works with the author on any changes for an undefined amount of time.
- Option to print a hardcover version of the book for an additional $250
- Limited distribution: This means the book will be available through Wasteland's online bookstore only. For $50, authors have the option to purchase an ISBN and bar code.
- Choice of trim size:
  5" x 8"
  5.5" x 8.5"
  6" x 9"
- Unlimited black-and-white photos throughout the book

Silver Plan: This package is priced at $350 ($440 for a 200-page book). In terms of services, the Silver Plan is identical to the Basic Plan with the exception that it includes a total of twenty-five paperback books, shipping included. It also offers a higher royalty (see royalty section for details).

Gold Plan: At $650 ($925 for a 200-page book), this package includes everything in the Basic and Silver Plans, plus:

- A total of seventy-five paperback books, shipping included
- ISBN
- Bar code
- Full-service marketing: Includes a press release written and distributed by Wasteland to more than one thousand media outlets, alerting them to the release of your book and providing follow-up information. It only includes two review copies of your book, but since this is basically an untargeted blast, that may not be an issue.
- Full distribution: Makes your book available on major online retailers, as well as available to order via brick-and-mortar stores. It does not provide online tracking of your book sales, but that information is available via an email query to the publisher.
- Five hours of copyediting: Can include formatting, structuring, and spelling and grammar check, but does not include rewriting or restructuring the author's work.
- Option of a three- or six-month payment plan
- Bookseller Returns Program

Platinum Plan: This package is priced at $995 ($1,400 for a 200-page book). Wasteland promotes this package to "career-minded writers." It includes everything in the Basic, Silver, and Gold Plans, plus:

- A total of 150 books, shipping included
- Ten total hours of copyediting
- Five total review copies as part of the marketing plan described in the Silver Plan

Titanium Plan: This package is priced at $1,250 ($1,700 for a 200-page book) and is for authors who want their book published in hardcover and paperback versions. It includes everything in the Platinum Plan, plus:

- A total of five hardcover copies of your book, shipping included
- Fifteen total hours of copyediting

Ultimate Plan: This package is priced at $1,995 ($2,750 for a 200-page book). Wasteland bills this package as its "most cost efficient." It includes everything in the Titanium Plan, plus:

- A total of five hundred paperback copies of your book, shipping included
- Twenty-five total review copies as part of the marketing plan (details under Gold Plan)
- Twenty total hours of copyediting

RETURN OF DIGITAL COVER AND INTERIOR FILES: The contract states: "Upon request, Wasteland Press will provide all files to the Author at no charge."

RETAIL PRICE OF AUTHOR'S BOOK: Wasteland authors determine the price of their books within a range limit set by the publisher based on page count. For example, I queried the Wasteland help desk with a 200-page paperback book and was told that the retail price range for my book would be $8.95 to $20.95. When I asked about the large discrepancy, it was explained that there is a balance between pricing your book too high to attract any buyers and too low to make a substantial royalty. Publisher Timothy Veeley suggested looking at similar books to find a competitive price, which is excellent advice.

PRICE AUTHOR PAYS FOR BOOKS: Although the website assures potential authors that their author discounts start at 50 percent off the retail price and then get higher based on the quantity ordered (http://www.wastelandpress.net/Prices_paperbacks2.html), that is true only if you set your retail price at a certain amount. Let's assume that you set the retail price for a 6" x 9", 200-page paperback at $13.95. Here are the numbers:

Quantity	Author Price	Markup
1–99	$6.50	67%
100–199	$6.25	60%
200–499	$6.00	54%
500–999	$5.50	41%
1000+	$4.55	17%*

The 17 percent printing markup presumes that Wasteland is printing such a large order on-demand. If it's printing the job with an offset printer, the printing markup will be more like 55 percent.

One reason Wasteland is a great company is that it has drastically lowered its printing markups since 2006. An author now pays $6.50 per book (for a 200-page paperback in quantities less than one hundred). Wasteland used to charge authors $8.25 for that same book. This change is great for Wasteland's authors.

ROYALTIES PAID TO AUTHOR: Royalties are 15–30 percent, depending on which plan the author buys, and are based on net sales, which Wasteland defines as: Retail price – 55 percent of retail (Ingram's fee) x 0.15 to 0.30 = Profit x 0.15 to 0.30 = Author royalty.

Royalties for each of the packages are:

Basic Plan: 15 percent
Silver Plan: 20 percent
Gold Plan: 25 percent
Platinum, Titanium, Ultimate Plans: 30 percent

So, on the same 200-page, paperback book, if the retail price is $13.95 and you are under the Gold Plan, you would make:

$13.95 Retail price
<u>–$7.67 Ingram discount (55%)</u>
$6.28 Gross profit (without backing out printing expense)
<u>x 0.25 Author royalty percentage</u>
$1.57 Author royalty

Is that reasonable? Well, let's look at what Wasteland makes:

$6.28	Gross profit
–$1.57	Author royalty
–$3.90	Printing cost
$0.81	Wasteland royalty

Wasteland is one of the few self-publishing companies that makes less in royalties than its authors. Because Wasteland calculates the author's royalty before deducting the printing cost, the actual royalty is much higher than 25 percent.

NOTABLE PROVISIONS OF THE PUBLISHING AGREEMENT: The publishing agreements can be found at http://www.wastelandpress.net/Compare.html. Although the Wasteland website posts different agreements for each of its publishing plans, they all offer the same legal information; the only differences between them are the individual plan details.

The "Right To Your Work" section gives the author all rights to the work, and all related cover images and other book-related files, and rights to use them elsewhere.

In the "Warranties" section, the author agrees that she is indeed the author of the book and that she has not engaged in plagiarism or libeled anyone in the writing of it. This is standard language.

In the "Right To Your Work" section, Wasteland states that it does not own the book and that it is not responsible for editing its content. In other words, if your book goes to print with a massive typo in the first paragraph, you are responsible. This is fair and standard language.

The "Book Royalties" section explains that Wasteland will pay the author a royalty, which differs depending on which publishing plan you purchase, and will be based on Wasteland's "payments actually received" in each sale less any shipping and handling, taxes, or returns. The payments actually received means just that—it's the amount Wasteland receives after Ingram/Lightning Source takes out its trade discount and the actual print costs.

In the "Indemnities" section, the author agrees that, in the event that a lawsuit arises from the book for any reason, neither Wasteland Press nor its employees will be held responsible, including any attorney fees. This is a fair clause.

The "Disclosure of Royalties" section simply states that the royalty checks are sent out every quarter, if there is a royalty to send, within thirty days of the end of the quarter. Royalty reports are available by emailing the publisher at webmaster@wastelandpress.net.

The "Shipping and Handling" clause basically says that Wasteland Press is not responsible if the books they are shipping on your behalf go astray. However, under the Basic Plan, the author can insure the arrival of her books by paying an extra $12, which would then guarantee a refund of any fees (i.e., the cost of the books ordered) if the books are lost. This fee is built into all of the other plans.

"Terms and Exclusivity" states that the author retains the copyright and may enter into any other publishing agreements at any time. It also states that either party can choose to terminate this agreement at any time. Refunds are based on who terminates and when:

1. If the author terminates before the book is printed, she will receive a full refund less 30 percent for pre-publication services, not to exceed $999.
2. If the publisher terminates before the book is printed, and no breach of contract has occurred, the author will receive a full refund. If a breach of contract has occurred, then the author will not receive a refund.
3. If either party terminates the agreement after the book has been printed, the author does not receive a refund. However, the agreement does make it clear that the author retains the copyright and can choose to enter into other publishing agreements.

In "Worldwide Distribution," the author gives Wasteland, Lightning Source, Ingram, and "any other distributor on behalf of Wasteland Press" permission to distribute her book. Note that not all publishing packages contain all of this distribution—this is a catch-all clause for any package. Distribution at all levels is included in all of the publisher's plans for one year. After one year, the author must pay $25 per year in order to keep the book in circulation. This section also says that if the author terminates, Wasteland has up to three months to clear the book from its database, which makes sense because the publisher needs time to fulfill any outstanding orders.

AUTHOR-FRIENDLY RATING: Wasteland is doing it right. The packages are a great value. When you include the number of free books, the value is unbelievable (in a good way).

The actual royalties are better than the percentages Wasteland states on its website. It's a rare moment in this industry when a publisher understates and over-delivers, but this one does on the royalty percentages.

Wasteland has smartly and aggressively lowered its printing markup, making its packages some of the best values in self-publishing. In an impressive, full-color informative packet that I received upon request, which included a sample Wasteland Press book, I learned that the bulk of the services are the same no matter which plan you purchase; the main difference between the plans seems to be more copyediting time, more review copies, and more author copies. Wasteland has a live chat window and the website is very easy to use and, though it could provide a greater level of detail, relatively useful.

Wasteland is one of the outstanding self-publishing companies. I'm a huge fan.

XULON PRESS

http://www.xulonpress.com

FORMAT OF BOOK: Paperback and hardcover

GENRES ACCEPTED: Xulon only accepts books that support its core Christian beliefs and values, but it publishes in many categories, including Christian living, theology, church growth, discipleship, Bible study, fiction, poetry, and biography. For more on the specifics, go to http://www.xulonpress.com/faith_statement.php.

PUBLISHING FEES: Xulon has several publishing packages, the details of which you can find at http://www.xulonpress.com/prices_programs.htm.

Basic Package: Priced at $799, this package includes:

- Custom book cover: Author can choose from Xulon's gallery or provide up to three of her own photos. Includes only one design with minimal changes. If unsatisfied, additional cover designs cost $300 each.
- Back cover design (author still needs to provide back cover copy)
- Professionally formatted text
- Electronic proof
- Choice of trim size:
  5" x 8"
  5.5" x 8.5"
  6" x 9"
  8.25" x 11"
- PDF review copy of the book: Includes twenty minor changes, after which changes are around $2 per change.
- ISBN
- One free author copy
- Personal template-based webpage via Xulon's online bookstore
- No distribution or royalty

Note: this package doesn't include distribution or royalty. Without these things, you are just paying to have your book printed. If you want to go with Xulon, this package makes no sense.

Premium Package: At $1,199, this package includes everything in the Basic Package, plus:

- Two free author copies
- R.R. Bowker's Books In Print registration

- Order/Pack & Ship Service: Offered twenty-four hours a day, seven days a week (toll-free order service takes phone orders and ships books to customers). Books are delivered seven to ten days from order. This service applies to sales that might come, for example, from your personal website. Xulon will handle fulfillment on individual sales if you don't want to deal with shipping, etc. It is part of the package, so there is no extra charge.
- 100 percent royalties on bookstore sales, 70 percent for sales through Xulon.com (royalties calculated after backing out print cost and distribution fees)
- Distribution through Ingram and Spring Arbor (Christian-book distributor): Includes a quarterly report of how many books sold and where they sold.
- Special-order availability in 25,000 bookstores, including 2,500 Christian bookstores
- Listing on Amazon.com
- Marketing to thousands of Christian bookstores and churches in the publisher's catalog, *Christian Book Browser*
- Access to additional fee-based services:
  International distribution for $89
  Returns service for $149

Best-Seller Package: At $2,099, this package includes everything in the Premium Package, plus:

- Five author copies
- Professionally written press release, posted on Newswire and distributed to three thousand Christian broadcasters and journalists through Xulon's Christian Media Alert publication
- Showcasing your book at one of four annual Christian book trade shows, with promotional handouts letting attendees know where they can order the book
- Submission to Google Books
- Free one-year marketing plan: All I was able to find out about this program is that it is a "clearly devised strategy for a person to follow that will take the guesswork out for how you will market your own book."

Elite Package: At $4,299, this package includes most add-ons that Xulon offers and everything in the Best-Seller Package:

- Twenty-five author copies
- Xulon Elite special logo on your book
- Christian Books TV video commercial for books posted on Xulon's YouTube channel
- Professionally written press release viewable by 250,000 newswire subscribers
- Three Christianity.com home page ads with 10,000 page views or more
- Copyright registration
- International distribution
- Rush (forty-five days to publish)
- Three years of paid paperback returns
- Two ads in Xulon's full-color seasonal catalog, *Christian Book Browser*, mailed to thousands of Christian bookstores & media (digital version on crosswalk.com)

For more information about the Elite Package, visit http://www.xulonpress.com/Elite.php.

OTHER SERVICES OF INTEREST: Xulon offers fewer à la carte services than many publishers, but those it offers are reasonably priced.

Editing: Xulon no longer offers its own editing services, but does have a list of freelance editors that it suggests.

Graphic Insertion: $15 per image ($25 if it needs to be scanned). Ten free insertions are included with the Elite Package.

International Distribution: This does not put your books on European bookshelves, but rather makes them available to be ordered overseas. This service is $89. It isn't available with the Basic Package, but is included with the Elite Package.

Bookstore Returns Program: Marks books returnable. All returned books are deducted from author's royalty. This service is $199 with the Premium and Best-Seller Packages, but included in the Elite Package.

Rush Service: Your book can be produced in forty-five days (rather than ninety) for $299.

Hardcover Edition: This will cost an additional $169 with any package.

Copyright Service: Xulon will register your book with the U.S. Copyright Office for $179. This is free with the Elite Package.

Marketing Services: Xulon offers an array of marketing services, the details of which can be found by clicking on each service at http://www.xulonpress.com/prices_programs.php. The offerings include book trailers, ads on Christianity.com, and inclusion in a catalog.

RETURN OF DIGITAL COVER AND INTERIOR FILES: Xulon will give departing authors a press-ready PDF file of their interior for a $100 fee; if you want both the interior file and the cover file together, the cost is $200. These files can be either layered or flat.

RETAIL PRICE OF AUTHOR'S BOOK: A book's retail price is determined by page count.

Page Count	Retail Price
48–104	$10.99
105–124	$11.99
125–199	$14.99
200–249	$15.99
250–299	$16.99
300–349	$18.99
350–399	$20.99
400–449	$22.99
450–500	$24.99

This retail pricing is a bit high.

PRICE AUTHOR PAYS FOR BOOKS: Xulon authors receive a discount on books, depending on how many they buy, with the scale ranging from 35 percent off the retail price for one to twenty-five books, to 70 percent off for more than one thousand books. There is a book cost calculator at http://www.xulonpress.com/order_copies.php. Let's assume you have a 200-page, 6" x 9" paperback that, per the previous section, retails for $15.99. Here's the math:

Quantity	Discount	Author Price	Markup
1–25	35%	$10.39	166%
26–50	40%	$9.59	146%
51–150	45%	$8.79	126%
151–250	50%	$7.99	105%
251–500	55%	$7.20	85%
501–1,000	60%	$6.40	64%
1,001–1,500	70%	$4.80	92%*
1,501+	Call	?	?

For print runs of one thousand copies or more, I assume Xulon uses an offset printer, hence the asterisk. Xulon's wholesale cost for the sample book would be far less than $2.50 a copy, but using this figure accounts for swings in offset print prices (which can be all over the place).

Xulon does offer free shipping on some orders and some marketing incentives from time to time, which certainly would lower the overall cost of printing.

ROYALTIES PAID TO AUTHOR: As I was writing this edition of the book, I pointed out to Xulon that the royalties page on its website (http://www.xulonpress.com/royalties_discounts.php) was not clear. Xulon promptly updated the page and explained the royalties in an easier-to-understand way. Now, that's author-friendly. Xulon pays its authors 100 percent of net receipts (retail book price less the bookseller discount and the cost to print) from all sales to bookstores, libraries, and distributors. For books sold individually through Xulon's website or toll-free number, the author receives 75 percent of net receipts (full retail price less the cost to print the book).

What makes Xulon's royalties impressive is that when calculating them, Xulon only backs out the actual print cost of the book—not the print cost charged to authors when they buy copies of their books. Take the 200-page, paperback book as an example. Xulon retails it for $15.99. Assume this book is sold on Amazon. Amazon takes a 55 percent trade discount.

$15.99 Retail price
–$8.79 Amazon.com discount (55%)
–$3.90 Xulon printing cost
$3.90 Author royalty

This is a true 100 percent royalty. Xulon pays its authors everything it's paid for retail and/or library sales.

For sales made through Xulon's website or through its toll-free number, Xulon pays a 75 percent royalty after subtracting out print costs. This is more than fair. Xulon obviously incurs costs in the picking and packing of books sent to consumers, and must also pay the operators taking phone orders.

For our 200-page paperback sold through Xulon:

$15.99 Retail price
–$3.90 Xulon printing cost
$12.09 Net profit
x 0.75 Author royalty percentage
$9.06 Author royalty

In this transaction, Xulon makes $3.03 (25 percent royalty). The author royalty here is excellent, as it pertains to books sold through the Xulon site.

NOTABLE PROVISIONS OF THE PUBLISHING AGREEMENT: The publishing agreement is not easy to find without a little digging, but a sample agreement is listed on the site map at http://www.xulonpress.com/imgs/global/service_agreement.pdf.

The beginning of the contract has checkboxes relating to certain aspects of the publishing process that the author must check, indicating that they agree to and acknowledge those specific stipulations. For example, one states that the author agrees to comply with Xulon's manuscript preparation guidelines. When publishers make it very clear to authors what is expected of them, the result is a better working relationship.

After the checkbox portion, there are additional paragraphs. "Author Right to Ownership" establishes that the author must provide the complete manuscript within one year. The author holds complete control of the work at all times.

"Term and Termination" specifies that either the author or the publisher may cancel at any time, and that the author may enter into another publishing agreement at any time. The percentage of money the author will be refunded upon termination is tiered, with 150 days as the point at which the author will receive no refund.

"Xulon Press Reservation" says that while the publisher will not conduct a formal review of the work, it has the right to refuse (or assign to an alternate imprint) any books containing anything not consistent with traditional Christian values, including New Age, occultist, or sexual references.

"Cover Design" says that the author receives an original cover using stock photos or images, and that designers will consider artwork submitted by the author but are not obliged to use it. It also states that Xulon controls what the cover looks like; the author has no option to decline. While you may not think this clause is fair—it is. In fact, more self-publishing companies should have it. What authors think should be on a book cover is what often leads to amateurish, unsellable covers.

"Text Format" states that all interior text will be formatted, according to the publisher's template, in Times New Roman font, although additional font choices are available to authors and are set forth in the manuscript guidelines.

"Annual Renewal Fee" imposes a $29.95 fee each year from the date that the author first uploaded his work; if not paid, the author is subject to a $20.00 late fee or cancellation of his contract.

AUTHOR-FRIENDLY RATING: The best things about Xulon are its contract and the fact that it is owned by a company with a significant online Christian presence. The contract clearly spells out the duties of both the author and the publisher. Less is not always more when it comes to contracts. Authors need to understand the process before they sign a contract. Xulon's specific contract does that.

Xulon is a division of a company that owns Christianity.com. Xulon promotes authors who pay for this service through that site and others. A large web presence can never hurt.

The royalties are great—some of the best in the business. Xulon claims that it is the only company that pays 100 percent net royalties. It isn't, but it's one of the very few that does. The way Xulon calculates royalties, using the actual print cost instead of the marked up printing costs, is why Xulon remains an "Outstanding" publisher in this book.

Xulon's one negative is the printing markups. They are among the highest I've seen at just about every quantity printed. I have a hard time with these printing markups, but I know that Xulon often provides complimentary shipping and offers marketing programs for free to offset printing fees. This isn't anything the company has to do or anything you should expect, but it's a nice touch. You have to balance Xulon's good qualities against the printing markups when deciding if Xulon is the company for you.

Xulon's website is clear and most of the fees and services are explained up front. Xulon representatives are friendly and don't use any pressure tactics to make sales. That is another plus.

I believe that authors who select Christian publishers are under the impression that such a company would never provide inaccurate information. That is why Xulon and other religion-focused publishers need to be held to a higher standard in the way they present information about their services. Authors inherently believe them. Xulon is very up front about its services and fees. If your book's main target audience is Christian, Xulon has some nice book promotion programs. If you can handle the printing markups on copies that you purchase for your own events, Xulon does provide solid packages and promotional opportunities.

CHAPTER 9

PRETTY GOOD SELF-PUBLISHING COMPANIES

How do you separate an "Outstanding" publisher from a "Pretty Good" one? It's usually a razor-thin distinction. As you've already read, some of the companies listed in the "Outstanding" category have elements of their services that are problematic for me. But, they've overcompensated for those deficiencies in other ways. Publishers that earned a "Pretty Good" rating typically had one aspect about their service that wasn't great (printing markups too high, royalties too low, or a clause in their contract that wasn't author-friendly and that the publisher would not change) and didn't compensate for it in some other way (e.g., free shipping for book orders, great contract terms, etc.).

The publishers in this section are good companies and provide a solid service. In fact, many of these publishers are one mere tweak away from the "Outstanding" category. I would feel comfortable using any one of the publishers listed in this chapter.

CREATESPACE

http://www.createspace.com

FORMAT OF BOOKS: Paperback. (Authors interested in creating ebooks are forwarded to the Kindle section of Amazon.com.)

GENRES ACCEPTED: CreateSpace, an Amazon.com company (now combined with BookSurge, another previously distinct Amazon.com brand), operates much the same as Lulu.com and is more of a content manager and printer than a publisher. Therefore, it does not discern genres or quality of writing; it only asks that you not use the site to print books that are disturbing (i.e., pornographic or hateful).

PUBLISHING FEES: CreateSpace offers a variety of services, available for review at https://www.createspace.com/pub/services.home.do. There are do-it-yourself publishing packages where it is free to upload your book (https://www.createspace.com/Products/Book/Index.jsp#content2), but you need to create your own cover and interior and submit them correctly to CreateSpace. CreateSpace only recommends its do-it-yourself packages for people with design experience. (See "Submission Requirements" at https://www.createspace.com/Products/Book/#content5.)

For those who want more services, CreateSpace offers packages that resemble publishing packages offered by other self-publishing companies. A list of these packages can be found at https://www.createspace.com /Services/PublisherSolutionServiceTable.jsp. They range in price from $299 to $4,999. An example is the Total Design Freedom Essentials package ($1,798), found at https://www.createspace.com/Services /TotalDesignFreedomEssentials.jsp. The following items are included in this package:

- One round of copyediting (based on a 60,000-word manuscript; additional fees may apply to longer works)
- ISBN
- LCCN
- Interior digital proof
- Unique book cover: Includes five hours of design time and two initial concepts, consisting of one central image, selected by the designer, as the focal point for the cover (more details at https:// www.createspace.com/Services/UniqueBookCover.jsp).
- Custom interior, including up to ten images
- The ability to sell your book on CreateSpace.com and Amazon.com

All of the services included in the Total Design Freedom package are also offered individually. You can also pay an additional $39 for the Pro Plan, which makes your book available at places other than CreateSpace and Amazon and gives you lower printing costs (https://www.createspace.com/Products/Book/ProPlan.jsp). If you plan on using CreateSpace, this extra $39 (and $5 per year after that) is a must. The savings are huge.

ADDITIONAL SERVICES: At https://www.createspace.com/pub/services.home.do, click the "Marketing" tab and you can view the marketing and PR services. These consist of mostly basic services, like press release writing and distribution, collateral materials (i.e., bookmarks), and two types of video trailers (https://www.createspace.com/Services/VideoBookTrailers.jsp).

RETURN OF DIGITAL COVER AND INTERIOR FILES: You might assume that this is a nonissue because, in the CreateSpace model, you provide all of the files and the book prints exactly as submitted. However, the CreateSpace agreement says that while the author owns all the rights to his content, the publisher owns all of the files created using its proprietary templates, including "source files, future-proof archive files, and packaging materials."

When I asked the CreateSpace help desk if I would own the source files created using CreateSpace templates, I was told, "We own the sources [sic] files we create for our printer."

If you want to sell your book outside of CreateSpace.com and Amazon.com, in addition to creating all new files, you'll need to purchase your own ISBN. CreateSpace owns the ISBN it offers with printing, and its contract states that you can only sell books imprinted with its ISBN on Amazon.com affiliated sites.

RETAIL PRICE OF AUTHOR'S BOOK: CreateSpace allows authors to set the price for their books, with the caveat that authors may not sell books on CreateSpace.com or Amazon.com for more than they charge elsewhere. Authors must also acknowledge that Amazon and its affiliates have the option to reduce the price of the book.

PRICE AUTHOR PAYS FOR BOOKS: There is a pricing calculator under the "Pricing" tab at https://www.CreateSpace.com/Products/Book/#content4 so potential authors can determine how much they will pay for books. For a standard 6" x 9", 200-page paperback the cost is $0.02 per page and $1.50 per cover, or $5.50 per copy. If the author has joined the Pro Plan, the cost for each book is $0.012 per page and $0.85 per cover, or $3.25. The printing costs don't vary by quantity, so if you order one copy or one thousand copies, the price per book is always the same (depending on whether you're in the Pro Plan or not). Without the Pro Plan, the markup is 41 percent. With the Pro Plan, the printing costs are actually less than the standard $3.90 per book because CreateSpace owns its own printer (which was once BookSurge).

While the printing costs for low quantities are great, the markups become high when you get into larger quantities, but are still much less than most other publishers in this book.

ROYALTIES PAID TO AUTHOR: To determine how royalties are calculated, visit https://www.CreateSpace.com/Products/Book/ and click on the "Sales & Royalties" tab; then, go to https://www.CreateSpace .com/Products/Book/Royalties.jsp. CreateSpace royalties are dictated by the retail price the author chooses, what CreateSpace charges for its printing services, and the trade discount given to each reseller (whether it's CreateSpace, Amazon, or third-party retailers). For sales on CreateSpace, it takes a 20 percent trade discount. For sales on Amazon, Amazon takes a 40 percent discount. For sales anywhere else, a 60 percent trade discount is given. The total royalties also change if the author is part of the Pro Plan.

For a 6" x 9", 200-page paperback that retails for $14.95, here is how the math looks:

Where Book Is Sold	**Standard Royalty**	**Pro Royalty**
CreateSpace	$6.46	$8.71
Amazon.com	$3.47	$5.72
Third Parties	n/a	$2.73

Since CreateSpace and Amazon are essentially the same thing, when calculating what CreateSpace/Amazon really makes on each sale, you need to factor in the trade discount it gives itself. For example, if our sample book sold through CreateSpace's eStore for $14.95 and you were in the standard program, you'd make:

$14.95	Retail price
–$2.99	Trade discount (20%)
–$5.50	Print cost
$6.46	Author royalty

Assuming the print cost is $3.90, CreateSpace/Amazon nets about $4.59 on this sale. If the print cost is under the Pro Plan, CreateSpace/ Amazon nets about $2.99, and the author makes $8.71. It's clear that CreateSpace prints massive amounts in house and isn't jobbing this out to a third party like Lightning Source, so it's impossible for an outsider to even guess at the actual profit.

Assuming everything is the same but the book is now being sold on Amazon, you'd make:

$14.95	Retail price
–$5.98	Trade discount (40%)
–$5.50	Print cost
$3.47	Author royalty

This is where CreateSpace/Amazon really makes out. CreateSpace is making money on the printing and is essentially giving itself a 40 percent trade discount to sell the book.

Assuming everything is the same but the book is now being sold through third-party retailers, you'd make:

$14.95	Retail price
–$8.97	Trade discount (60%)
–$3.25	Print cost
$2.73	Author royalty

The wild card here is that we don't know how much of the 60 percent CreateSpace/Amazon keeps and how much the third party actually takes as trade discount. I doubt that the full 60 percent of the trade discount is given to Amazon's competitors, as this would enable them to sell the book for less than Amazon.com's sales price. However, that is pure speculation (and some common sense) on my part.

NOTABLE PROVISIONS OF THE PUBLISHING AGREEMENT: The publishing agreement can be found at http://www.CreateSpace.com/Help/Rights/MemberAgreement.jsp.

Section 1 says that CreateSpace can change the terms of the agreement, its policies, and its service offering at any time. It will post a notice of changes for up to thirty days, but it's up to the author to check the site for changes; the author's continued use of the site after the changes take effect signifies agreement.

Section 3 outlines what services authors are eligible for once they have registered on the site, including book order fulfillment and a listing on the CreateSpace eStore, Amazon Properties, and other sales channels. It also says that CreateSpace has the ultimate say on bar code placement.

Section 4 deals with how CreateSpace handles titles. Basically, it says that if an author violates the company's guidelines, CreateSpace can remove the content and the author will still be held responsible for any outstanding fees. It also says that the author can remove content at will; however, CreateSpace has thirty days after receiving notice from the author to remove the content, and can continue to fulfill any orders placed up to the end of that thirty days.

Also included in Section 4 is Subsection 4.2, "Pricing; Legal Title," which says that CreateSpace is the "seller of record" for the author's book. This means that it ultimately has the power to set the selling price. It also says that, while the author sets the retail price, it must be set at or below the price the book is selling for elsewhere. This clause is bad if you intend to sell the book from your own website. Normally you could sell the book on your website for less than on CreateSpace, since you wouldn't have to pay any portion of the trade discount to anyone. Unfortunately, Subsection 4.2 prohibits this, which may limit some of your sales avenues. However, you could always terminate the contract and publish elsewhere.

Subsection 4.3, "Customer Returns and Refunds," allows CreateSpace to handle returns in several ways, on a case-by-case basis:

1. The company can resell a returned book, with no additional royalty to the author.
2. The company can destroy the book.
3. The company can refuse all returns.
4. The company can accept the return and, if it has already paid the author a royalty, charge the return against future royalties or bill the author for the royalty amount.

Section 5 deals with taxes and fees, and states that CreateSpace will pay author royalties within thirty-one days of the end of the month in which the book was sold. This section states: "If you are unable to make Electronic Funds Transfer ('EFT') payments, we will pay by check, but we may charge a per check fee and accrue and withhold payments until the total amount due meets a minimum dollar threshold." That minimum dollar threshold is unspecified.

Section 5 also holds the author responsible if a buyer uses a fraudulent credit card to purchase the author's book, meaning that the earnings from the fraudulent sale will be deducted from future earnings. Authors are also responsible for paying their own taxes on royalties; CreateSpace will not withhold a deduction.

Section 6 covers content, licenses, and feedback. In part, it allows CreateSpace to create digital versions of your content, or book, for the purpose of advertising and display, and to allow Search Inside! feature.

Subsection 6.4, "Ownership," says that while you, the author, own all the rights to the content, CreateSpace owns all of its own templates and the resulting files it creates, including source files, future-proof archive files, and packaging materials.

Subsection 6.5, "Cover Images," says: "We may agree to provide you a file containing an image of the cover of your Title ('Cover Images'). Contingent upon your receipt of such Cover Image, we hereby grant you, during the term of this Agreement, a worldwide, royalty-free right to use the Cover Image for any lawful purpose related to promoting your Title." This is not the same as returning the production files to you for your own use when you're no longer in the agreement.

All that Subsection 6.5 says is that, during the term of the agreement, CreateSpace lets you use the cover image to promote your book. When you terminate with CreateSpace, you no longer have the right to use that cover image. Now, if you provided the image that was used on your book cover and then terminated your publishing agreement, while you couldn't use CreateSpace's rendition of the cover (containing that image), you could create a similar cover using the same image. Subsection 6.6, "Feedback," says that if the author sends CreateSpace information or a suggestion, all rights to that information or suggestion belong to CreateSpace, even if it leads to a change in the way the company provides service. That means that if you send them a great idea and they implement it, you won't get paid. This is not unreasonable.

Section 7, "Representation and Warranties," is basically standard language stating that your content is not breaking any laws—you didn't steal it, it isn't libelous or otherwise injurious to someone else, and as far as you know it is based on fact (where appropriate).

Section 8, "Indemnification; Maintenance of Rights; Copyright Infringement," basically states that CreateSpace will not be held responsible if a claim is brought against the author for his or her book, including attorney's fees. Further, it states that if the author learns of a claim against her title, she will remove the title from the site and accept financial responsibility for any books that are returned as a result of the claim.

The title of Section 9, "Disclaimer of Warranties; Limitation on Liability," is written in full capitals to show importance, one presumes, and states that CreateSpace makes no guarantees that your content or its website will always be available. It also protects the company from damages if it should lose any hard copies of your content. If it does lose content, the author is only entitled to the lesser of $100 or the cost to replace the disk or other media the content was stored on. The lesson here: don't ever send a publisher the only copy of your book.

Section 10 gives both CreateSpace and the author the ability to terminate the contract at any time by giving each other written notice. Upon termination, the author must pay any outstanding fees, and CreateSpace is obligated to fulfill any outstanding book orders.

Section 15 states that the agreement is governed by the laws of the

State of Washington, and that any disputes claiming over $7,500 of relief will be settled in Seattle, Washington.

Section 16, "Miscellaneous," allows CreateSpace to sublicense any of its rights per the agreement, but it specifically states that the author may not assign any of her rights. This can be a problem if you want your business to own the copyright to your book or wish to assign any royalties to your corporation. It also states that CreateSpace will not be held responsible if anything, such as an act of God or foul weather, keeps it from fulfilling its responsibilities per the contract. That means that if a hurricane wipes out the printing press on the eve of a book signing and your books are not delivered, you cannot hold CreateSpace liable for any money you lose as a result. This is a standard clause.

AUTHOR-FRIENDLY RATING: CreateSpace has come a long way since taking over floundering BookSurge. Its offerings are easy to figure out and make sense—unlike Lulu's, whose site is difficult to maneuver, and whose sheer volume of offerings nearly require a degree in instructional design to figure out.

CreateSpace (in my opinion) is primarily geared toward the author who is bringing a completed cover and interior to the table. But, the company does offer reasonably priced packages for those who aren't.

CreateSpace's book prices are competitive. There are no setup fees (unless you're paying for CreateSpace to help you design and format your book), but they make up for that in the printing markups. There is no cost savings to the author on volume, so whether you order ten copies of your book or one thousand, you pay the same price per unit. If you're participating in the Pro Plan, the printing costs are much more favorable, even without the volume discounts. Even though CreateSpace gives no quantity discount, its prices still beat Lulu's quantity discounts across the board.

One negative is that CreateSpace has a clause in its contract that prohibits you from setting your list price (on your own website or at other retailers) lower than the list price on CreateSpace or its affiliates' sites (i.e., Amazon.com). This can get murky. Does it mean that if Amazon discounts your book from $15 to $10 in order to sell it, you can't sell your book for the same discounted fee? Or, does it mean that you are stuck with the original retail price? Certainly, if you set the list price at $15 and an online retailer decides to sell it for $9 through no control of your own, it is hard to imagine that you would be liable to Amazon.

Overall, CreateSpace provides a good service. While the distribution seems wide, certainly the concentration is on sales through CreateSpace, Amazon, and any of their affiliates. If you're a do-it-yourselfer, CreateSpace blows Lulu and WordClay away. If you're like the rest of us and want some help getting through the process, CreateSpace does offer it for a fee. With good pricing to authors for copies of their own books and decent royalties, CreateSpace is finally a publisher to consider. Impressively, Amazon has tamed its own beast.

OUTSKIRTS PRESS

http://www.outskirtspress.com

FORMAT OF BOOKS: Ebook, paperback, and hardcover

GENRES ACCEPTED: All

PUBLISHING FEES: There are five publishing packages ranging from $199 to $1,099, the most expensive of which is for books with a full-color interior. A side-by-side comparison of all the packages can be found at http://outskirtspress.com/publishinginformation.html. It's not especially descriptive, so if you want to know more about the various services look here: http://www.outskirtspress.com/help.php.

The four packages for the black-and-white interiors are outlined below:

Emerald Package: Priced at $199, this package (http://outskirtspress.com/emerald.php) includes:

- Choice of two full-color cover templates
- Digital author review: Includes up to twenty-five minor changes, after which every change is $0.50. Additional rounds are $49.00 plus $0.50 per edit.

- One free author copy
- Black-and-white interior layout template
- Interior graphics: First ten graphics are placed for a $49.00 fee (if uploaded; if mailed, the fee is $99.00).
- Template-based author webpage
- Marketing toolkit
- Local radio contacts
- One book size: 5.5" x 8.5" trim size, must be between 30 and 800 pages in length

Sapphire Package: For $399, this package (http://outskirtspress.com/sapphire.php) includes everything in the Emerald Package, plus:

- Three copies of the book
- Choice of nine full-color cover templates
- Choice of trim size:
  5"x 8"
  5.5" x 8.5"
  6" x 9"
- Author website, with choice of two background colors and link to purchase book from Amazon
- Ability to set the royalty
- Distribution through Ingram, Amazon.com, and BarnesandNoble.com
- Manuscript evaluation
- Below-wholesale pricing for author
- ISBN
- Bar code

The promise of "below wholesale pricing" (stated in the pop-up next to the "Great Author Discounts" line on the side-by-side package comparison) for authors who want to purchase copies of their own books is simply not true. In fact, the printing is marked up at least 50 percent over the actual wholesale price.

Ruby Package: At $699, this package (http://outskirtspress.com/ruby.php) includes everything in the Sapphire Package, plus:

- Worldwide distribution
- Choice of sixteen full-color cover templates
- Six free author copies
- Author website with three background options, author photo, and link to listing on Amazon
- Choice of nine book formats
- R.R. Bowker's Books In Print registration
- Listing on Outskirts' website
- Access to other fee-based services (http://outskirtspress.com/publishing/OutskirtsPress.pdf), including:
    - LCCN
    - Ingram Publishing announcement
    - U.S. Copyright Office registration
    - Custom cover, which includes a copy polish and custom interior, and choice of photos from the image gallery with one round of changes (additional changes available for $15/hour)
    - Retail returns program
    - Ebook

Diamond Package: For $999, this package (http://outskirtspress.com/diamond.php) includes every feature of the Ruby Package, plus:

- Fifteen available formats for the book
- Ten free author copies
- Twenty-five customizable cover choices, including free cover image gallery
- Author website with choice of four background colors, author photo, author contact information, and a link to purchase from Amazon or Barnes & Noble
- Professional interior layout, including drop caps
- Free ebook version
- Loyalty program: If author publishes a second book through the Outskirts Diamond program, the author will receive a 10 percent

discount. A third book gets 19 percent off, which becomes the publishing price moving forward.

- Audio excerpt: A three-minute recording of the author's voice either talking about or reading from the book.
- Press release distribution: Book release written and distributed by an Outskirts PR professional to 100,000 media outlets.
- Qualification for EVVY nomination: The EVVY Awards are sponsored by the Colorado Independent Publishers Association and recognize excellence in self-published and independently published books. According to Outskirts, it nominates approximately 5 percent of its authors for this award.

OTHER SERVICES OF INTEREST: Outskirts offers a smattering of à la carte services, which can be found at http://www.outskirtspress.com/outskirts_pricelist.pdf. Here are a few of note:

Editing: Basic copyediting corrects typos, spelling, and syntax at $0.014 a word with a minimum of 15,000 words. Books of poetry are $50.00 an hour with a minimum of four hours. More extensive editing services are available and charged by project.

Custom Designed Professional Cover: Offered with three of the four black-and-white interior packages; the author works with a designer to create a 100 percent original cover. The cost is $299. The designer will provide two options and one round of changes, after which all changes are charged by fifteen-minute increments at $50/hour.

Hardcover Edition: Only available with the Diamond or Ruby Package, the price is either $199 or $298, depending on whether the hardcover edition is the same size as the paperback edition.

Standard Press Release: For $99, Outskirts publicity professionals create a standard book release announcement, which is then distributed to a database of 100,000 media contacts. But, since it's not targeted, you're taking a $99 gamble that one or two people out of 100,000 will respond. (I didn't see anything to indicate the publisher has 100,000 media contacts interested in romance novels and 100,000 interested in self-help books, for example.)

Custom Press Release: For $199, Outskirts' publicity professionals write a customized press release, which is then distributed to the 100,000 media contacts. Here, you're just sending a better-written press release to a non-targeted list. The results won't be much different.

Returns: For a $499 annual fee, this program, which is only available with the Diamond or Ruby packages, allows retailers to return unsold books to Ingram.

RETURN OF DIGITAL COVER AND INTERIOR FILES: Departing authors may take their interior and cover files with them for a fee of $499 per file. The cover file is a flat PDF, not a layered, editable PDF. If you decide to re-publish your book yourself, you can take a press-ready PDF to any printer and print it. However, you can't sell the book through any third-party retailer or wholesaler without an ISBN and bar code. Unless you have the design software to do it yourself, a new publisher would need to be able to get into these PDFs and replace the ISBN. So, you're paying $998 for files that have little value to you—or to Outskirts, for that matter—unless you want to print the book for your personal use.

RETAIL PRICE OF AUTHOR'S BOOK: Outskirts allows authors to choose one of three pricing plans, each with its own pros and cons. Detailed information can be found at http://outskirtspress.com/publishing/guide/BookPricing.pdf.

Plan 50: Meets most brick-and-mortar's 30 to 35 percent retail margin, which means a higher retail price and lower profit.

Plan 40: Described as a "comfortable compromise," this plan gives most bookstores only a 10 to 25 percent retail margin (Most prefer—or require—40 percent).

Plan 25: Outskirts cautions that this should be used for online sales only, since the plan's low retail price and comparably high author profit leaves no room for trade discounts to bookstores.

The $13.95 (retail price) pricing calculator is a nice touch. Outskirts does a much better job than in the past of informing authors that low trade discounts mean virtually zero retail sales. Some of the ways authors turned "the publishing industry upside down" (see "The Custom Difference" on http://www.outskirtspress.com/calculator.php) need more explanation. Short discounting of 20 percent means that an author will only get online sales. Disallowing retail returns means that almost no retailer will ever think about ordering a copy. There are certainly books and book marketing strategies these might work for, but for most they won't.

As for the pricing plans themselves, the Plan 50 that Outskirts recommends for the most retail availability, in fact, doesn't really offer that. According to http://www.outskirtspress.com/publishing/guide/BookPricing.pdf, under Plan 50 retailers are offered a 30 to 35 percent trade discount—but in an article by Brent Sampson at http://www.outskirtspress.com/articles_retailmargin.html, he says (correctly): "Physical offline retailers typically expect a margin of at least 40 percent." Something seems to be a bit off here.

Plan 40 is not really a compromise, because under it off-line retailers only get a 10 to 25 percent trade discount. They won't be ordering books at that discount level. Plan 25 is the only one that is accurately described on the website. Brick-and-mortar retailers will not buy your book with a small trade discount.

PRICE AUTHOR PAYS FOR BOOKS: The price the author pays to buy copies of his book is determined by the page count, publishing package, retail price, and selected pricing plan. There are a lot of combinations here, so the only way to really get a feel for this is to play around with the calculator at http://www.outskirtspress.com/calculator.php.

One thing that is absolutely certain is that the author is not paying "below wholesale pricing" (as stated both on the website and in the contract). For example, a 200-page, 5.5" x 8.5" paperback costs $3.90 to print on demand. Just using the suggested pricing model on the calculator page (for the 200-page book), if you bought the Diamond Package, chose Plan 50 for royalties, and went with the suggested retail price of $13.95, you'd get a 55 percent discount off the retail price. Outskirts requires that you purchase books in groups of five. Whether you order five, one hundred, or one thousand, you pay the same price per book. Under the plan above, you'd pay $6.27. That's a 61 percent markup over the actual printing cost—obviously not below wholesale. Once you order in quantities over five hundred, Outskirts pays even less for printing, so the markup will rise. Remember, by choosing the other pricing plans but keeping everything else the same, the author price per book is even higher.

ROYALTIES PAID TO AUTHOR: Royalties depend on the publishing package, the price plan chosen, and the retail price. One thing that is certain is that they aren't 100 percent. Since only Plan 50 would give an author a shot at being picked up by brick-and-mortar retailers, let's use it when calculating the royalty. According to the Outskirts Publishing Guide, Plan 50 provides stores with a 30–35 percent trade discount. The calculation also assumes the purchase of the Diamond Package and a retail price of $13.95, $14.95, or $15.95.

To see the actual royalty amount and percentage, simply use the Outskirts calculator at http://www.outskirtspress.com/calculator.php. The numbers don't lie, and don't add up to 100 percent royalties:

$13.95	Retail price
–$4.88	Trade discount (35%)
–$3.90	Actual cost to print book
–$0.82	Author royalty
$4.35	Outskirts Press profit

The Outskirts contract says, "AUTHOR RECEIVES 100 PERCENT OF THE ROYALTIES PROFIT for each wholesale print copy sold for which Outskirts Press receives payment. Royalties profit is defined as the difference between the Base Price and the Wholesaler's Price." That's simply not the case. On the example above, Outskirts Press makes a royalty/profit of 31 percent of the retail price, and the author actually makes 6 percent of the retail price.

If everything is the same except the retail price is set to $15.95, the math looks like this:

$15.95 Retail price
–$5.58 Trade discount (35%)
–$3.90 Actual cost to print book
–$1.82 Author royalty
$5.55 Outskirts Press profit

Outskirts Press comes out even better in this scenario, making a royalty/profit of 35 percent of the retail price, while the author actually makes 11 percent of retail price.

This is not 100 percent royalties. No way. No how.

NOTABLE PROVISIONS OF THE PUBLISHING AGREEMENT: There are four contracts, one for each of the publishing packages. They are identical except for the specifics outlined in "Attachment A." A sample contract is available at http://www.outskirtspress.com/Contract_OutskirtsPress.pdf. The review below covers all four contracts.

Section 1, "License," Subsection 3 gives the publisher a worldwide, nonexclusive license to print and distribute the work as an ebook or print book.

Section 2, "Royalties & Pricing," Subsection 5 states, in all capital letters, "AUTHOR RECEIVES 100 PERCENT OF THE ROYALTIES PROFIT for each wholesale print copy sold for which Outskirts Press receives payment." As discussed previously, that statement is only true because the base price to print the book is a marked up amount.

Section 3, "Publisher Services," Subsection 13 states that publication takes place within ninety days of "author's approval to proceed with production." That term is undefined, however.

Section 4, "Author Warranties," and Section 6, "Indemnification," are standard and reasonable.

Section 5, "Termination," Subsection 22 allows either party to cancel the contract with thirty days written notice, which is good. Upon cancellation by the author, he or she will pay any outstanding fees, plus an administrative fee of $49. Subsection 25 allows Outskirts to terminate the contract if it has "irreconcilable differences" with the author. If Outskirts terminates before publication, the author receives a 100 percent refund of the package fee. If it's within the first year of publication, the author is refunded 50 percent of the package fee. If it's within two years of publication, there is a 25 percent refund of the package fee.

Section 6, Subsection 29 states that if the publisher cannot fulfill its obligations under the contract in a timely manner due to reasons out of its control, it is not liable. For example, if a tornado destroys the facility housing the printing press, which delays publication of the book within the time required by the contract terms, the publisher is "excused" from the time requirement. This clause is standard in most commercial contracts.

Section 6, Subsection 30 also contains a clause often found in such publishing agreements. The publisher does not warrant its services, which are provided on an "as is" basis. Damages owed to the author are limited to fees "actually paid by the author to the publisher for the one month period prior to publisher's act" that gives rise to the liability. The publisher also rejects liability for any damages that could possibly result from publisher error. This clause has little to do with any intentional acts by the publisher, such as refusal to pay royalties or refusal to cease book sales after termination. Instead, it covers situations like Outskirts failing to send you copies of your book in time for a scheduled book signing. You wouldn't be able to sue Outskirts for damages that resulted from the inability of people to purchase the book at the book signing.

Section 6, Subsection 32 specifies Douglas County, Colorado, as the venue for all legal proceedings.

AUTHOR-FRIENDLY RATING: Although Outskirts' package fees are in the ballpark, you'll need to add $299 for a custom-designed cover to any package you choose if you want something more than a basic cover. Paying to publish with a template cover is throwing money away, because you'll never have a professional-looking book without a custom cover.

Outskirts allows authors who terminate their contracts to take press-ready PDFs with them, albeit for a $998 fee. These aren't editable files and aren't worth anything close to $998 ($499 for the cover files and $499 for the interior). As you know, I believe that authors pay for this right initially, so to see that Outskirts' fee for the return of these files has gone from $198 to $998 in just two years concerns me.

The royalties paid to authors are low; Outskirts makes more on each sale than the authors do in most cases. The author price for books isn't as high as other publishers, but it's still at least 50 percent more than the actual printing costs.

What keeps Outskirts in the "Pretty Good" category is that it provides some really low entry points to get your book published—but that's it. The printing prices are not "below wholesale," so that statement on its website is false. Outskirts would be better served to remove that statement, since its printing markups are much less than most companies. The royalties are not really 100 percent as stated in the contract. And, you have to pay nearly $1,000 to get your files back. If you have a few hundred dollars and really want to publish your book, Outskirts is a good company for you. But, understand you are not getting "below wholesale printing" or 100 percent royalties (even under a definition that would back out actual production costs and wholesaler/retailer fees).

CHAPTER 10

PUBLISHERS WHO ARE JUST OKAY

If none of the "Outstanding" or "Pretty Good" publishers discussed in this book fits your needs or will publish your work, then by all means comb the "Just Okay" group to see if a publisher meets your requirements.

What does "Just Okay" mean? It means just what you think it means—slightly below average, but not horrible.

There are many publishers far better than those covered in this chapter. These "Just Okay" publishers offer deficient and overpriced products and services and have issues that preclude them from inclusion in the better categories.

Like I said, consider a publisher in the "Just Okay" category only if you can't get a publisher in either the "Outstanding" or "Pretty Good" group to accept your work (which is next to impossible).

LULU
http://www.lulu.com

FORMAT OF BOOKS: Ebook, paperback, and hardcover

GENRES ACCEPTED: All

PUBLISHING FEES: Lulu charges no up-front publishing fee for authors willing to do all of their own cover design and formatting. In that case, there are distribution fees only. (See http://www.lulu.com/services/distribution for details.)

For authors who need design and formatting services, Lulu bundles together their most popular services, previously offered à la carte, into three publishing packages (for black & white interiors), which can be found at http://www.lulu.com/services/pre-publishing/.

Best Seller: Priced at $629, this package includes:

- ISBN
- One galley (review) copy for author
- Customized, template-based cover, based on author-provided images, blurbs, etc.; designers can also use images from Lulu's free image library
- Inclusion in Lulu's globalREACH distribution service, making your book available to online bookstores and allowing brick-and-mortar bookstores to order your book upon customer request
- Email support (no phone support)
- Template-based formatting, including your choice of 6 interiors
- Up to fifteen images
- Table of contents
- Editorial Review, in which an editor will suggest an editing level and provide you with a sample edit and price quote.

Masterpiece: Priced at $1,429, this package includes everything in the Best Seller package, plus:

- Premium cover (includes two custom cover designs)
- Phone support (three phone appointments throughout the publishing process)
- Conversion of your book to the ePub format (ebook)
- Ultimate formatting (an expansion of basic formatting, ultimate formatting includes unlimited images, but doesn't include resizing the images)

Laureate: Priced at $4,729, this package includes everything in the Masterpiece, plus:

- Three additional phone calls during the publishing process

- Twenty-five hardcover books (black-and-white interior, 6" x 9" trim size only)
- One hundred paperback copies (black-and-white interior, 6" x 9" trim size only)
- Editing up to 100,000 words

These packages are well-priced, however it's hard to understand how three (or even six) phone calls during the publishing process would be sufficient. The lack of allowed communication is problematic, but if you understand these limitations, proceed—but use your calls wisely.

There is a children's book publishing package (not covered in this review) described at http://www.lulu.com/services/pre-publishing/childrens-imagination-package.

Lulu's à la carte services can be found at http://www.lulu.com/services/pre-publishing (by scrolling down the page).

OTHER SERVICES OF INTEREST: In addition to offering many of the individual services included in the publishing packages à la carte, Lulu offers a variety of marketing services. A complete list can be found at http://www.lulu.com/services/packages/marketing/.

One marketing package is the "Book Lover's Bonanza" for $1,895. I thought that the "Triple Blog Book Blitz" sounded interesting. I emailed Lulu's customer service department and asked for a description of the entire service. The "Triple Blog Book Blitz" is a short piece written by Lulu about your book and posted on three online book review sites. Lulu wouldn't tell me what those blog sites were, but the rep did tell me that I should Google the book *Wheat of Weeds* by Glenda Turner to see how effective the Book Lover's Bonanza package is. What I found was a link on the *Fascinating Authors* radio show site (see the paragraph below) and mentions on two blogs, www.iheartbookreviews.com and www.bookreviewstation.com. My company works with a lot of book bloggers, and not many hide their identity in their domain name registration (which is an option). But both of these blog sites had private registration. Even more interesting, both URLs were registered on November 2, 2009. What are the chances that two independent bloggers who post real reviews registered their sites on the exact same day, month, and year, through the same registrar, and hid their identities?

The package also includes one appearance on a internet radio program called "Fascinating Authors Radio," a press release, listings of some media contacts for you to contact yourself, syndication through an article of parts of your book, and inclusion on the Virtual Book Review Network. Problem is that Lulu doesn't tell you what level of service you get from that network (the Virtual Book Review Network has packages as low as $125). I visited the Virtual Book Review Network website. I emailed them to ask what sites their network consisted of, but I never received a response. If a website that touts promotion through a directory of sites doesn't tell you on its own site what websites are actually included, something isn't quite right.

In describing its "Wow-The-Media" press release, Lulu says, "[a] well-crafted press release that sings your praises will increase the likelihood of big book sales." While there isn't anything technically misleading about such a line, the unsuspecting author may believe that a great press release alone actually increases the chances of big book sales. You need a lot more than a polished press release.

The Virtual Author Tour is another marketing package where the some of the services delivered are far from the promises made on Lulu.com. The Virtual Author Tour costs $3,790 (http://www.lulu.com/services/marketing/virtual-author-tour) and, among other things, promises a blog tour. To me, a blog tour consists of authors providing guest articles for a blog, being interviewed by the blogger, or something that has a level of substance. I emailed Lulu to ask about this. A very nice woman, April Flora, responded to my email. She told me about how the author of *Handbook of Financing and Growth* purchased the Virtual Author Tour package, and then listed some sites on which his book was featured, including NYTimes.com, HuffingtonPost.com, BusinessWeek.com, and others.

I was thinking that Lulu must be good to get someone featured on these major sites. I went to the sites and searched them for both the title of the book and the author's name. Nothing. I emailed April and told her that I couldn't find anything on these sites and asked if she could please send the actual links to where the posts are. She responded that she wasn't provided any information with the actual links. She did tell me, "Final analysis: On the internet the numbers never lie. Results are always trackable, measurable, and definable. As you're looking for a company to market you online, make sure you're looking at the numbers. They'll matter to your success!" She also told me that the question had been escalated to her manager to find out where the links were for this campaign. That was on July 23, 2010. I never heard anything again. I think I know why.

So, the NYTimes.com blog—well here is the link: http://dealbook.blogs.nytimes.com/2010/02/02/galileo-sets-up-lgbt-capital-for-gay-market/. Nothing in the actual blog posting itself is about the book or the author. There is a comment by "Melissa" that provides a link to the book's website. Same thing with HuffingtonPost.com (http://www.huffingtonpost.com/gregory-bedrosian/2010-the-year-of-the-entr_b_433086.html). No mention in the blog posting itself, but another comment with a link. Is this really a "blog tour?" You be the judge. Can links, no matter how irrelevant (and in comment sections of major websites), help search engine rankings? Not in this case. Major sites like these usually put "no follow" tags on links pasted in comment sections. In both of my examples, that's what happened. Are authors paying nearly $4,000 for this service because they envision serious mentions of their books on major websites? Probably.

Lulu has a large number of service offerings. The marketing and PR services that I reviewed seemed way overpriced for what you actually get. The sales copy was so over-the-top that I found it insulting to my intelligence. The email response, while not technically inaccurate, was misleading. What worries me is that many new authors could read this copy and not understand what they'll really get. Again, Lulu doesn't make any literal false statements, but the overall tone suggests an outcome that isn't achievable by most authors.

RETAIL PRICE OF AUTHOR'S BOOK: Authors set the price for their books, thus determining their own royalties as well. The retail cost calculator is at http://www.lulu.com/en/includes/calc_retail_inc.php.

RETURN OF ORIGINAL PRODUCTION FILES: Lulu uses its own formatting system, so there aren't any original production files that would be useful to you. Not using a standard formatting program like Adobe InDesign limits your options should you ever decide to publish your book elsewhere in the future.

PRICE AUTHOR PAYS FOR BOOKS: On http://www.lulu.com/publish/books, there is a book cost calculator. You can click on it to see how much it costs to buy copies of your book. There is a chart on https://support.lulu.com/View.jsp?procId=49bbc167ce33751cc301faf089b32b5f&authToken=10fb59282a01ecec21d9f593bbcbb140&forceLogout=true&locale=en_US. This chart also provides another way to view what the author pays for books. For a 6" x 9", 200-page paperback with a black-and-white interior, here is how the math breaks down to purchase a single copy:

$8.50 Author purchase price
-$3.90 Actual printing cost
$4.60 Lulu profit

Lulu makes $4.60 per copy printed. This is a 118 percent markup. The price does drop the more books you buy. For example:

Quantity	Price Per Copy	Printing Markup
10	$8.08	107%
25	$7.65	96%
100	$6.80	74%
200	$6.38	64%
500	$5.65	45%
1000	$5.53	121%*

The markup for one thousand copies is an estimate. Most publishers would print one thousand copies offset, which is cheaper than print-on-demand. If you went to an offset book printer you found online, you could get one thousand copies of your book printed for around $2.00–$2.50 per book. I used $2.50 to get to the 121 percent markup.

ROYALTIES PAID TO AUTHOR: For royalties from sales of a book through third-party retail sites, the author makes 75 percent of the net (retail price, less printing costs, less trade discount, less Lulu royalty). If the author selects a $13.50 retail price and a $1.00 royalty on a 200-page, 6"x9" paperback with a black-and-white interior, the breakdown is as follows:

$13.50 Retail price
– $5.50 Manufacturing cost
– $6.75 Trade discount
– $0.25 Lulu commission
$1.00 Author royalty

Because of the printing markup, Lulu actually makes $1.85 in this transaction.

Interestingly, if you want to make an extra dollar per book, the numbers look like this:

$16.00 Retail price
– $5.50 Manufacturing cost
– $8.00 Trade discount
– $0.50 Lulu commission
$2.00 Author royalty

For royalties on books sold through Lulu, the "manufacturing cost" that is $5.50 for retail sales purposes suddenly jumps to $8.50. I spent an hour on Lulu's live support and no one would tell me why they were different or which pricing was correct. I was told that someone would get an answer to me within one business day. It's been much longer than one business day, and I still haven't heard anything.

I then found a chart at https://support.lulu.com/View.jsp?procId=49bbc167ce33751cc301faf089b32b5f&authToken=10fb59282a01ecec21d9f593bbcbb140&forceLogout=true&locale=en_US that shows the manufacturing/printing costs for books sold through Lulu and sold through other retail channels. This chart confirms that the "manufacturing cost" for a book sold on Lulu.com is $8.50 per book, while the "manufacturing cost" for that same book sold through retailers is $5.50.

For the same 200-page book used before, here is how the numbers break down for sales on Lulu.com:

$4.00 Page cost ($0.02 per page)
+ $4.50 Binding fee
$8.50 Manufacturing cost
+ $4.00 Author Royalty
+ $1.00 Lulu commission (20% of profit or 25% of royalty)
$13.50 Retail price

So, on this transaction, back out the actual printing cost of $3.90 and Lulu makes $5.60 while the author makes $4.00, much more than the commission percentage it claims.

The markups are high either way, but this type of pricing model isn't the worst. Yes, Lulu is making a lot more on books that you buy for your own purposes and/or sell through Lulu.com. But, for retail sales, Lulu is cutting you a break. Most other self-publishing companies don't.

It should be noted that the only type of distribution that Lulu offers is through online retailers. Brick-and-mortar stores can, however, order your book if a customer requests it. See www.lulu.com/services /marketing/retail_listing/?cid=publish_portal.

NOTABLE PROVISIONS OF THE PUBLISHING AGREEMENT: Lulu publishes two agreements. One is the general publisher agreement that all authors and users must use, and the other applies to those who sign on to one of Lulu's two distribution programs.

Member Agreement: This agreement can be found at http://www.lulu.com/about/member_agreement.php. Although it is used by authors and website users, only the portions relevant to writers are discussed here.

Section 3 states that Lulu makes no claim to the copyright in your work but has permission to post and sell an author's work. This section lists all author representations and warranties, which are reasonable.

Section 5 discusses payment terms and agrees to pay you the "creator revenue" or royalty amount you chose. This section is general and refers back to the "publishing portal" (where the pricing is actually set). This section does tell you how you will be paid and when.

Section 8 explains Lulu's return policy for both print-on-demand and "trade print" items. This section is more for the consumer who buys a book from Lulu.com than it is for authors.

Section 10 is significant because it explains how an author removes his or her work for sale from the publisher's website. It's a simple process that can be done at any time.

AUTHOR-FRIENDLY RATING: Trying to find answers to my questions on Lulu's website and dealing with the live support operators was extremely frustrating. There is no phone support (unless you purchase the more expensive publishing packages, and even then the support is limited). The live support operator couldn't answer any question effectively. When I asked why the manufacturing/printing costs for the same book were so much higher when selling my book on Lulu as opposed to selling it on a third-party website, an incident ticket was created for me, but no one ever got back to me.

While the royalty Lulu pays for books sold on its site aren't bad, Lulu's income per book sold is much more than the 20 percent of the author's royalty as is stated on its website. You can't hide your profit inside print costs and pretend it's not there. Obviously, it doesn't cost $3 more to a print book sold on Lulu.com than it does to print the same book and sell it on Amazon.com. It's the same book being printed at the exact same printer.

Lulu actually punishes authors who sell a lot of books because of its high printing costs, which result in artificially high retail prices. Lulu requires that you do a lot of the legwork yourself, and without much phone support, Lulu can be frustrating for the inexperienced author. I felt like I was going in circles and getting nowhere.

Most of the packages only include very basic covers and interiors. If you are a skilled designer, a basic book meets your needs, or you simply don't have enough money to publish any other way, Lulu is a company to consider, so long as you keep your sales expectations in check. And Lulu is well suited to the experienced author whose book is already designed and formatted and who only needs a simple distribution package.

Lulu has much more going on than just books (CDs, calendars, yearbooks, etc.), and in trying to be all things to all people, it's easy for one to get confused. There are simply so many offerings and packages. I've been doing this self-publishing stuff for a long time, and I still had a hard time sorting out the offerings and pricing models (especially when it came to printing costs).

If you want to dip your toe in the publishing waters, Lulu is a fairly low risk venture where, in some cases, you can publish without any up-front fees. Lulu also has a basic publishing package for $629. You won't get much for that, but you aren't paying much either.

While allowing an author to set his own retail price seems great in theory, without guidance most authors will way overprice their books in order to make a large royalty. Overpriced books don't sell, so a large part of nothing is nothing. Understand what other books in your genre sell for when considering how to price yours.

The agreement is as author-friendly as they come. The ability to set your retail price is a great feature, but since so many authors don't understand how to properly price their books, it can also be a feature that leads to disaster. Being able to set your royalties as high or low as you want can be great, yet also problematic for the same reasons.

I found the slick marketing copy to be a turnoff. I think that many authors will be sucked in by it without understanding what they are actually getting. The description that I received (via email) of the "Blog Tour," touting all of the major blogs, was as close to a bait-and-switch as a company can do without actually doing it. Was a link to the book's website on the NYTimes.com blog? Yes. Was the author or book really featured or discussed? No. The way the sales rep avoided providing real answers to my questions was annoying and maddening (although I don't think she was given the real information herself).

My overall interaction with Lulu made me feel like I was at a used car lot. While I don't know a lot about cars, I do know a lot about self-publishing, and I was able to ask the right questions. I'm not sure every other author will.

MAGIC VALLEY PUBLISHING
http://www.magicvalleypub.com/

FORMAT OF BOOKS: Paperback

GENRES: All

PUBLISHING FEES: Magic Valley offers one pared-down package.

Publishing Package: Priced at $379, plus $45 for a proof, this package includes:

- ISBN
- Bar code
- Listing with online booksellers, including Amazon.com and BarnesandNoble.com
- Cover design, which includes a total of four hours of design time (The website says two hours, but the contract says four.)
- Typesetting
- Choice of trim size:
  5" x 8"
  5.5" x 8.5"
  6" x 9"
- Inclusion in catalog—free for first year, $22 for each year after that
- Copy of Mark Ortman's *A Simple Guide to Marketing Your Book: What an Author and Publisher Can Do to Sell More Books*, a $10.95 value

RETURN OF DIGITAL COVER AND INTERIOR FILES: Magic Valley's author agreement says that the "Publisher will retain possession of all materials submitted by Author. Publisher will have no obligation to provide Author any submitted materials or production files at anytime [sic] or for any reason." I never received a response to my email query asking if there was a fee that I could pay in order to take the files with me.

RETAIL PRICE OF AUTHOR'S BOOK: Magic Valley allows its authors to set the price of their books but asks them to keep in mind a 40 percent Amazon.com discount.

PRICE AUTHOR PAYS FOR BOOKS: Wholesale or author orders are charged a $2.00 cover charge per unit, plus $0.015 per page. So, your price on a 200-page, 6" x 9" paperback would be:

$2.00	Cover charge
+$3.00	Per-page fee ($0.015 x 200 pages)
$5.00	Wholesale price

Here the printing markup is a respectable 28 percent.

ROYALTIES PAID TO AUTHOR: Oddly, the author agreement references a royalty, but nowhere on the website or the agreement does it mention how much of a royalty the author will receive. In the previous edition of this book, I reported that the publisher had told my research assistant that the royalties were 100 percent of the net sales. This time, Magic Valley didn't return our calls or respond to our emails. Since the website and contract are both silent about the actual royalties paid, your guess is as good as mine.

NOTABLE PROVISIONS OF THE PUBLISHING AGREEMENT: The publishing agreement can be found at http://www.magicvalleypub .com/publishingagreement.pdf.

Paragraph 1 states that the author is responsible for sending the publisher the agreement, payment, and his work in a ready-to-publish format.

Paragraph 2 states that if the author does not submit the work in an acceptable format (note that "acceptable format" is not defined in the contract) or requests subsequent revisions, the publisher will apply an unspecified fee.

Paragraph 3 covers the ownership of the production files and states that the publisher has no obligation to return any files to the author. It is fairly standard for a publisher to decline responsibility for the safekeeping of the author's materials, but not providing the production files is another thing. If the author decides to leave Magic Valley and cannot take his production files with him, he will have to pay another designer to create a cover and typeset the book.

Paragraph 5 is a fairly standard warranty section in which the author agrees that he is the author of the book, that it does not contain libelous or hateful material, and that he has the right to publish it. It also states that there will be "no recipe, formula, or instruction contained in the Work that may be injurious to the reader or user."

Paragraph 6 is also a standard clause, stating that Magic Valley Publishers does not own the work and assumes no responsibility for reviewing the work. It also says that either party can terminate the agreement at any time, without cause. The publisher is not responsible for errors introduced by its distributors, and "Publisher shall be held harmless for any damages Publisher sustains by distributing the Work." This means that if an author defames someone in her book, and that person sues Magic Valley (since it is the publisher), the author agrees that any damages assessed against Magic Valley will be the author's responsibility. This is a fair and reasonable clause.

Paragraph 7 states that the publisher agrees to prepare the work for distribution, assign an ISBN, and register the book with distributors so it is available via print-on-demand. It also says that the publisher "shall keep records of all book sales and distribute Author royalties quarterly."

Paragraph 8 deals with pricing and says that it will be determined per title and subject to change without notice, which means that if you publish a second book with the company you will not necessarily pay the same fees. The breakdown of the fees is as listed previously. This clause also guarantees an original book cover, which includes either stock photography or an image created by the author and up to four hours of design production time. The clause also states that the publisher will typeset the book. Additional time with the design department is available for purchase at an hourly rate of $75. The author is responsible for the "about the author" section and any back cover content.

Paragraph 9 states that the author will pay an annual catalog fee of $22 and that the first year's catalog fee is included in the package price.

AUTHOR-FRIENDLY RATING: The publishing options here are simple. The contract is simple. The printing markups are quite reasonable. But the publisher didn't respond to phone calls or questions about its royalty calculations. My research assistant emailed our first query and received no reply. She re-sent the email three different times. She then called on a Saturday and left a clear, detailed voicemail message, giving the company her email address so that it could respond. Guess what happened? Nothing.

I'm guessing that this publisher is a mom-and-pop operation. Such publishers need to be supported, but not responding to four emails and a phone call is just too much. If you can't get a publisher to ever respond to you when you want to do business with them, forget about them. Plus, authors don't get the original production files back. Despite good printing prices, I can't think of any compelling reason to consider Magic Valley.

WORDCLAY

http://www.wordclay.com

FORMAT OF BOOKS: Paperback

GENRES ACCEPTED: All

PUBLISHING FEES: Wordclay is owned by Author Solutions, Inc. (parent company of AuthorHouse and iUniverse). It is similar to Lulu and CreateSpace in its offerings; authors pay nothing to upload files and sell their books on the Wordclay website. Wordclay offers authors a host of publishing services, from editing and design to distribution. Wordclay's services are offered à la carte, so out of the individual services offered at http://www.wordclay.com/ServicesStore/ServicesStoreHome.aspx I've assembled what might make up a typical publishing package:

- Cover design: $275 for a template-based cover with stock photos (includes one round of corrections and five hours of design time), $999 for a custom cover
- Custom typesetting: $325, includes up to five hours of design time

- Returns insurance: $799 (most places charge around $200)
- Copyright registration: $150
- ISBN and channel distribution: $99

So, what amounts to a pretty basic publishing package is $1,648.

OTHER SERVICES OF INTEREST: The downside to the free-upload model is that the templates the publisher provides will only take authors so far, and then they need to find service providers to help them create a cover, edit content, and the rest of it. The Wordclay model is different than others in this category, such as Lulu and CreateSpace, in that it offers these services, for a price, in house. Below is a sampling of the basic services needed to get a book out; the full service listing is available here: http://www.wordclay.com/ServicesStore/ServicesStoreHome.aspx.

Copyediting: Correcting basic spelling, grammar, punctuation, and syntax costs $0.03 a word and takes from forty-five to sixty days. For those in a hurry, Wordclay offers an Express Edit, which takes one–two weeks and costs $0.04 a word. Content editing, which includes grammar, flow, content, and organization, takes up to seventy-five days and costs $0.06 a word.

Content Editing: In addition to basic copyediting, an editor will help you reorganize your book's chapters and paragraphs. This takes seventy-five days.

Editorial Review: For $275, an editor will review either your first chapter or 1,650 words, whichever comes first, and suggest a level of editing.

Personalized Website: Wordclay will set up a template-based website for you for the hefty fee of $479, plus a $29 per month hosting fee. You will then "customize" your own website with your choice of eleven layouts, eleven color options, and three hundred header graphics.

Softcover Distribution: This package is $99 for one year, $129 for two years, and $139 for three years.

Marketing: The basic marketing package costs $399 and includes a professionally written press release, distributed to media outlets in three cities of your choice, and a list of contact information so that you, the author, can follow up with those media outlets that received the press release.

Expanded Book Marketing: For $799, your press release will be delivered to media contacts in five cities. You'll also receive thirty press kits, each containing two full-color flyers and a copy of your press release, and the contact information for each of the media outlets.

RETURN OF DIGITAL COVER AND INTERIOR FILES: When I asked Wordclay via email if I could have my production files, the representative responded:

> "When you upload your manuscript online you will be given a preview files [sic] (.pdf and .doc form) in order for you to review your work, you can save this filess [sic] on your end for your record. In addition, you may also request for us to send you the files after the completion of your work."

RETAIL PRICE OF AUTHOR'S BOOK: Wordclay allows authors to set their own price for the book as long as it is higher than the base price. I inquired about a 200-page paperback with a black-and-white interior, and I was told the base price would be approximately $13.17, which includes a $3.74 royalty for books sold through Wordclay's website.

PRICE AUTHOR PAYS FOR BOOKS: I was told that author discounts are equivalent to Wordclay's cost to print. The Wordclay representative told me in an email, "For a 200-page book, the print cost is $8.43." Since Wordclay has a printing calculator on its home page (right-hand side of the page), it's easy to see if that statement is true or not. For a 200-page, 6" x 9" paperback, the printing charges are:

Quantity	Author Price	Markup
1–24	$8.43	116%
25	$8.01	105%
50	$7.76	99%
100	$7.59	95%
250	$7.42	90%
500	$7.17	84%
1000	$6.74	189%*
2000	$6.74	250%*

The asterisks above are there because I assume that quantities this large are printed offset, which is cheaper. If you went to any printer to get these quantities printed, it would cost you approximately $2.33 per copy for one thousand copies and $1.94 per copy for two thousand. If Wordclay isn't printing these offset, then my markup percentages don't apply. If these larger quantities are printed on-demand, then the markup would be 73 percent.

When my research assistant sent a few questions in an email to the customer service representative, all of her questions except "Where do you print your books?" and "How do you come to the $8.43 print cost?" were answered. Since we know the actual print costs, we know that the rep's statement about not marking up printing was inaccurate.

ROYALTIES PAID TO AUTHOR: Wordclay allows the author to set the price of his or her book, and therefore the royalty, so long as the price set exceeds the base price.

Let's say you sold the 200-page, paperback book for $14.99 on Amazon.com:

$14.99	Retail price
–$13.17	Wordclay base price (includes printing/distribution)
$1.16	Author royalty

For the same book sold through Wordclay for $14.99, the math looks like this:

$14.99 Retail price
–$9.43 Wordclay base price (includes printing/distribution)
$5.56 Author royalty

I had trouble finding this information on the site; but, when I chatted with a live operator via online chat, that was the information I was given. I have it in writing, just in case.

NOTABLE PROVISIONS OF THE PUBLISHING AGREEMENT: The publishing agreement can be found at: http://www.wordclay.com/TermsOfUse.aspx.

In the "Agreements" section, the author agrees to take full responsibility both for the content that is published and any materials used to create the content; if anything is misspelled, lost, or damaged, Wordclay will not be responsible. Furthermore, Wordclay does not guarantee the quality of its printing (e.g., colors may appear differently in the print and online versions).

Section 1.4 of the agreement says, "You acknowledge that you may not utilize the formatted Work and cover with any other publisher, if we cease publication of the Work." In other words, if you determine to print your book elsewhere, any interior design and/or cover design you create using Wordclay's templates or by hiring its designers will need to be redesigned. So exactly what do you get for the $999 cover design fee if, in the end, you don't really own the cover?

The "Your Legal Responsibility" section says that Wordclay will not publish works that are plagiarized, libelous, illegal, or written in language that is pornographic, hateful, or obscene. This is reasonable.

In "Our Legal Responsibility," it says that Wordclay cannot be held liable for your work (i.e., if you get sued for something you publish, you are on your own). Wordclay also asserts its right to withhold service if an author violates the terms of the agreement. It also reserves the right to change promotional offers and substitute offers of the same or greater value. And Wordclay does not promise that its site will be error-free or even available. This is reasonable. The website availability language really means that if the site goes down for a while, you won't have a cause of action against them.

The "Indemnification" section is basically more of the same and simply says that neither Wordclay nor its employees can be held liable for the author's work. If a lawsuit does arise as a result of an author's work, Wordplay can hold the author's royalties and stop publishing the book. Further, it will not refund any of the fees the author has paid. Again, this is reasonable.

The "Pricing and Royalty Agreements" section, namely 5.2, has a red flag buried in it. In fact, if I hadn't read it I wouldn't have believed it, so here is a direct quote cut and pasted from the actual document: "If your account is inactive or terminated and we are unable to contact you using the contact information provided, we may also, at our discretion, charge a termination fee equal to the amount of unpaid royalties to cover administrative costs."

The "Termination" section states that either party can terminate with thirty days notice but that authors will not be eligible for any kind of refund upon termination.

The "Force Majeure" section basically states that Wordclay is not responsible for acts of nature that might keep it from providing its services. If inclement weather or an act of war keeps it from providing said services for ninety days, the author can terminate his contract.

The "Governing Law" section simply says that any arbitration arising from this contract will take place in Bloomington, Indiana, which is fair but not advantageous to the author, unless he or she happens to live in Bloomington.

AUTHOR-FRIENDLY RATING: Wordclay is AuthorHouse's answer to Lulu and CreateSpace. CreateSpace is far superior to Wordclay. But, of all the Author Solutions companies, Wordclay is the best. The prices seem the most reasonable and the printing markups, while high, are not as bad as some of its related companies. The royalties, while not spectacular, are not bad. If I had to use one Author Solutions company, this would be it.

CHAPTER 11

PUBLISHERS TO AVOID

If you choose to publish with any of the companies listed in this chapter, picture me whispering in your ear, "I told you so." It is harder to make the "Avoid" list than it is to make the "Outstanding" list. It is not my goal to tear down any company, but these publishers make the process of self-publishing frustrating and financially unviable. I spent a lot of time trying to get these publishers to answer my questions, provide copies of their contracts, and explain why they do what they do. You will see the results of my efforts as you read this chapter.

Any publishers that refused to provide me a copy of their publishing contract automatically ended up on this list. If they don't want prospective authors to see a contract, there must be a good reason. Perhaps there's something in it that's not author-friendly, and they assume that by not providing a copy they are ensuring that the bad contract terms will never be discovered.

Other publishers ended up on this list because clauses in their contracts were absolutely horrible. Some clauses required authors to give up rights for many years, to give up their ancillary rights to movies and television, or to engage in other unsavory practices (at least in my opinion), like forcing authors to pay a lot of money to get their original production files.

I have no vendetta against these companies. I know how important your book is to you, and my goal is to assist you in having a positive publishing experience. If you want to increase your chances of having a good experience, go with one of the publishers described elsewhere in this book.

ARBOR BOOKS INC.

http://www.arborbooks.com

FORMAT OF BOOKS: Ebook, paperback, and hardcover

GENRES ACCEPTED: All

PUBLISHING FEES: Arbor Books is both a self-publishing and ghostwriting service. The publisher's website does not provide detailed information about its services or fees. However, I filled out Arbor's "request a quote" form and received the following information regarding a 200-page paperback book.

There are several different tiers of publishing fees, each providing you with subsequently more books: (1) for $2,500, the author gets one hundred copies of the book; (2) for $3,500, the author gets two hundred copies; (3) for $5,500, the author gets five hundred copies; (4) for $6,500, the author gets one thousand copies; and (5) for $10,500, the author gets three thousand copies. The sample contract sent to me was for the thousand-copy package, which includes:

- Five hours of phone or email consultation, after which representatives bill at $115 an hour
- Custom-designed cover: Includes up to three rough drafts. (A representative told me, "Generally we don't charge for minor changes, font choice, color, contrast, etc. Charges are more for when you approve of something and then change your mind.")
- Proofs, alterations of which cost $150 for cover, $50 for interior
- Typesetting (add $10 for every graphic insertion, $20 per page to recreate charts)
- ISBN
- Bar code
- Library of Congress Control Number (LCCN)
- U.S. Copyright Office registration
- Printing, for the number of books of your choice, plus shipping

OTHER SERVICES OF INTEREST:

Ghostwriting: Arbor Books is a jack-of-all-trades, but of its many services, perhaps the most interesting is that it will actually write your book for you for $8,000–$25,000.

Editing: Proofreading costs $0.04 per word; a "commercial-quality edit" costs $0.07 per word. This is quite high.

Contacting Agents and Publishers: Arbor Books has four different "strategies" for contacting agents and publishers, ranging from $1,500 to $4,995. On the lower end, Arbor Books will simply query agents for you. On the higher end, they will help you find endorsers, query agents and publishers, write a book proposal, and provide you with sample books for reviewers.

Ebook: For $1,995, Arbor Books will design your ebook.

Marketing and Publicity Program: This costs $2,000 and includes:

- Promotional kit with the following parts: cover letter; press release; talking points; cover letter for speaking engagements; and back-cover copy, which includes a blurb, a biography, and "other elements."
- Outreach to 150 retail distributors; library distributors; national book chains, including Borders and Barnes & Noble; internet booksellers, including Amazon.com, Borders.com, Target.com, VirginMega.com, and Waldenbooks.com; book clubs and other specialty organizations and their catalogs; and key reviewers and media outlets, including *Kirkus Reviews*, *Publishers Weekly*, *The View*, *The Oprah Winfrey Show*, *Good Morning America*, *The Today Show*, *Live With Regis and Kelly*, *USA Today Book Club*, C-SPAN, *Imus in the Morning*, *New York Times Book Review*, *Time*, *Newsweek*, *Library Journal*, and many more.

Note: What that last service really means is that your book will be carried by at least one wholesaler that makes your title available for sale through internet retailers, and also makes it available to some traditional retailers should they wish to special order it. This does not mean that your book will be in bookstores. While the list of media outlets to which press kits are sent looks impressive, keep in mind that anyone can send a book to these outlets. "Outreach" to media outlets means sending information about your book to them. These major media outlets are besieged with unsolicited press releases, review copies, and other materials. These venues find you after your book has generated significant buzz, not the other way around.

The services in general are grossly overpriced and not in line with the self-publishing market in general.

RETURN OF DIGITAL COVER AND INTERIOR FILES: Arbor Books provided me with a total of two contracts, each for a different print volume. One contract specifically mentions that the layered application files cost $350; the other contract didn't mention those files at all. Beware.

RETAIL PRICE OF AUTHOR'S BOOK: The author sets the price of the book. "The publisher usually sets the price. In case of self-publishing, you can charge whatever you wish. You're the boss!" said the publisher's representative.

PRICE AUTHOR PAYS FOR BOOKS: In the sample contract for one thousand books, reprint prices were not listed. In the sample contract we received for a one-hundred-book run, reprints were listed as:

Quantity	Price Per Book	Markup
100 copies	$9.50	144%
300 copies	$9.33	139%
500 copies	$7.00	80%
1,000 copies	$4.20	110%*

Because the initial book order is included in your contract, it's hard to determine what the printing markups are. But, using the reprint figure provided by the company, the markups appear to be high. Once print runs exceed five hundred copies the books are usually printed offset, which is cheaper than print-on-demand. Arbor's cost for five hundred books is probably much less than $3.90 a book, but I used $3.90 (which gives them a huge benefit of the doubt of here). At one thousand copies, pricing can be anywhere from $2.00 to $2.50 per unit at a book printer you'd find online. The markup percentage I used is based on $2.00 per book at one thousand copies, hence the asterisk.

ROYALTIES PAID TO AUTHOR: Arbor Books does not pay author royalties, because it doesn't actually sell books. The company does not have a bookstore, nor does it provide its authors with websites to sell their books. It is hard to tell whether Arbor's $2,500 marketing program (http://www.arborbooks.com/index.php?id=marketing.html) provides some level of distribution. It says that it contacts certain retailers and wholesalers, but it is very unclear. If you buy the program that includes distribution, you will make 45 percent of sales through Amazon.com and BarnesandNoble.com. If Arbor Books is involved in the book fulfillment, they keep approximately 15 percent, plus shipping, of the wholesale price.

So, it appears that after the initial books that come with the package, you would need to order more from Arbor Books and then have them sent to a wholesaler (if you have the marketing program), to yourself, or to whomever you have fulfilling the books for you. If you sell the books directly, you will be able to sell your book at reasonable price and still make a profit. For example, if you purchase a small number of books (e.g., one hundred copies) for $9.50 a book, you can sell it for $13.95 and still make $4.00 per book. The real problem here comes in when you have to price your book to sell on Amazon.com and other online retailers. Since Arbor inflates the printing costs, you'll have to price your 200-page book at $22.00 just to make $0.40 per copy. The math is not pretty:

\$22.00	Retail price
–\$9.50	Author price per book
–\$12.10	Amazon.com discount (55%)
\$0.40	Author profit

That isn't going to cut it. There are few, if any, 200-page paperbacks that can command a \$22 retail price.

NOTABLE PROVISIONS OF THE PUBLISHING AGREEMENT: Arbor Books does not post its author agreement on its website but readily presented one with the price quote.

The "Ownership of The Work; Author's Grant" clause says that the work belongs to the author, but that she grants the publisher the nonexclusive right to print, publish, and distribute the book globally. It also states that the publisher has not read the book and is relying on the author's representation with regard to the author's ownership, right to publish it, and so on.

The "Production, Manufacturing, Design and Delivery" clause says that the author must send all of the necessary content to the publisher and that the publisher is not responsible for loss or damage. It also outlines the proofing and printing process, most notably stating that the author has three days to review the printer's proof, which may vary from the design proofs, and that the author will be charged 80 percent of the per-copy book price for an overrun. Overruns by printers are common. The author will receive a complete refund for books that are not printed in the event of an underrun.

The "Marketing, Distribution and Sales" clause reiterates that Arbor Books will not be responsible for the marketing, distribution, or sale of the work unless the author pays for the marketing package. In no event, it says, is Arbor Books responsible for the success of the book. It does not pay royalties.

In the "Representations, Warranties and Covenants" clause, the author agrees that she is the owner of the book and that she has the right to enter into the publishing agreement. Further, she warrants that the book is not libelous or scandalous and does not infringe on anyone else's rights.

In the "Indemnity" clause, the author agrees not to hold Arbor

Books or its employees responsible, legally or financially, in the event of a lawsuit resulting from any alleged breach of a representation or warranty by the author.

The "Term and Termination" clause states that the agreement is effective until the book has been delivered, unless Arbor Books has agreed to market the book, in which case it lasts until completion of those services. But, either party may terminate the agreement for any or no reason with thirty days notice. Upon termination, the author must pay all outstanding fees. If the publisher terminates, it will account for the time spent on production and refund the author the difference between the amount paid by the author and the value of any time Arbor Books spent on the project, at a value of $115 an hour.

The "Pricing" clause says that the prices quoted in the agreement are good for only 180 days after the effective date.

In the "Non-compete" clause, the author basically agrees to pay $50,000 if she hires any of Arbor Books' editors, typesetters, or other staff outside of the contract during a five-year period. This is a ridiculous clause, and the extended time period probably makes it unenforceable. But, I wouldn't chance it.

The "Notices" clauses states that all notices, requests, and demands under the publishing agreement must be made in writing and delivered via a tracked system (i.e., registered mail, fax, email).

The "Governing Law, Jurisdiction and Venue" clause simply states that the agreement is governed by the laws of the State of New Jersey and that any litigation must be brought in Newark or Bergen County.

The "Miscellaneous" clause says that the agreement can only be amended in writing, and any amendments require a signature from both parties. It also says that while Arbor can transfer all rights, interests, and obligations stated in the agreement, the author may not (without prior consent from Arbor Books).

AUTHOR-FRIENDLY RATING: When I look at Arbor's website, I feel like I'm in the middle of Times Square outside of Crazy Eddie's Electronics, and some guy wearing a huge gold chain is trying to entice me to come inside. The website is stuffed with content, images, words, and dozens of links, but no useful information (i.e., fees, service descriptions, or what the publisher's packages include). The books posted in the most prominent spot on the home page are all bestselling books, but by other publishers. There is small type that explains that these books (e.g., *The Bridges of Madison County*) were originally self-published. But, at first glance, the website gives the impression that Arbor is somehow connected with these major bestsellers. It isn't.

From a services standpoint, this publisher charges way too much. For $3,800, all you get is cover design, typesetting, and one hundred copies of your book. For $5,800, you get distribution, but no fulfillment other than through online retailers. Sure, you get one hundred books, but that's worth about $390 (assuming it's a 200-page paperback). Other services, like ebook creation, are way out of whack with the rest of the market.

I have a feeling that Arbor Books is sort of a money pit, where you keep paying in but don't get anything out of it. For $5,800, you get what most other companies reviewed in this book provide for about $1,000–$2,500. The grossly inflated printing markups further reinforce why this publisher should be on any writer's avoid list.

I encountered a humorous and revealing story about Arbor Books on a particular blog. The blogger was dismayed to discover that Arbor was telling its authors to buy advertisements in the *New York Times Book Review* for the sole purpose of then quoting their own ads on the back of their books and attributing the quotes to the *New York Times*—as if the *Times* had reviewed the book! For this post, see http://robnyc.blogspot.com/2007/07/grab-your-credit-card-and-buy-glowing.html. This post prompted Arbor to remove the instructions on how to do that, and what remains is much subtler (see http://www.arborbooks.com/index.php?id=getreviewed.html).

AUTHORHOUSE

http://www.authorhouse.com

FORMAT OF BOOK: Ebook, hardcover, and paperback

GENRES ACCEPTED: All

PUBLISHING FEES: AuthorHouse offers a variety of publishing packages, including children's books and poetry, but only the standard paperback and hardcover packages are discussed here. (Visit http://www.authorhouse.com/ServicesStore/ChoosePackage.asp for details.)

Foundation Package: This package costs $599 and includes:

- Custom-designed, full-color cover
- Custom interior design
- Electronic proof
- One copy of the book
- Ebook in PDF format
- Listing with online booksellers (i.e., Amazon.com, BarnesandNoble.com, and Borders.com)
- Professional marketing consultation
- Bookstore availability (meaning that a bookstore could order a copy—this doesn't mean that a bookstore will *have* a copy)
- ISBN

Legacy Package: This package costs $799 and includes everything in the Foundation Package, plus:

- Ten image insertions
- Copyright and Library of Congress Control Number (LCCN)
- Five complimentary copies

Legacy Hardcover Package: This package costs $1,099 and includes everything above, plus:

- Personalized back cover
- Ten complimentary paperbacks
- Five complimentary hardcovers

Discovery Package: This package costs $1,399 and includes everything above, plus:

- Book-buyer's preview and Barnes & Noble's "See Inside the Book"
- Marketing kit, including bookmarks, postcards, and business cards

- Submission to Google Book Search and Amazon Search Inside! programs
- Fifteen complimentary paperbacks
- Ten complimentary hardcovers

Pinnacle Package: This package costs $1,999 and includes everything in the packages listed previously, plus:

- Booksellers return program
- Book-signing kit
- Forty complimentary paperbacks
- Twenty complimentary hardcovers

OTHER SERVICES OF INTEREST: AuthorHouse offers a host of optional services, including everything from copyright registration to editing and marketing services, but at a higher price than you'll find elsewhere. For a complete list of services, see http://www.authorhouse.com/Services/default.aspx. For the sake of comparison, here are a few of the services:

Line Editing: Includes grammar, syntax, and spelling for $0.029 per word. This is about double the going rate for this level of editing by an experienced editor.

Developmental Editing: Includes grammar, syntax, and spelling, plus an in-depth review of the work's character development, content, and flow. The editor works closely with the author during the course of the editing process. This service costs $0.064 per word, which is about 50 percent higher than you can find elsewhere.

Custom Cover Illustration: The author works with a design consultant and illustrator to create original artwork for the book's front and back cover. Up to twenty-five changes are included.

Stock Art Placement: $12 per image

Image Scanning: $5 for black-and-white images

Image Insertion: $5 per image

Library of Congress Control Number: $75 (The LCCN registration is free and takes about five minutes to do. You are simply paying for the service of having it done for you.)

U.S. Copyright Office Registration: At $170, this is overly expensive. Also, the sales rep emailed my researcher and implied that AuthorHouse can register a copyright faster than one could on his own. That is absolutely false. The rep stated that if you register a copyright on your own, "it can take up to one year! AuthorHouse is able to do this as we publish your book project, which can be as fast as ninety days or even thirty days with our Rapid Release service." Since an expedited registration from the U.S. Copyright Office costs $760 per work filed, I doubt AuthorHouse is expediting registration and charging only $170 for it. AuthorHouse cannot make the process go faster, unless they (or you) are paying the $760 to expedite the copyright filing.

Rapid Release: For an extra $500, AuthorHouse promises to have your book in your hands within thirty days.

Hardcover: For $350, you can add an embossed spine and dust jacket.

Author Website: For an initial $399 and $29 per month, AuthorHouse will set up and host your website. The publisher wouldn't provide any information with regard to whether or not this fee entitles the author to ownership of the website and/or the domain name. I emailed the same question to AmericanAuthor .com, the company that provides this service for AuthorHouse. The rep from AmericanAuthor.com responded quickly and told me that the author always owns the content on the site, but doesn't own the website layout. So long as the author continues to pay $29 per month for hosting, the author can continue to use the layout. Also, the author can supply his or her own domain name. The $29 per month for hosting is expensive. You can get hosting for $5–$10 per month. However, the best part of my experience dealing with AuthorHouse was the response of its third-party website provider.

RETURN OF DIGITAL COVER AND INTERIOR FILES: The AuthorHouse contract states: "You acknowledge that you may not utilize the formatted Work, International Standard Book Number (ISBN), and cover with any other publisher." When asked whether a departing author could pay a fee for the files, the AuthorHouse representative said, "We will not be able to release any sort of master file of the book to you."

If an author leaves to seek a more affordable and profitable self-publishing alternative, then the author will have to pay to have everything recreated, even though he or she has already paid AuthorHouse to create these files.

RETAIL PRICE OF AUTHOR'S BOOK: AuthorHouse does not publish the exact pricing chart for its books, although it has a sample structure here: http://www.authorhouse.com/GetPublished/BookSales.aspx.

AuthorHouse allows its authors to set the royalty for their books at 5–15 percent for books sold via retailers like Amazon.com, and 5–50 percent for books sold via AuthorHouse's online bookstore—books will be priced accordingly. AuthorHouse has a minimum price scale and, obviously, a low-priced book equals a low royalty.

Although the sample chart shows slightly different page-count increments, an AuthorHouse representative quoted me the retail price spread for a 178–271-page paperback book sold on AuthorHouse.com. The retail prices ranged from $9.90 for a 5 percent royalty to $18.70 for a 50 percent royalty. (One should also note that AuthorHouse's online bookstore doesn't publish the page count of its books!) While a 50 percent royalty sounds great, it's doubtful that a 200-page paperback will sell for $18.70, especially one written by an unknown author.

PRICE AUTHOR PAYS FOR BOOKS: Author discounts are based on the size of the book and the quantity ordered. No pricing chart is available on the AuthorHouse website. My researcher had to request the information three times via email before she got someone to send her details. For a 200-page, 6" x 9" paperback, the discount would be:

Quantity	Author Price	Markup
1–24	$9.31	139%
25–50	$9.25	137%
50–99	$9.15	135%
100–249	$8.85	127%
250–500	$8.75	124%
501–749	$8.50	118%
750–999	$8.25	111%
1,000–1,499	$7.45	272%*
1,500–1,999	$6.50	225%*
2,000–2,999	$5.85	227%*
3,000–3,999	$4.85	232%*
4,000–4,999	$4.30	216%*
5,000	$4.00	300%*

So, why all the asterisks? Well, at quantities like these for the book described above, I'm assuming that AuthorHouse is not printing them digitally, but rather using an offset printer, which is much cheaper. You could get 1,000–1,499 books printed almost anywhere for around $2.00 per book. You could get 1,500–1,999 copies printed for about $1.78 per book. If you ordered 3000–3,999 copies, you could get them for $1.46 per book. For runs of 4,000–4,999 the print cost would be around $1.36 per copy. And for 5,000 books, the cost per book would be about $0.99.

Now you know why AuthorHouse doesn't have the pricing chart available on its website.

ROYALTIES PAID TO AUTHOR: AuthorHouse calculates its paperback and hardcover royalties from the retail price of the book. It allows authors to choose a royalty rate between 5 and 50 percent for books sold on retailers like Amazon.com, and between 5 and 15 percent for books sold on the AuthorHouse website. This is explained at http://www.authorhouse.com/GetPublished/BookSales.aspx. The author can also choose to set the royalties at different percentages for sales on the AuthorHouse website versus third-party sales. Authors receive their payment scale, which is determined by the size of the book, after they sign the publisher's contract. The royalty for ebooks is 25 percent of the purchase price.

Because AuthorHouse uses a 250-page, 6"x 9" paperback to demonstrate its royalty structure, so will I. (Remember, I usually base these calculations on a 200-page paperback.) The website page on royalties is very confusing. At first glance, the dollar figure under the royalty amount looks like the actual royalty, but it's actually the retail price on which the royalty is based. The AuthorHouse profit is calculated after backing out the actual printing cost of $4.65 per book (250 pages x $0.015 per page + $0.90 per cover). The royalties for selling this 250-page paperback on the AuthorHouse site are as follows:

Retail price	Royalty	Author profit	AuthorHouse profit
$9.90	5%	$0.50	$4.75
$11.70	20%	$2.34	$4.71
$13.40	30%	$4.02	$4.73
$18.70	50%	$9.35	$4.70

For books sold through third-party retailers, the book prices go up to accommodate a 40 percent wholesale discount. Even though AuthorHouse wouldn't disclose the trade discount, it was ascertainable from the example given on the website. The royalty paid to the author is based on the retail price of the book. So, for the 250-page paperback that retails for $14.99 (as detailed on the publisher's website), the author makes $0.73 per copy sold, while AuthorHouse makes $3.35, almost five times more than the author. Here is the math:

$14.49 Retail price
–$5.76 Trade discount (40%)
–$4.65 Actual print cost
–$0.73 Author royalty (5%)
$3.35 AuthorHouse profit

The more accurate depiction of the royalty chart for sales through third-party retailers on http://www.authorhouse.com/GetPublished/BookSales.aspx should look like this:

Retail price	Royalty	Author profit	AuthorHouse profit
$14.49	5%	$0.73	$3.45
$15.99	10%	$1.60	$3.34
$18.49	15%	$2.77	$4.79

In every sales scenario above, AuthorHouse makes a lot more money on each sale than the author does. What is AuthorHouse doing to sell your book? Nothing. If it's providing marketing services, it's because you've paid for them. Almost all sales that result will be because of your efforts. So, when you get someone to purchase your book, why on earth should this publisher make so much more than you do?

NOTABLE PROVISIONS OF THE PUBLISHING AGREEMENT: A copy of the contract can be found at http://www.authorhouse.com/uploadedFiles/AuthorHouse_US/Packages/Agreement_Order_Forms/AH_Terms_and_Conditions_10_16_09.pdf.

The printing markups and royalties aren't pretty. The contract isn't either. Sections 1.4 and 1.5 make it clear that the author will not receive the production files (book cover, layout, etc.) from the publisher upon termination: "We will have no obligation to provide to you any submitted materials or production files at anytime [sic] or for any reason." Further, "You acknowledge that you may not utilize the formatted Work, International Standard Book Number (ISBN), and cover with any other publisher." Section 1.5 also gives the publisher the final say in your work's appearance, price, style, and formatting.

Section 1.6 gives AuthorHouse 180 days from the date on which it receives your work to have your work published. This does not include copyediting or the time that the work is in your hands for any reason.

Section 1.8 makes it clear that AuthorHouse provides no promotional assistance unless the author purchases those additional services.

Section 5.6 is particularly troubling. AuthorHouse will not allow the author to transfer ownership interest or royalty rights to someone else without the express, written permission of AuthorHouse, which can be withheld at its "sole discretion for any reason." My guess is that this clause exists to prevent disgruntled authors from transferring their rights to a third party and is held like a club over the disgruntled author's head.

Section 6.1 is also fierce; it severely limits the author's legal remedies. You will either allow AuthorHouse to fix the problem ("use commercially reasonable efforts to cure") or to return your fees for the service at issue. Any author claim must be made within thirty days of the problem occurring. An author who is ready to make a claim or threatens legal action probably wants to get his money back and walk away from the publisher. My guess is that in 99 percent of the cases, AuthorHouse will "fix" the issue instead of refunding you a dime. If you plan on signing a contract with AuthorHouse, reread this paragraph many times. The drafter of this contract has anticipated author lawsuits and has tried to prevent the types of suits and claims authors can make. The last sentence says, "To the fullest extent legally possible, you agree not to allege that the remedies in this Section fail their essential purpose." Even though there is an arbitration clause, given the language in 6.1, the only way you could initiate an arbitration action would be if AuthorHouse failed to fix the problem or return your money for that particular service. Since Section 6.1 doesn't provide a time period within which AuthorHouse will act to fix the problem, you are basically screwed.

Section 7.2 is the bright spot in an otherwise dismal contract. It allows the author to terminate the contract with thirty days written notice. The author, however, won't be entitled to a refund or to the book's interior and cover production files.

Even if you are unhappy, the most you will ever get back is what you paid for the services. You will not receive lost profits or damages for pain and suffering (see Section 4, "Disclaimer"). Such a clause is standard. The author who decides to sue, however, must file the claim for arbitration in AuthorHouse's hometown of Bloomington, Indiana. The prevailing party will be awarded legal fees.

AUTHOR-FRIENDLY RATING: If after reading this book you are still considering AuthorHouse, then good luck.

While the publishing fees are not unreasonable, the printing markups and low royalties are egregious. Further, any disagreement with AuthorHouse is a lost cause. The publisher's contract makes it difficult to complain and see results. In fact, nothing about the AuthorHouse contract favors the author, with the exception of being able to terminate the contract quickly.

If you don't mind paying a 139 percent markup on printing and receiving puny royalties, then AuthorHouse is probably okay for you. But before you choose this publisher, rent the movie *Boiler Room*. Almost every email inquiry was answered with some type of request to speak on the phone, despite repeated explanations that my research assistant is unavailable during business hours. Why so eager to speak on the phone? Because it's easy to sell the sizzle that way with no accountability. Don't be fooled by the hype and slick sales techniques. The numbers don't lie.

CROSSBOOKS

http://www.crossbooks.com

FORMAT OF BOOK: Paperback and hardcover (ebooks are included in some packages)

GENRES ACCEPTED: CrossBooks is a division of Lifeway Christian Stores and only accepts books that are in line with its "Statement of Faith," which is found at http://www.crossbooks.com/AboutUs/SoF.aspx.

PUBLISHING FEES: CrossBooks offers a variety of publishing packages. The standard packages range from $1,099 to $6,999. A full description of them can be found at http://www.crossbooks.com/Publish/PublishingPackages.aspx. CrossBooks also has color book packages and "Pro" publishing packages ranging from $11,999 to $36,999 (http://www.crossbooks.com/Publish/ProPackages.aspx).

Classic: This package costs $1,099 and includes:

- ISBN
- Template-based custom cover
- Book design and interior layout
- Distribution through Ingram's Lightning Source (which includes Amazon.com and BarnesandNoble.com)
- Ebook creation and distribution
- Ten complimentary copies

Classic Plus: For $1,899, this package includes everything in the Classic Package, plus:

- Twenty free paperback copies and five free hardcover copies
- Copyright registration
- Cover copy polish
- Editorial review

Publisher's Choice: For $2,999, this package includes everything in the Classic Plus, plus:

- Library of Congress Control Number (LCCN)
- Listing on Google Books, Amazon Search Inside!, and BarnesandNoble.com's "See Inside"
- Author website
- Returns Program
- Three hundred bookmarks, postcards, and business cards

Marketing Plus: For $4,299, this package includes everything in the Publisher's Choice package, plus:

- Inclusion in CrossBooks' catalog
- Social media prep

Home Life: For $6,999, this package includes everything in the Marketing Plus package, plus:

- An ad in *Lifeway* magazine
- Expanded promo (which, according to http://www.crossbooks.com/Publish/AdditionalServices.aspx?serviceId=126, is creation of a press release and then distribution to the media in five cities of the author's choice)
- *Foreword Clarion* book review

OTHER SERVICES OF INTEREST:

Author Website: For $479 plus $32 per month, CrossBooks will set up and host your website, through AmericanAuthor.com (http://www.crossbooks.com/Publish/AdditionalServices.aspx?serviceId=148)—essentially the same deal that CrossBooks' cousins, Trafford and AuthorHouse, have with AmericanAuthor.com. Interestingly, the same package at Trafford is $399 plus $29 per month. My guess is that the additional amount is the cut taken by CrossBooks/Lifeway. The $32 per month for hosting is expensive. You can get hosting for $5–$10 per month.

Email Marketing Campaign: This service is also similar to the campaigns offered by Trafford (so read Trafford's review in this book for more details). There are several options here. One campaign sends an email to 500,000 people, and costs $1,915 with CrossBooks (http: //www.crossbooks.com/Publish/AdditionalServices.aspx?serviceId=179). Yet, the nearly identical program with Trafford costs $1,596.

A complete list of all additional services can be found at http://www.crossbooks.com/Publish/AdditionalServices.aspx.

RETURN OF DIGITAL COVER AND INTERIOR FILES: Like its cousin iUniverse, CrossBooks allows authors to purchase the text and cover digital production files for $750 each if the request by the author is eighteen months or less from the book's release date. If it is after eighteen months from the release date, it's $150 per file. It should be obvious that producing the files in the first eighteen months doesn't take any more time or effort on the publisher's part than providing them after eighteen months.

RETAIL PRICE OF AUTHOR'S BOOK: The publisher has final say over the retail price (which is a good thing). I took a random sampling of some of CrossBooks' titles and I found:

- *A Pastor's Guide To Conducting A Funeral: Things Every Pastor Needs To Know, But May Have Been Afraid To Ask* (116 pages / paperback / $12.99)
- *Bill Wallace of China* (256 pages / paperback / $16.99)
- *Rocked: How to respond when life's circumstances rock you to your core* (140 pages / paperback / $11.95)

PRICE AUTHOR PAYS FOR BOOKS: CrossBooks says up front that it prints its books with Lightning Source (http://www.crossbooks.com/help/printondemand.aspx#where). Authors receive a 50 percent discount off of their first order, provided it is more than 150 books. After this, as shown at http://www.crossbooks.com/help/royalties.aspx#volumediscount, the discounts vary based on volume ordered and are calculated at a discount off of the retail price. To get an example, I used *The Day the Chicken Cackled: Reflections On A Life in Pakistan*, which is a 232-page paperback and retails for $16.99. Lightning Source charges $4.38 to print this book in very small quantities.

Quantity	Discount	Author Price	Markup
1–24	30%	$11.83	170%
25–49	35%	$11.04	152%
50–99	40%	$10.19	133%
100–249	45%	$9.34	113%
250–499	50%	$8.49	94%
500–999	55%	$7.65	75%
1,000–1,999	60%	$6.02	141%*
2,000+	65%	$5.26	173%*

For large print runs, I am assuming CrossBooks prints the books offset, which is much cheaper than print-on-demand—hence the asterisks. If you went to any online book printing company you could get 1,000 copies of the mythical 6" x 9", 200-page paperback for around $2.50 per copy. The cost for 2,000 or more would be around $1.93 per copy. However, offset pricing can vary a lot; so again, the printing markups for the big runs are estimates only.

ROYALTIES PAID TO AUTHOR: This publisher pays a 50 percent royalty equal to what the publisher earns on each book sold after backing out print costs and trade discounts. Here is an example directly from the website at http://www.crossbooks.com/help/royalties.aspx/. After reviewing the site, it was unclear to me what the COGS (cost of goods sold) was based on. It is the "cost" to print the book. A sales rep emailed me that it was based on a 200-page, paperback, 6" x 9" book.

If we price our book at the suggested retail price ($17.95), sold through a retailer, the math looks like this:

$17.95 SRP (suggested retail price)
–$8.62 Retail discount (48%)
$9.33 Net retail discount
–$4.97 COGS (cost of goods sold)
$4.36 Net COGS
x 0.50 Royalty rate percentage
$2.18 Author royalty

The math for a web sale looks like this:

$17.95 SRP
–$4.97 COGS
$12.98 Net COGS
x 0.50 Royalty percentage
$6.49 Royalty earned

A few notes of interest here. The COGS for this 200-page book is actually $3.90, not $4.97, thus CrossBooks has marked up the printing by $1.97, or 27 percent (one of the lowest markups on record). In the "Retail Sale" example, the author doesn't truly make a 50 percent royalty because CrossBooks's $1.97 printing markup is hidden in the print costs. In that example, the author makes $2.18 and CrossBooks, with its printing markup, makes $4.15.

The same holds true for the "Web Sale" example, when the book is sold through the CrossBooks site. Here the author makes $6.49 per sale and CrossBooks makes $8.46.

Another big question for me is: why is the cost to produce the book (used to calculate royalties) so much less than the cost to produce the same book, should the author want to buy a copy of it for his own use? It shouldn't be.

NOTABLE PROVISIONS OF THE PUBLISHING AGREEMENT: The publishing agreement is only accessible after you start the publishing process. So, if you want to see one prior to actually paying CrossBooks any money, you'll need to select a package and begin the ordering process.

The first thing you will need to agree to is the "Statement of Faith." You agree to the following: "By checking 'I accept' and initialing this page, I accept that CrossBooks only publishes books that uphold the Statement of Faith. CrossBooks will perform a Theological Review to verify that my book upholds the Statement of Faith, and I accept that the $150.00 cost for the review is nonrefundable."

It is unclear if that $150 is a separate fee or included as part of the package. Once you've accepted the Statement of Faith, you move on to the contract itself.

Section 6 states that the term is for three years from the date the publisher first sends the files to the printer for the first print run. But, per Section 7, the author can terminate by giving thirty days written notice.

Section 11 gives CrossBooks up to 180 days to publish the work. Section 12 gives CrossBooks control over the details of publication, including price, online presentation, whether or not to use DRM (digital rights management) on any ebook version, and so on. These are generally good ideas. While it's important for authors to have control, so long as the publisher is doing things (such as retail pricing) in a way that helps the project, this control is better left in the hands of the publisher.

One portion of Section 12 worth noting is that the author is prohibited from utilizing "all, or portions of the WORK, the International Standard Book Number (ISBN), and identical or similar cover with any other PUBLISHER." I emailed CrossBooks and asked what this meant. I received the following response: "The content remains always yours. You can reuse your own artwork as well. The only thing we do not release are [sic] the files we created with our process for the final design and formatting of your work. So...no problem, sir."

Now, that isn't exactly what the contract says. Clearly, another cover with the same image on it could be interpreted as being "similar" to CrossBooks'. If I were you, I'd get email confirmation about this clause if I were considering this publisher.

Section 18 gives the publisher to the right to terminate and refund all fees less a $150 setup fee.

Section 24 allows the publisher to amend the agreement at any time, with thirty days written notice. If the author doesn't object in writing and terminate the contract within thirty days, the terms are deemed accepted. The only thing an author can do if she disputes the amendment is terminate the contract. So, the publisher could change the royalty structure, and if you don't like it, all you can do is terminate the contract.

Next is Schedule A.

Section 1 sets forth the royalties, as described previously. It also includes ebook royalties, which are 50 percent of the actual payments CrossBooks receives from the sales.

Section 4 sets forth that CrossBooks has final say over the retail price of the book and that all ebooks will have a default price of $9.99.

Section 5 sets forth a refund schedule, should an author back out during any part of the process. This is a nice touch, and not many companies do it.

Section 6 outlines the author discounts for purchase of their own books. That schedule is set forth within this review.

Section 8 sets forth that authors who terminate can purchase their production files (interior and cover) for $750 each if the termination is within eighteen months of the release date of the book. The files are $150 each if the termination is after eighteen months from the release date. This is contrary to the email I received from the sales rep about return of production files.

AUTHOR-FRIENDLY RATING: It sort of feels like Lifeway wanted to get into self-publishing and either approached or was approached by Author Solutions, Inc. So, they created CrossBooks by taking Lifeway's existing Statement of Faith and slapping some publishing packages around it, then marked everything up more than the comparable services in Author Solutions' other companies (like iUniverse, Trafford, Xlibris, and AuthorHouse). And, voilà—you have a publishing company. The packages are okay. They're priced bit high for what you get, but I've seen worse. The printing markups are shameful, but not much different from Author Solutions' other companies.

Judging by the example of the royalties, it appears that CrossBooks doesn't mark up the actual printing costs for the purpose of calculating royalties as much as the other Author Solutions companies do. That's a good thing. CrossBooks also has a fair refund schedule, something the others don't either. But, like with other Author Solutions companies, just when you think something is getting better, there's the whammy from left field. This one is the $1,500 to get back the production files you already paid to have created.

If you really want to use CrossBooks' services, it's cheaper to use one of Author Solutions' other companies. If you really want a Christian publisher, there are better ones.

Since many authors who read this are probably also looking at WestBow, you should know that both CrossBooks and WestBow have the EXACT same address: 1663 Liberty Drive, Bloomington, IN 47403 (http://www.crossbooks.com/ContactUs/Default.aspx and http://www.westbowpress.com/ContactUs/Default.aspx), because they are both being operated by Author Solutions, which is also at 1663 Liberty Drive in Bloomington, IN.

DORRANCE PUBLISHING

http://www.dorrancepublishing.com

FORMAT OF BOOKS: Paperback, hardcover, and ebook

GENRES ACCEPTED: All

PUBLISHING FEES: Dorrance has been around since the 1920s and offers both traditional subsidy and self-publishing packages. The difference, according to the publisher, is that traditional subsidy means the publisher will keep your book in stock and provide marketing, distribution, and fulfillment. Self-publishing means that the company will produce and print your book, and you will be responsible for storage and sales. Package details are not available on the website, which also looks like it has been around since the 1920s.

Publishing package fees—or any details at all—will not be discussed until a book is submitted for review and accepted. After my editor submitted a manuscript for a 202-page, perfect bound, paperback book, we were accepted to the Subsidy Package, which costs $11,500 and includes the following:

- Basic mechanical editing for grammar, spelling, and punctuation
- Typesetting (font determined by the designers), proofreading, and interior layout design
- Custom cover, which can incorporate artwork provided by the author if she chooses
- U.S. Copyright Office registration
- LCCN ("If your book qualifies.")
- Book warehousing, fulfillment, and distribution for two years
- Twenty-five author copies
- Specified amount of fees, determined on a case-by-case basis, put toward a promotion budget, the highlights of which include:
    - Listing in Dorrance's online bookstore, DorranceBookstore .com

- Preparation of a "digital interactive press kit" featuring book synopsis, author bio, publicity release, high-res copy of cover, and links to your listing in Dorrance's online bookstore, sent to three hundred media outlets
- Publicity release distributed to online news media: Google News, Yahoo! News, blogs, radio programs, and newspapers
- Google AdWords search engine marketing campaign, linking to your listing on Dorrance's online bookstore
- Inclusion in Google Book Search and R.R. Bowker's Books In Print; Amazon.com listings
- Announcements about your work sent to wholesalers and distributers
- Telephone calls to up to twelve booksellers to introduce your work and offer to set up an author signing
- Direct mail marketing postcards, sent to your personal mailing list

Dorrance also offers an assurance program, which allows authors who lose their income within a year of paying/signing to cancel their payment plan and walk away from their additional payment obligations. A 100 percent credit is applied if and when the author resumes services.

While the marketing sounds extensive, the contract explicitly states that Dorrance only agrees to provide $1,000 of total marketing in employee time and actual out-of-pocket expense.

RETURN OF DIGITAL COVER AND INTERIOR FILES: When we queried Dorrance about their policy regarding ownership of the working cover and typeset files, we received this answer via email: "Regarding the production files, we will hang on to those while we continue to print copies of the book. Should you decide to terminate the contract for some reason, we can give you the files–no charge."

That's great, but the contract does not address this issue.

RETAIL PRICE OF AUTHOR'S BOOK: According to the contract, "Dorrance shall determine the retail price of the Work based on the final page count of the desired Work." Details are not specified in the contract.

PRICE AUTHOR PAYS FOR BOOKS: The author receives twenty-five books as part of the package's purchase price. If the author exhausts that supply, he or she may purchase additional copies at 45 percent off the retail price.

Based on Dorrance's online bookstore, here are some retail prices of recent books:

- *What's Left? What's Right? A Political Journey via North Korea and the Chinese Cultural Revolution* (180 pages / paperback / $18.00)
- *8442 Eastwick Avenue; The Soul of Ellenwood Lives in the House Where Life's Long-Lasting Memories Blossomed* (122 pages / paperback / $14.00)
- *Adventures of Timmy and Sherry, Book I: Losing Their Marbles* (342 pages / paperback / $28.00)

So, if the author of the $18.00 (180-page) book wanted to buy copies, he would pay:

$18.00 Retail price
–$8.10 Author discount (45%)
$7.90 Per book (based on $0.015 per page plus $0.90 for the cover)

The cost to print this book is $3.60, so the printing markup is 119 percent.

If the author of the 342-page book wanted to purchase copies, he would pay:

$28.00 Retail price
–$12.60 Author discount (45%)
$15.40 Author cost per book

Since the cost to print this book is $6.03, the printing markup is 155 percent.

ROYALTIES PAID TO AUTHOR: The author royalty is 40 percent of the retail price for books sold through the Dorrance online bookstore, and 20 percent of the wholesale price for books sold through third-party retailers and wholesalers. For ebooks, the author earns 80 percent of the retail price for sales through the Dorrance online store, and 40 percent of the amount paid to Dorrance by a third-party reseller.

For the 180-page book that sells for $18.00, the author would make the following amount from a sale on Amazon.com:

$18.00	Retail price
–$ 9.90	Amazon.com discount (55%)
$8.10	Wholesale price
x 0.20	Royalty percentage
$1.62	Author royalty

On this same sale, Dorrance makes:

$18.00	Retail price
–$9.90	Amazon.com discount (55%)
–$3.60	Actual print cost
–$1.62	Author royalty
$2.88	Dorrance profit

For the sale of the same 180-page book from the Dorrance online bookstore, the author would make the following:

$18.00	Retail price
x 0.40	Royalty percentage
$7.20	Author royalty

On this same sale, Dorrance makes:

$18.00	Retail price
–$7.20	Author royalty
–$3.60	Actual print cost
$7.20	Dorrance royalty

NOTABLE PROVISIONS OF THE PUBLISHING AGREEMENT: Dorrance does not provide copies of its contract on its website and will not even answer any questions about it for prospective authors—until the author submits a manuscript. We had to literally go undercover in order to obtain the following information.

Section 1 gives Dorrance, for the full two-year term of the contract, the exclusive right to publish the book and "all other right to and in the work," which refers to subsidiary rights covered later in the contract. This is something you never see in self-publishing contracts. Under the contract we received, we pay them $11,600 and we're stuck for two years.

Section 3 covers what and how the author will pay Dorrance for its services, which in this case is in three separate installments. It also says that Dorrance "makes no contribution to the cost of the initial publication."

Section 4 states that Dorrance has 160 working days (nine months) after the contract is signed to complete the book, unless prevented by the author, acts of God, or other circumstances beyond its control. The author agrees to review any edits or production proofs within six days of receiving them.

Section 5 provides the technical specs for the author's book and states that, while Dorrance will consult with the author, the "content, style, design, and format of the cover/jacket will be entirely at the discretion of Dorrance." It also says that the author will pay for any changes made to the book after the author has approved the proofs. In this section, Dorrance also states the level of editing provided.

Section 6 says that if the author would like any of her materials returned (i.e., any cover art she has provided) she must make a written request for it within thirty days of signing the contract. Otherwise, the original manuscript and all other materials submitted will not be returned. This is not the same as getting the original production files returned. There is nothing in the contract that provides for that, despite the information we received from the representative.

Section 7 details the author's royalty and the retail price of the book. Royalties are paid biannually, on January 31 and July 31. Dorrance has the right to increase the retail price of the author's book; in such a case, royalties would be adjusted accordingly.

Section 8 states that the author's package includes twenty-five copies of the work at no extra charge. This section also provides the author's cost to purchase books at a 45 percent discount plus the cost of shipping.

Section 9 outlines the publisher's promotion plan, with a caveat that the publisher will spend no more than $1,000 (or the equivalent in labor) on promotion. The details are listed in the package description of this review. However, I don't know how they can actually provide all of that promotional work for $1,000.

A paragraph in Section 9 also states that the author must tell Dorrance when she is undertaking promotional efforts on her own so that Dorrance may approve the wording and information.

Section 10 permits Dorrance to sell any subsidiary rights (which include book club, paperback, hardcover, reprint, serial, dramatic, motion picture, television, radio, translation, and other such rights) during the term of the agreement. Should Dorrance sell any subsidiary rights, the author earns 80 percent while Dorrance keeps the other 20 percent. Again, this is something you shouldn't have to give away when you are paying to publish.

Section 11 says that Dorrance will secure a copyright for the book in the author's name.

In Section 12, the author agrees that she has the right to publish the book, that it is her work, and that it is not libelous or fraudulent. It also says that Dorrance will not be held legally or financially liable if litigation arises due to copyright or other issues.

Section 13 extends the contract terms to the electronic form of the book, stating that they will "strive to make the work available" as an ebook thirty days from the publication date of the physical book. Dorrance will determine the retail price, and the author will receive 80 percent of that price for ebooks sold.

Section 14 details the term of the contract. It says that after two years, either party can terminate the contract with a thirty-day written notice. It also specifies that if the author fails to pay any of the fees outlined in the contract, the contract will be terminated and any fees that have been paid will not be returned.

If the author terminates the contract during the production process and Dorrance is not in breach of contract, then all fees will be forfeited.

If after publishing the book, Dorrance determines that the book is libelous, obscene, or otherwise injurious or unlawful, it can terminate the contract and the author must forfeit all fees.

Section 16 says that the contract is complete and that any additions must be made in writing and signed by both parties.

Section 18 says that the contract is subject to the laws of the County of Alleghany and the Commonwealth of Pennsylvania. Any disputes will need to be settled there, and under no circumstance will litigation resolve with either party paying the other more than the payments made in the course of the contract. However, the non-prevailing party must pay all lawyers' fees. One other goody from this section: neither party can reveal the results of any arbitration without the consent of the other. So, if Dorrance does you wrong and you win, you can't warn others.

If the author thinks the publisher has not performed its duties according to the contract, she must present her case in a certified or registered letter to the publisher and give the publisher an unspecified "reasonable" amount of time to correct its mistakes; otherwise, the author cannot claim a breach of contract.

Section 19 says that the contract applies to the heirs, executors, administrators, and assigns of the author and the successors and assigns of Dorrance. That basically means that if you die, or Dorrance sells its business to PublishAmerica, the contract is still binding.

AUTHOR-FRIENDLY RATING: The $11,600 is not the worst deal I've seen for the services provided, but the marketing services that are included at that price are pretty lame. The printing markups are through the roof. The retail price of the books seem to be higher than market (at least the three books I looked at). The royalties are okay, but after paying $11,600, should the publisher get to make more than you do on every sale? I'd say no. You can't get back your production files. On top of that, add a contract with a two-year term, the assignment of your subsidiary rights, and an arbitration clause that prevents you from speaking about the results, and I can't think of any reason to use this publisher.

And, in the cover letter Dorrance sent to us, they stated, "To the best of our knowledge, we are the only full-service subsidy publisher to offer our authors the opportunity for simultaneous publication in bookstore quality traditional format, and also in an online electronic ebook format." Either they have been using the same cover letter for years, or they don't know what's happening in the industry today.

iUNIVERSE
http://www.iuniverse.com

FORMAT OF BOOKS: Paperback, hardcover, and ebook

GENRES ACCEPTED: All

PUBLISHING FEES: iUniverse has six publishing programs, a side-by-side comparison of which can be viewed at www.iuniverse.com/Packages/PackageCompare.aspx. Interestingly, all prices given below are for online submissions; add $100 per package for mailed submissions.

Select Package: This package (http://www.iuniverse.com/Packages/Select.aspx) costs $599, and includes:

- ISBN
- Ebook setup
- Webpage in the iUniverse online bookstore
- PDF proof and one round of corrections
- Books shipped after three days of production time
- Distribution through Ingram and Baker & Taylor
- Volume discount for authors
- Twenty-five black-and-white images
- Your choice of trim size:
  5" x 8"
  5.5" x 8.5"
  6" x 9"
  7.5" x 9.25"
  8.25" x 11"

- Custom cover design
- Access to myuniverse.com, the publisher's online distribution and royalty monitoring system, and quarterly sales reports
- Five free copies of the book

Premier Package: This package (http://www.iuniverse.com/Packages/Premier.aspx) is $1,099. It includes everything in the Select Package, plus:

- Editorial evaluation: the publisher will recommend an appropriate level of editing, which you can then purchase.
- Editor's Choice Recognition Program, which makes you eligible for the Star Program, Rising Star, and Reader's Choice programs (detailed below)
- iUniverse's Star Program eligibility, which, if you are selected for the Editor's Choice program and sell more than five hundred books, includes:
  - Professional cover reassessment, back cover revision
  - Professional edit
  - LCCN
  - Listing in separate Star Program section of iUniverse's website
  - Presentation to traditional publishers, book clubs, international publishers, audio book publishers, and large print publishers
- Barnes & Noble's "See Inside" listing
- Ten free copies of the book

Premier Pro Package: This package (http://www.iuniverse.com/Packages/PremierPro.aspx) is $1,549. It includes all products and services in the Premier Package, plus:

- Twenty free paperback books
- One free hardcover book

- Cover copy polish: The publisher simply goes over your cover, using your input, and makes the book more marketable.
- Eligibility for the Rising Star Program, which, if chosen, includes:
  - Marketing Tool Kit and Marketing Success Workbook, which is a guide to marketing your book; a $49 value
  - Worldwide distribution
  - Featured in the Rising Star catalog and Rising Star section of iUniverse bookstore
  - Booksellers Return Program (softcover only)

Bookstore Premier Pro Package: This package (http://www.iuniverse.com/Packages/BookstorePremierPro.aspx) is $2,099 and includes all services and products in the Premier Package, plus:

- Booksellers Return Program

Online Premier Pro Package: This package (http://www.iuniverse.com/Packages/OnlinePremierPro.aspx) costs $3,150 and includes all services and products in the Bookstore Premier Pro Package, plus:

- Forty free paperback books
- Ten free hardcover books
- Author website
- Copyright registration
- LCCN
- Google/Amazon Book Search
- Social media marketing setup, in which iUniverse sets you up with a blog, as well as a profile on Facebook, Flickr, Myspace, and other online social networking sites

Book Launch Premier Pro Package: This package (http://www.iuniverse.com/Packages/BookLaunchPremierPro.aspx) costs $4,200 and includes all services and products in the Online Premier Pro Package, plus:

- Sixty free paperback books
- Twenty free hardcover books
- Author website

- Copyright registration
- Email marketing campaign: Email outreach to individuals who have indicated interest and have given permission to receive commercial emails. You will also receive a report of how many emails were opened and how many purchases were made as a direct result.
- One hundred each of bookmarks, postcards, and business cards for your own use

OTHER SERVICES OF INTEREST: As you can imagine, a giant company like iUniverse offers myriad add-on services. Here are a few worth noting:

Editorial Services: All levels of editing are available, including basic copyediting at $0.022 per word; line editing, which covers syntax, word choice, and light structural changes for $0.029 per word; content editing, which focuses on plot and flow, at $0.035 per word; and "content editing plus," for manuscripts that require more work than basic content editing, at $0.042 per word. These fees are almost double industry standard, and you can find competent editors for much less.

***Kirkus Discoveries* Book Review:** iUniverse charges $360 for this service. If you worked directly with Kirkus, you would pay $350, but you would still need to send in two copies of your book. *Kirkus Discoveries* is a respected publication. Its writers are the same folks who write the impartial reviews you'll find on *Kirkus Reviews*, which means your payment doesn't guarantee a stellar review. (If you receive a bad review, you can decline from having it posted.) A *Kirkus Discoveries* review lends your book legitimacy.

Ghostwriting: An iUniverse "professional writer" takes your first draft and/or notes and writes a manuscript in consultation with you for $72/hour. There is a $299 fee to obtain a cost estimate and writing sample, which can be applied to the total cost if you choose to purchase the ghostwriting service.

Developmental Edit: This is a thorough reading of your book with feedback and constructive criticism intended to create a strong rewrite. For nonfiction writers, editors will look at concept development, organization, and illustration. Fiction writers will get feedback on plot, pace, characterization, and dialogue. The fee is $0.064 per word. You are paying a lot for something that doesn't include copyediting. A publishing-ready edit, which would include copyediting and notes like these, in addition to further rounds of editing after the author has made his changes, can likely be found elsewhere for less.

Co-op Advertising: Your book will be included in a group ad with other iUniverse authors. Journals include the *New York Times Book Review*, *ForeWord Magazine*, and *BookMarks Magazine*. Prices vary from $450 to $875 per book. This kind of advertising falls into the "flush your money down the toilet" category. Your co-op ad will feature a number of other unknown authors. Industry insiders and literary enthusiasts are not going to pass over ads for books by well-known authors and zero in on your book's tiny cover image and blurb (especially when they're in a group ad that everyone in the industry knows is from a self-publishing company). If you buy this service and make your money back from it, I will let you watch me rip out each page of this book and eat it.

Booksellers Return Program: This service can be purchased for $699 with any of the packages that do not already include it.

RETURN OF DIGITAL COVER AND INTERIOR FILES: As stated in the FAQ section applicable to its contract (http://www.iuniverse.com/faqs/agreements.aspx), iUniverse makes it clear that, unless an author submits a completed cover, iUniverse owns the cover it creates for you. If you submit a photo that you own and iUniverse creates a cover based on that photo, iUniverse owns the cover. Period. At least the company states it in black and white.

Similarily, iUniverse does not return the original production files. Period. If you terminate your contract with the publisher, you will have the "right to purchase" your digital files in press-ready PDF format with the iUniverse logos and ISBN removed. The fee for the files is based on when you terminate. If you terminate at eighteen months or later, you'll pay $150 each for the cover art and interior files. If you terminate any earlier, you'll pay a whopping $750 each for the cover and interior files. The problem is that you can't really sell your book anywhere without an ISBN, so you will need to have a new ISBN, a new bar code, and other information inserted throughout the book. While this is possible with only the press-ready files, it's harder than if you had the original production files. With iUniverse, you are paying extra for something you already paid them to create. I don't understand why publishers insist on charging for these files.

Charging $1,500 for the press-ready PDFs is so wrong. If you decide you want to publish your book with a company that offers higher royalties and lower printing markups, you should be able to take your production files to such a company. Otherwise, it's like publishing from scratch. You have already paid to have these production files created. They are of no use to the publisher if you terminate your relationship.

RETAIL PRICE FOR AUTHOR'S BOOK: iUniverse sets the price for all of its books, loosely based on a sliding scale. I say loosely because while the chart (found at http://www.iuniverse.com/faqs/bookproduction.aspx#Question2) indicates that a 200-page paperback would retail for somewhere between $15.95 and $18.95, it's possible to find a 360-page, 6" x 9" paperback selling on the publisher's website for $29.95 and another 160-page, 5" x 8" paperback selling for $7.95. The following is from the publisher's pricing chart:

Page Count	Retail Price
75 or less	$8.95–$10.95
120	$10.95–$13.95
180	$13.95–$16.95
240	$15.95–$19.95
300	$17.95–$21.95
360	$20.95–$23.95
420	$22.95–$26.95

The retail pricing is higher than it should be. In an email, the iUniverse rep stated, "Print-on-demand (POD) books are priced slightly higher in the marketplace than traditionally published books because traditionally published books are printed thousands of copies at a time, which allows for a lower cost per unit."

That statement is often true, but it sums up the biggest problem with print-on-demand books. Retailers don't care how a book is printed (so long as the quality is there). What they do care about is wholesale price. Retailers won't overpay for your book because you didn't get your printing costs low enough to make the book competitive with similar books in your genre.

Ebooks are priced at $9.99, unless the retail price of the print version is less than that, in which case the ebook will adopt the lower price.

PRICE AUTHOR PAYS FOR BOOKS: Authors may purchase their first 150 books at a 50 percent discount from the listed retail price. After that, discounts are on a sliding scale. Assume that we are printing our standard 200-page, 6" x 9" paperback. With a retail price of $17.95, here is how the math looks:

Quantity	Discount	Author Price	Markup
1–24	30%	$12.57	222%
25–49	35%	$11.66	199%
50–99	40%	$10.77	176%
100–249	45%	$9.87	153%
250–499	50%	$8.97	130%
500–999	55%	$8.07	107%

Because of the retail price ranges iUniverse uses to determine the final retail price, the actual markup percentages could be higher or lower (depending on a different retail price). For example, if the retail price were $16.95 instead of $17.95, the printing markup for one hundred copies would be 139 percent instead of 153 percent.

When I asked why the retail prices and print costs for authors were so high, considering the substantial fees authors pay to get their books in print and the low royalty, an iUniverse representative provided this response: "We set cover price based on page cont; until the book completes the design phase, we can only estimate the price. Cover price of a paperback book with 160,000 words would be estimated at $25.95 to $29.95 with nonfiction books averaging $1.00–4.00 higher than fiction."

This answer is otherwise known as dodging the question. The markups are staggering. These are just about the highest I've seen—ever.

ROYALTIES PAID TO AUTHOR: iUniverse allows the author to choose one of two royalty rates and one of two bookseller discounts (http://www.iuniverse.com/faqs/booksellerdiscount.aspx). Their standard royalty rate is 20 percent of net sales, which includes a bookseller discount of 36 percent; however, you can also choose a 10 percent royalty, which allows you to increase the bookseller discount to 50 percent. The only chance you'll have to get your books into stores is to choose the 10 percent royalty with the 50 percent discount. Online retailers are different, and if you chose the 20 percent royalty with the 36 percent trade discount, online retailers would still sell your book.

Here's the math on the mythical 200-page book when sold through Amazon using both 36 percent and 20 percent royalty figures:

$17.95 Retail price
–$6.46 Amazon.com discount (36%)
$11.49 Net profit
x 0.20 Royalty percentage
$2.30 Author royalty

Since this book costs $3.90 to print, iUniverse makes $5.29 (after printing costs) on this sale, more than double what the author does.

If the author chooses the 50 percent trade discount and 10 percent royalty, it looks like this:

$17.95	Retail price
–$8.98	Amazon.com discount (50%)
$8.97	Net profit
x 0.10	Royalty percentage
$0.90	Author royalty

Again, since the book costs $3.90 to print, iUniverse makes $4.17 per book—almost 4.5 times more than the author.

When the book is sold directly on iUniverse's site, the numbers become really unfavorable, despite the unchanging percentage. Here's how that math works if the 200-page book used in the previous example is sold on iUniverse's website with the author earning a 20 percent royalty:

$17.95	Retail price
–$3.90	Actual print cost
–$3.59	Author royalty (20%)
$10.46	iUniverse profit

iUniverse makes nearly three times what the author makes. If you have the 10 percent royalty program, it's even more grim:

$17.95	Retail price
–$3.90	Actual print cost
–$1.80	Author royalty (10%)
$12.25	iUniverse profit

The author makes $1.80 per sale and iUniverse makes $12.25. You need to ask them why. A royalty of 20 percent, no matter where books are sold, is low by self-publishing standards. When you do the math, you should wonder why you pay them to publish your book and they end up making more on each sale than you do.

NOTABLE PROVISIONS OF THE PUBLISHING AGREEMENT: The contracts can be found on each package's description page. With the exception of Schedule A, the contracts and the paragraph numbers discussed below are the same regardless of the program. For a sample contract, I used the one at http://www.iuniverse.com/uploadedFiles/iUniverse/Packages/Agreements/Online_Premier_Pro_Publishing_Agreement_11_02_09.pdf.

Paragraph 2, "License to Publish," and Paragraph 5, "Terms," give iUniverse nonexclusive print rights in English for three years from the book's release date. However, the author can cancel any time during the term by giving thirty-days notice. Additionally, if the author has not given thirty-days notice by the end of the term of the contract, the contract automatically renews for another year.

Paragraph 6, "Author's Right of Termination," gives the author the right to purchase the digital interior and cover files of his work in PDF format upon termination, the details of which are discussed earlier in this review.

Paragraph 11, "Publication," allows the publisher 90–180 days to release the book.

Paragraph 12, "Publication Format," gives the publisher total control over price, appearance of your book, and more. Prices for books can be found at http://www.iuniverse.com/why-iUniverse/publishing-the-iUniverse-way/selling-your-books/pricing-your-book.aspx. As already mentioned, a book of 240 pages prices at $15.95–$19.95. Also of note in Paragraph 12: "Author acknowledges that author may not utilize the formatted work, International Standard Book Number (ISBN), and cover with any other publisher."

Paragraphs 19 and 20 cover author warranties and indemnifications, which are reasonable and standard.

Paragraph 21, "Notices," explains the manner in which the author or publisher must give notice to terminate the agreement. These requirements must be precisely followed for the termination to be effective and valid.

Paragraph 23, "Copyright Infringement," gives the publisher the right to commence action for copyright infringement on behalf of the author. Any recovery made will be split by the parties after expenses.

This section also gives the publisher the option of not commencing a suit for infringement, in which case the author is free to do so. Upon any recovery by the author, the monies will be split after the author recovers his attorney's fees.

Paragraph 24 gives iUniverse the right to amend the agreement, including the royalty payment structure and timing, by giving authors a thirty-day notice. The author will then have thirty days to notify iUniverse that he doesn't accept the amendment, at which time his contract will be terminated. If an author doesn't respond within thirty days, the author's silence is deemed acceptance.

Paragraph 27, "General Provisions," is stuffed with legalese, but don't be intimidated. It says that if a legal dispute arises, such as an issue over contract interpretation, the statutes and case laws of Indiana will be used to interpret the provisions. It also prohibits the author from assigning rights in the contract to anyone else without the publisher's consent. For example, if you decide to incorporate a business, you must obtain the publisher's permission before assigning the contract rights to your new corporation—although, because the contract language says the publisher can't "unreasonably" withhold consent, such an assignment shouldn't be an issue.

The final portion of Paragraph 27 says that any promises or representations made to the author prior to signing the agreement are unenforceable if they are not mentioned in the agreement. If the written contract doesn't resemble the oral agreements you made, don't sign it. Once you've signed the agreement, the only way to alter it is in writing, or it doesn't count. An oral agreement that you and iUniverse made before or during the term of the contract is invalid unless it's memorialized in writing. This is not a negative. All agreements should be in writing.

In Schedule A, found at the end of the contract, you'll want to note the following:

1. Section 1, "Royalties," outlines royalties for paperback and hardcover books, stating that on books sold through Barnes & Noble, the author will receive the author-selected royalty (either 10 or 20 percent) plus 5 percent of the payments the publisher receives from the book, less taxes, shipping charges, and returns. For all other books, the publisher will pay the 10 or 20 percent

of net sales, less any taxes, shipping charges, and returns. Ebooks garner 50 percent of the net sale, less distribution and technology fees, taxes, and returns. I would ask the publisher to define "technology fees," as they could be a way to whittle away at your ebook profit.

2. Section 4, "Free Copies," states that the author will receive a certain number of free copies of her book, as specified by the publishing package.
3. Section 7, "Title Maintenance," says the author agrees to pay an annual fee to maintain the book title, which is posted on the website. The fee is subject to change but will never exceed $25.
4. Section 8, "Production Files," states that the author has the right to purchase the digital interior and cover files of the work in PDF format upon the effective date of termination of the contract. The fee is based on when you terminate. At eighteen months or later, you'll pay $150 each for the interior and cover files; any earlier and you'll pay a whopping $750 each. As I outlined previously, this is patently unfair and a strong reason for not doing business with iUniverse.

AUTHOR-FRIENDLY RATING: The first warning flag appeared when my assistant contacted iUniverse via their website email form; she didn't receive an emailed response to her basic questions for almost three weeks, and when she did, her questions were only half answered. For instance, when she sent a detailed email request for clarification on a specific service, the rep's sole answer was a link to the website description of the service—which is what the question was asking for elaboration on.

Another perfect example of deliberately obscuring information came when she asked about the possibility of purchasing the interior files. She was told, "The cost depends on when you decide to purchase them. You can find the prices in each of the contracts in the packages." Instead of getting a straight answer, we had to dig through *six* different contracts to find our answers—discovering in the process that the information is the same for all packages, which would have made answering her question very simple.

iUniverse is the 900-pound gorilla of self-publishing. In the distant past, iUniverse was rated an "Outstanding" publisher in this book. However, all the strides toward author-friendliness were wiped away when the publisher started charging authors the outrageous fee of $1,500 for their digital interior and cover files. Add in one of the lowest royalties in the business and huge printing markups, and there isn't much left to do but shake your head. Plus, when asked about these issues, the response was nothing more than doublespeak.

iUniverse is owned by Author Solutions, Inc., which also owns AuthorHouse, Trafford, and Xlibris.

The iUniverse site is easy to use and the packages themselves are not bad. The "Rising Star" and related features are good ones. I wish that iUniverse would continue that good stuff moving forward. Instead, it pays puny royalties, has printing markups that would make most dictators feel guilty, and won't give its authors their original production files without a king's ransom. It's too bad. iUniverse is still wallowing in the murky swamp of self-publishing companies to be avoided.

LLUMINA PRESS

http://www.llumina.com

FORMAT OF BOOKS: Ebook, hardcover, and paperback

GENRES ACCEPTED: All

PUBLISHING FEES: Llumina has three publishing packages: $799 for paperback, $899 for hardcover, and $999 for paperback and hardcover. If you want to sell your book as an ebook, add another $65 to any package.

All packages (http://www.llumina.com/prices.htm) include:

- ISBNs for paperback and/or hardcover editions
- Library of Congress Control Number (LCCN)
- Bar code
- R.R. Bowker's Books In Print registration

- Listing with online booksellers: Amazon.com, BarnesandNoble .com and more
- Typesetting, including seven interior graphics; extra graphics are $5 each
- Physical proof, which is overnighted to you
- Four-color cover design: A designer will create up to two design options that use either author-supplied art or an image in the public domain. Includes two rounds of revisions. If neither of the options suit, the author can pay for another cover design at $75 an hour with a one-hour minimum.
- Choice of trim size:
  Paperback:
  5" x 8"
  5.5" x 8.5"
  6" x 9"
  7.5" x 9.25"
  7" x 10"
  8.25" x 11"
  Hardcover:
  5.5" x 8.5"
  6" x 9"
  7" x 10"
- Distribution through Ingram and Baker & Taylor
- A webpage on the publisher's website (see http://www.llumina .com/store/god.html for an example), which a representative assured me incurs no annual renewal fee

OTHER SERVICES OF INTEREST:

Marketing and Promotional Packages: All packages include twenty-four review copies of your book, a press release with an email blast of the release to thousands of media outlets, a sell sheet, and a listing in Llumina's e-zine. To review the packages, visit http://www.llumina.com/marketing.htm. Prices for black-and-white books range from $529 to $1,099.

Personalized Website: For $599, plus a $199 fee every six months, you will receive an eight-page, template-based website with your own URL. An example can be found at http://www.watersofthedancingsky.com/. (Keep in mind that you can easily purchase your own domain name for less than $10.) Two bad things about these websites are that the domains are owned by Llumina, and that these template-based sites look fine in some browsers (e.g., Internet Explorer) but terrible in others (e.g., Google Chrome). Authors are basically paying $600 up front, then $400 per year to rent a website. Because Llumina owns the domain, should the author decide not to renew this hosting plan, the website goes away and all of the time author spent marketing the website and getting others to link to the site becomes worthless.

Bookstore Distribution Program: This isn't really so much a distribution program as it is an assurance by Llumina that if a bookstore agrees to take a chance on your book, it can be returned if it doesn't sell (http://www.llumina.com/bookstore_returns.htm). This program costs $500 for the first year and $140 for each year thereafter. All it does is cover the cost of making your books returnable through Ingram, so you don't have to give up the royalty on returned books. It includes a listing in a catalog that Llumina sends to 2,500 book retailers. This is different than having your book distributed by a distributor that actively markets the book to the trade. But, if your books aren't marked as returnable, virtually no retailer will buy them.

RETURN OF DIGITAL COVER AND INTERIOR FILES: The contract states that the publisher owns the cover and interior files. When I emailed to ask if they would provide the files for a fee, the publisher told me that I could buy the high-resolution PDFs for $350 per file—this means that you'd have to spend $700 for both the cover and interior files. The rep pointed out that I would already have my low-resolution files because they would have been sent to me anyway for approval, but this doesn't help as far as reprinting the book elsewhere.

RETAIL PRICE OF AUTHOR'S BOOK: Llumina's book prices are based on page count and the discount you choose to give distributors. A calculator is available here: http://www.llumina.com/calculator.htm. For a 200-page, 5" x 8" paperback with a 50 percent trade discount, the retail price would be $15.95. At a 40 percent trade discount, the retail price of the book is $11.95. Authors can choose a trade discount between 35 and 55 percent.

PRICE AUTHOR PAYS FOR BOOKS: Author discounts are based on quantity. A calculator is available at http://www.llumina.com/calculator .htm. For the book example above, if it retails for $15.95, the author pays $11.17 to as low as $7.18 to purchase copies (depending on quantity). Here's the breakdown with a 50 percent trade discount and a $15.95 retail price:

Quantity	Author Cost	Actual Cost	Publisher Markup
1–24	$11.17	$3.90	186%
25–199	$8.77	$3.90	125%
200–399	$7.98	$3.90	105%
400–599	$7.18	$3.90	84%

Here's the breakdown with a 40 percent trade discount and an $11.95 retail price:

Quantity	Author Cost	Actual Cost	Publisher Markup
1–24	$8.37	$3.90	115%
25–199	$7.77	$3.90	99%
200–399	$7.17	$3.90	84%
400–599	$6.57	$3.90	69%

Well, the numbers aren't great. If you go with a more aggressive trade discount (needed, in my opinion, to have a shot at retailers today), the markups are over the top.

ROYALTIES PAID TO AUTHOR: The royalty structure is explained in detail here: www.llumina.com/royalty.html. For paperback and hardcover books, the royalties are: 30 percent of the retail price for copies sold through the publisher, and 10 percent of the retail price for copies sold through third-party retailers. So for that same 200-page paperback book, priced at $15.95, the royalty for a book sold on Amazon.com would be:

$15.95 Retail price
x 0.10 Author royalty percentage
$1.60 Author royalty

Llumina's profit on each book sold through Amazon.com or other third-party retailers is as follows:

$15.95 Retail price
–$7.98 Amazon.com discount (50%)
–$3.90 Actual printing cost
–$1.60 Author royalty
$2.47 Llumina profit

For sales through the publisher's website of that same 200-page paperback, priced at $15.95, the royalties would be:

$15.95 Retail price
x 0.30 Author royalty percentage
$4.79 Author royalty

Lumina's profit on a sale of this book through its website:

$15.95 Retail price
–$4.79 Author royalty
–$3.90 Actual printing cost
$7.26 Llumina profit

A complete description of the royalty structure can be found in the "Print Royalties" and "Electronic Royalties" sections of the author agreement.

NOTABLE PROVISIONS OF THE PUBLISHING AGREEMENT: The complete author agreement is at http://www.llumina.com/agree.htm.

"Term of License" calls for a three-year term, which starts from the date the book is first released for publication—not the date you sign the contract. The contract will automatically renew for a one-year term if the author doesn't give a thirty-day cancellation notice.

The author only grants nonexclusive print and electronic rights (see the "License to Publish" section) and can terminate at any time with thirty-days written notice (see the "Author Cancellation" section).

The "Author Cancellation" term needs to be understood before you consider signing the contract. Many publishers, and rightfully so, have clauses stating that the publisher is entitled to keep a portion of the initial publishing fee if an author cancels prior to the publishing process being completed. That is fair. What makes Llumina's cancellation clause tricky is that it states that all fees received will be refunded, less the cost of the work already completed, which is billable at $50 an hour. The publisher's personal time bills at $100 an hour. Again, I don't think this is unreasonable; you just need to be aware of it because you don't (and won't) know how much time has been spent until you attempt to cancel.

"Subsidiary Rights" confirms the author's rights to all film, television, and other rights.

"Royalties" states the terms I've outlined, adding that royalties will not be paid on returns.

"Author's Copies" gives the author a 30 percent discount on an order of fewer than twenty-five books, a 45 percent discount for an order of 25–199, a 50 percent discount for an order of 200–499, and a 55 percent discount for an order of 500 or more.

"Publisher Termination" gives the publisher the right to terminate the agreement at any time without refunding the author's publishing fees if the book has been printed.

"Author Warranties" and "Indemnification" are standard and reasonable.

"Author Agreements" states that all files created by the publisher will be retained by the publisher. While the representative did tell me via email that I could buy both files for a total of $700, that language is not in the contract.

"General Provisions" contains no language requiring that lawsuits and arbitration proceedings be held physically in Florida. The language, "This Agreement shall be governed by the laws of the State of Florida," only requires a court or arbitrator to refer to Florida case law and statutes when interpreting the contract and its terms and to resolve other similar issues.

AUTHOR-FRIENDLY RATING: While researching Llumina, I sent the same email three times to the first email contact I came across on their website and never received a response. However, when I forwarded the query to a different contact email address, the second representative responded in less than a day.

The prices of the publishing packages are acceptable, but the "custom" covers leave a lot to be desired. Of all the publishers reviewed in this book, Llumina produces the least impressive covers, some bordering on amateurish. Although the up-front fee includes cover art, you may be disappointed with the product.

The retail book prices are high. The retail price of the book directly affects what the author pays for copies. For orders of up to twenty-five copies of a book with a retail price of $17.95, the author pays $12.57 per book.

The site was hard for me to navigate, and there were a number of dead links and pages that didn't work in certain browsers. While the publishing packages are reasonably priced, it should be noted that the two lower-priced packages don't have any distribution. The printing markups are very high and royalties are pretty low. Based on the number of times we tried to contact the publisher without a response, the fact that many of the pages don't work in certain browsers, that the online bookstore relies on a Google search bar to find titles, and the overall feel I get from the site, my guess is that Llumina is a small operation and unable to keep everything running smoothly. That, plus the printing markups and royalties, really makes Llumina a company not worth your time.

Also, just as this book was about to go to print, I received emails from two people who have done freelance editing jobs for Llumina and claim to have not yet been paid, even though the jobs were done months earlier. I also received some emails from authors claiming they weren't paid royalties. The editors sent me a lot of documentation to support their claims. From what I can tell, Llumina, like many other businesses, may be having a rough time. Before I considered Llumina, I'd want to make sure that it was financially viable.

My head says that you should avoid them, but my heart says, "This is a small publisher fighting the man." Regardless, I know that you can find a better option for the money.

PUBLISHAMERICA

http://www.publishamerica.com

FORMAT OF BOOKS: Paperback

GENRES ACCEPTED: PublishAmerica considers most fiction and nonfiction, although it will not print theses, coffee table books, screenplays, textbooks, or books of quotations.

PUBLISHING FEES: PublishAmerica claims to operate like a traditional publisher and, therefore, assesses no publishing fees. However, the publisher's contract terms are so outrageous that, with the exception of not charging up-front fees, it really has little in common with traditional publishing.

I would love to tell you all about PublishAmerica's publishing services, but I can't. My research assistant emailed some basic questions using both their online email form under the "Contact Us" tab (twice) and a direct email to their Acquisitions Department (about which, for the record, the website says, "Use this address if you are a new author and would like to find more about PublishAmerica"—good luck with that). We received no response to any of these email inquiries.

RETAIL PRICE OF AUTHOR'S BOOK: The PublishAmerica website does not list the publisher's retail prices, but I found a few paperbacks by PublishAmerica on Amazon.com:

- *How To Upset a Goliath Book Biz: PublishAmerica: The Inside Story of an Underdog with a Bite,* by Willem Meiners (353 pages / paperback / $24.95)

- *Wounds and Scars: A Seventh Cross Novel, Book II*, by Brian L. Stowe (379 pages / paperback / $29.95)
- *A Katrina Moment*, by Alexandra Everist (156 pages / paperback / $24.95)

These retail prices are off-the-charts high. Retailers are not likely to carry these titles, even if they are the best books ever written, because the retail prices can't be supported by the marketplace.

Per the contract, PublishAmerica has full discretion and control over the retail price. At least from the three examples I saw, it's not setting the prices at a level that will garner any sales.

PRICE AUTHOR PAYS FOR BOOKS: PublishAmerica extends its authors a 20 percent discount on purchases of twenty or fewer books, and 30 percent on twenty-one books or more. Using the three examples above, let's see what each author will pay to buy copies. For *How To Upset a Goliath Book Biz*, if Meiners purchases more than twenty-one copies of his book, here's what he will pay:

$24.95 Retail price
–$7.49 Author discount (30%)
$17.46 Author price per book

Because this book is 353 pages, it costs $6.20 to print each copy ($0.015 x 353 pages + $0.90). So, after print costs, PublishAmerica is making $11.26. This is a 182 percent printing markup.

Using the numbers for Brian Stowe's 379-page book, if he purchases more than twenty-one copies, here is what he'll pay:

$29.95 Retail price
–$8.99 Author discount (30%)
$20.96 Author price per book

Because this book is 379 pages, it costs $6.59 to print each copy ($0.015 x 379 pages + $0.90). So, after print costs, PublishAmerica is making $14.37 per copy. This a 214 percent printing markup.

Finally, if Alexandra Everist purchases more than twenty-one copies of her book, here is what she'll pay per copy:

$24.95 Retail price
–$7.49 Author discount (30%)
$17.46 Author price per book

Because this book is 156 pages, it costs $3.24 to print each copy ($0.015 x 156 pages + $0.90). So, after print costs, PublishAmerica is making $14.22 per copy. This is a 439 percent printing markup.

To be fair, the publisher doesn't charge any up-front fees—but this pricing will make you wish they had.

ROYALTIES PAID TO AUTHOR: PublishAmerica's royalties are based on the number of copies sold and the sales price:

Quantity Sold	Author Royalty
Up to 2,000	8%
2,001–6,000	25%
6,001+	50%

If a 200-page book retails for $19.95, is sold through the PublishAmerica site, and sells less than two thousand copies, here is what the author makes per sale:

$19.95 Retail price
x 0.08 Author royalty percentage
$1.60 Author royalty

In the meantime, PublishAmerica makes:

$19.95 Retail price
–$1.60 Author royalty (8%)
–$3.90 Printing cost
$14.45 PublishAmerica profit

For books sold through third-party retailers like Amazon.com, the author makes the same royalty, but PublishAmerica makes less than it does through sales on its own site.

The acquisitions editor would not tell me what the booksellers' discount is, but the PublishAmerica FAQ shows a 40 percent discount for Amazon.com:

$19.95	Retail price
–$7.98	Amazon.com discount (40%)
–$1.60	Author royalty
–$3.90	Printing cost
$6.47	PublishAmerica profit

It might be acceptable for PublishAmerica to make this kind of profit from your book if it were putting a lot of money into marketing it, but it's not. Not to mention the fact that the book is so overpriced it will have a very hard time in the marketplace. Outside of your family and friends, you will have trouble selling a book at these retail prices to anyone.

NOTABLE PROVISIONS OF THE PUBLISHING AGREEMENT: PublishAmerica won't provide a copy of the contract until it has accepted your manuscript, but I was lucky enough to get a copy of one from an author trying to extricate herself from it.

After reading the contract, I know why this publisher doesn't want anyone to see it. The first big red flag is that the only address listed for the company is a post office box.

Section 1 grants PublishAmerica exclusive rights to publish the book in all formats for seven years worldwide. This seems reasonable at first glance because the publisher fronts all printing and publishing costs. But a closer look at the contract language makes it clear what's really going on here. Authors have a three-month window of time before the end of the first seven-year period in which they can terminate the contract; otherwise another seven-year term commences. Why is the seven-year term a big deal? Well, the only way an author is going to sell books is if that author is aggressively marketing his or her book. What happens if your book takes off and a big-time publisher approaches you? You're stuck in a seven-year contract. What happens if your book takes off and you realize that by publishing on your own you can make quadruple what PublishAmerica is paying you? You're stuck in a seven-year contract. What happens if you forget about and miss the three-month window, seven years from now? Another seven years.

Section 3(a) defines the royalty payments: 8 percent of the sales price for the first two thousand copies sold, 25 percent for the next four thousand copies, and 50 percent after six thousand copies.

Section 3(c) breaks down the division of profits for the sale of a bundle of rights that the author owns for his or her published book, such as translations, book club sales, motion picture, radio, serial, and television. Should the author allow the publisher to sell any of those rights, the author will receive only 50 percent of any monies earned. These are rights that are typically negotiated for between a traditional publisher and an author. Authors don't just give away 50 percent of these rights for the honor of having a publisher print copies of their book. Again, if the author's book takes off and third parties want to purchase these rights, the author is stuck with PublishAmerica as a partner. PublishAmerica, per Section 18, doesn't own these rights to sell them, unless the author specifically gives it the rights in writing. The only way an author's book will ever end up in a situation where these additional rights are even an issue will be if that author finds the opportunity. PublishAmerica is not out aggressively selling or promoting any of its authors' books. Why should you do all the work and give them half the money for the sale of any of the rights set forth in Section 3(c) of the contract?

Section 4 sets forth the price at which authors purchase copies from the publisher. The author receives a 20 percent discount off the retail price (which is set by the publisher) for orders fewer than twenty copies. For orders of more than twenty books, the author receives a 30 percent discount.

Section 7 gives the publisher up to one full year to commence publication. If publication has not yet commenced for reasons other than delays by the author or anything beyond the publisher's control, and the author terminates the agreement, they cannot recoup any of the money already spent.

Section 10 allows the publisher to edit an author's book as the publisher sees fit. This section of the contract actually makes sense, since technically authors assign the rights to the book to PublishAmerica for seven years. This section also allows the publisher to require an author to make revisions to the work as the publisher sees fit. If you sign this contract and PublishAmerica demands rewrites, either you do them, or your book doesn't get published for seven years. A clause like this is reasonable if a publisher plunks down a healthy advance and is going to spend money promoting an author's book, but that is not the case here.

Section 11 says that any changes the author wishes to make to the electronic page proof must be submitted within forty-eight hours of receiving the proof. It also gives the publisher the right to make all formatting decisions.

Section 13 states that the publisher has the right to set up a website for your book with a domain name that PublishAmerica will own. The section states that PublishAmerica will promote your book (or not promote your book) as it sees fit.

Section 15 of the contract explains that authors get royalty statements and payments (if sales were made) twice each year: February and August.

Section 17 does not permit authors to transfer or assign any rights to the contract without the written consent of PublishAmerica. There is no "reasonableness" clause here, so if you're on PublishAmerica's bad side, they can make it tough for you. However, authors always have the right to assign their royalty payments without publisher consent.

Section 18 states that the author agrees that PublishAmerica has the exclusive right, for the duration of the contract, to negotiate all movie, television, radio, and other rights on the author's behalf, only with the author's written consent. Further, "Approval of all terms, provisions and conditions of any and all contracts in connection with any such sale, assignment, lease, license, or other disposition under this paragraph or paragraph number 17 shall be given by the Author upon the recommendation of the Publisher; and, for that purpose, the Author agrees to duly execute any and all contracts, assignments, instruments and approved papers submitted by the Publisher."

Section 19 allows the publisher to sue someone for copyright infringement at its own discretion, and to keep 50 percent of the net proceeds of any recovery.

Section 24 states that all disputes will be submitted to a court in the state of Maryland. This is standard contract language, though it does benefit the publisher.

Note that the contract I read was quite recent, but as the company refuses to let potential authors see a contract, I have no way of knowing if changes have been made since that time.

AUTHOR-FRIENDLY RATING: Performing a Google search on PublishAmerica will call up several boards with ongoing discussion and criticism of the publisher. It's also worthwhile to check out the Wikipedia overview of PublishAmerica at http://en.wikipedia.org/wiki/PublishAmerica, which covers both authors' complaints and recent arbitration and provides links to news coverage of the publisher. For author case studies, check out http://www.wizardessbooks.com/html/PA_stories.htm.

Even without these postings, it doesn't take incredible insight to see that the books are way too expensive. For the price authors pay to buy their own books, they ought to go with a good self-publisher where they will at least get the services they've contracted.

The website is so poorly written and misleading that it should serve as a warning to writers who think that their book will get a strong edit from PublishAmerica. Also, the website explicitly states that the editor will determine whether the book needs editing and the level of editing required, and that—not surprisingly—in the interest of getting a book into print, sometimes the publisher will forego the edit. Never forego the edit!

If the author manages to hustle up a book signing, PublishAmerica may not be there with the books. One man successfully sued PublishAmerica because he spent thousands of dollars on publicity for his book only to find out that bookstores were unable to order it.

How this company keeps chugging along is beyond me. Don't be fooled into thinking that PublishAmerica is a "traditional" publisher and that its acceptance of your book is akin to acceptance by any other traditional publisher. It's not. One author who contacted me hired a lawyer and spent thousands of dollars to get out of her contract. She was more than willing to give us a copy of the contract, as well as valuable information about the way PublishAmerica treats its authors.

Finally, the best thing I can do is let PublishAmerica do the talking for me. Here is an excerpt from the FAQ section of PublishAmerica's website:

> **Question:** *Is this a great millennium, or what?*
> **Answer:** *Some writers tell us, incredulously, they can't believe their luck. After all, many of them have queried publisher after publisher, often without receiving any response at all, and always to no avail. So how can PublishAmerica do what other traditional publishers cannot do? The answer is quite simple. Other publishers could do exactly the same, if only they would. Our bet is that in the next few years more than a few of them will change their mind about "unmarketable writers," now that digital printing technology enables them to save substantially on overstocking. This new century promises to be the era of the yet-unnoticed writer.*

The funny part is: I don't think this is meant to be ironic—PublishAmerica sure didn't "notice" my research assistant, or her queries. If you don't have the money to publish your book and PublishAmerica is your only option, save up until you can afford a better option. You'll be glad you did.

TRAFFORD PUBLISHING

http://www.trafford.com

FORMAT OF BOOK: Paperback and hardcover (ebooks are included with some packages)

GENRES ACCEPTED: All

PUBLISHING FEES: Trafford Publishing offers seven publishing packages for books with black-and-white interiors, as well as several additional packages for full-color and children's books (which will not be discussed here). A side-by-side comparison of the seven packages can be found at http://www.trafford.com/Packages/BW.aspx.

Prime Package: This package costs $799 and includes:

- ISBN
- Template-based custom cover: Includes one free round of corrections. You can supply your own artwork if you wish, or select images or ideas from their image library.
- Book design and interior layout
- Worldwide distribution through Amazon.com and BarnesandNoble.com
- Personalized page in the publisher's online bookstore
- One round of proof corrections

Watermark Package: For $1,299, this package includes everything in the Prime Package, plus:

- Fifteen free copies
- Listing through publisher's online store
- Copyright registration
- Inclusion in Google Book Search and Amazon Search Inside!
- Cover copy polish, where editorial staff turns your ideas into "intriguing cover text"

Elite Package: For $1,899, this package includes everything in the Prime Package, plus:

- Library of Congress Control Number (LCCN)
- Twenty free paperback copies
- Fifteen hardcover copies

Signature Package: For $2,499, this package includes everything in the Elite Package, plus:

- Thirty free paperback copies

- Fifteen hardcover copies
- Barnes & Noble's See Inside program
- Book marketing program: According to the Trafford representative, "Marketing kits generally involve bookmarks, posters, postcards that you can give to anyone in your area. Internet marketing is also done through Trafford's website and making your book available to Amazon.com and other book sites."

Signature Bookseller Package: For $2,999, this package includes everything in the Signature Package, plus:

- Forty free paperback copies
- Twenty hardcover copies
- Bookseller's return program
- Book buyer's preview, allowing retailers to preview your first chapters before ordering

WebBlazer Package: For $4,999, this package includes everything in the Signature Bookseller Package (including the free copies), plus:

- Social media setup (profiles on Facebook, MySpace, and other more book-focused communities)
- Standard publicity: This is a press release and a list of three hundred targeted media outlets based on your topic and location. The way the description is worded sounds like you simply get the press release and a list of addresses, but in an email the publisher assured me that they send the press releases out themselves.
- Personalized WebBlazer website, which is separate from the page on Trafford's bookstore and contains information about your book
- Multiple book email campaign

Editorial Connoisseur Package: For $7,499, this package includes everything in the Signature Bookseller Package (and does *not* include the WebBlazer additions), plus:

- Fifty paperback copies
- Twenty-five hardcover copies

- Book-signing kit
- *ForeWord Clarion* book review and *ForeWord Magazine* ad
- Content editing, up to 70,000 words (after which add $0.035/word)
- Newswire Plus, which makes your press release available to over 17,000 media

The most shocking thing about these packages is that book returns aren't included until you spend $2,999. Also, the content editing fee of $0.035 per word is higher than most.

OTHER SERVICES OF INTEREST:

Author Website: For $399 down and $29 per month, Trafford will set up and host your website. Trafford is owned by Author Solutions, Inc. (the same company that owns AuthorHouse) and has the same deal with AmericanAuthor.com to provide this service. The rep from AmericanAuthor.com told me that the author always owns the content on the site, but doesn't own the website layout. So long as the author continues to pay $29 per month for hosting, the author can continue to use the layout. Also, the author can supply his or her own domain name. The $29 per month for hosting is expensive. You can get hosting for $5–$10 per month.

Email Marketing Campaigns: Trafford has several options, described at http://www.trafford.com/Servicestore/ServiceList.spx?Service=CAST-987. You can send an email to an opt-in list of 500,000 people up to 10,000,000 people. The prices range from $1,596 to $9,996. There are also packages where four books by four different authors are marketed in the same email, reducing the cost for each author. The problem with these emails is that the recipients aren't necessarily interested in a book like yours. You have to read what Trafford says on its website carefully here. It says that emails are sent to people who "have already opted-in to receive news about the book industry." If your book is a coming-of-age novel, can there really be 500,000 to 10,000,000 people in the U.S. who have expressed interest in receiving emails about your specific genre? Not likely. People who've signed up for some list to receive emails about the "book industry" will make up a pretty broad list. The percentage of people who open these emails is likely small, and the percentage of people who take action once they've opened them is even smaller. A good open rate would be 2 percent and a great action rate would be 2 percent (of those who open it). Assume Trafford sends an email to 500,000 people and 10,000 open it (2 percent). Assume 2 percent of those people (200) buy your book. You won't get close to making even a third of your money back. Without a highly targeted opt-in list, email marketing is simply not effective. Trafford is doing nothing wrong by offering this, but new authors see these huge numbers and assume that such volume will turn into sales. It rarely does.

Book Trailers: Trafford has offerings from $19,999 to $1,859 at http://www.trafford.com/Servicestore/ServiceList.aspx?Service=CAST-977. I can't comment on the "Hollywood" book trailers with "Hollywood" producers and actors, but I wouldn't pay $20,000 for one. As for the basic book trailer, you can get something comparable for under $1,000.

RETURN OF DIGITAL COVER AND INTERIOR FILES: File ownership is not covered on the Trafford website or its author agreement, but I emailed the publisher, asking who owns production files for the formatted book, and received this reply: "You will be sent PDF proofs via email to approve or fail. If you want electronic files, this would be the only way to keep them. We do not sent [sic] electronic files of your book to you. They are property of Trafford. The content is absolutely yours, but the files are ours. We send them to the printer to create your book."

RETAIL PRICE OF AUTHOR'S BOOK: When my research assistant emailed Trafford, a representative informed her that the base retail price for a 200-page paperback with a black-and-white interior would be $15.04. An author can raise the retail price of his book if he "believe[s]the content of the book warrants a higher price than the average." There do not seem to be any restrictions or requirements pertaining to raising the retail price.

PRICE AUTHOR PAYS FOR BOOKS: Authors receive a 50 percent discount off of their first order, provided it is more than 150 books. After this, as shown at http://www.trafford.com/FAQ/BookSalesOrdering.aspx#Discount, the discounts are as follows:

Quantity	Discount	Author Price	Markup
1–24	30%	$10.53	170%
25–49	35%	$9.78	151%
50–99	40%	$9.02	131%
100–249	45%	$8.27	112%
250–499	50%	$7.52	92%
500–999	55%	$6.77	74%
1,000–1,999	60%	$6.02	141%*
2,000+	65%	$5.26	200%*

For large print runs, I am assuming that Trafford prints the books offset, which is much cheaper than print-on-demand, hence the asterisks. If you went to any online book printing site you could get one thousand copies of the mythical 6" x 9", 200-page paperback for around $2.50 per copy. The cost for two thousand or more would be around $1.75 per copy. However, offset pricing can vary a lot; so again, the printing markups for the big runs are estimates only.

ROYALTIES PAID TO AUTHOR: The author selects a royalty of either 10 or 20 percent for print copies, calculated as follows: retail price less the trade discount to booksellers and less the single copy printing cost. With a 20 percent royalty, the discount for online retailers is 36 percent. Let's base our example on a 200-page book priced at the minimum retail price with the 20 percent royalty. The math would look like this if the book were sold from Trafford.com:

$15.04	Retail price
–$5.41	Trade discount (36%)
$9.63	Net profit
x 0.20	Author royalty
$1.93	Author royalty

Trafford makes $7.70 on this sale. Back out the printing cost of $3.90, and Trafford earns $3.80, almost 100 percent more than the author.

If you select a 10 percent royalty rate, the trade discount offered to retailers (both brick-and-mortar retailers and online retailers) is 46 percent. In this situation:

$15.04	Retail price
–$6.92	Trade discount (46%)
$8.12	Net profit
x 0.10	Author royalty
$0.81	Author royalty

Trafford makes $7.31 on this sale. Back out the printing cost of $3.90, and Trafford earns $3.41, more than four times what the author does.

If the book is sold through the Trafford website, the author presumably earns 10 or 20 percent of the retail price, so in the examples above, either $1.50 or $3.00 per book. Those numbers might look good, until you look closer. Back out the actual printing cost of $3.90 and Trafford makes $12.03 to $13.54 per sale, while the author earns a tiny fraction of that.

You should know that if you choose the 20 percent royalty option, the chances of ever having your book ordered by a brick-and-mortar bookstore are practically nil. This type of retailer demands at least a 40 percent trade discount. Online retailers will accept much lower trade discounts.

NOTABLE PROVISIONS OF THE PUBLISHING AGREEMENT: The publishing agreement can be found at http://www.trafford.com/uploadedFiles/Trafford/Packages/Order_Forms_and_Agreement/Trafford_Terms_and_Conditions_11_02_09.pdf.

Section 1.4, under "Agreements," states that Trafford has no obligation to provide the author with any submitted materials or production files for any reason.

Section 5, "Pricing and Royalty Agreements," states that Trafford makes royalty payments on a quarterly basis, assuming you are owed at least $25 for that quarter; any outstanding royalties are then paid in full within sixty days of December 31st.

Section 13 says that the agreement is nonexclusive and that either party may terminate it at any time, without cause, with written notice. It also says that the agreement is subject to the laws of Bloomington, Indiana, and that any arbitration will take place there. Also, per the contract, the arbitrator is required to award costs and attorneys' fees to the prevailing party in any arbitration. This section also waives the Supplementary Procedures for Consumer-Related Disputes, instead making the standard business disputes from the American Arbitration Association applicable. The AAA decides whether the case is a consumer or business case, unless there is a clause like this one that precludes them.

Guess what the principal difference is between a business and consumer case? The fees. Consumers who file cases under $10,000 pay a $125 filing fee. For a business dispute, the filing fee is $750 plus another $200 if a hearing is held. The Trafford contract requires a hearing, so if you have a dispute and want to arbitrate, you're $950 down before the case is even heard. These guys don't miss a beat. Wow.

AUTHOR-FRIENDLY RATING: The old adage "A fool and his money are soon parted" comes to mind when I think of the author who chooses this publisher—especially after reading this review. Trafford charges a premium for many of its services, yet it still triple-inflates the printing costs and has a royalty structure where, in every scenario, it ends up with most of the money from the sales of a book.

Trafford's business model will bury you and your book. You will pay more up front than you need to. The printing costs are so overinflated that the retail price of your book will make it uncompetitive. Finally, after all the money you paid to publish, Trafford will be making most of the money each time you sell a book. And, if you have a dispute that requires arbitration, you have to pay $950 just to start the arbitration proceedings. It's a bad deal and keeps getting worse.

WESTBOW PRESS

http://www.westbowpress.com

FORMAT OF BOOK: Paperback and hardcover (ebooks are included with some packages)

GENRES ACCEPTED: WestBow Press is a division of Thomas Nelson and only accepts books that are in line with its "Editorial Standards," which are found at http://www.westbowpress.com/AboutUs/EditorialStandards.aspx.

PUBLISHING FEES: WestBow offers a variety of publishing packages. The standard packages range from $999 to $6,499. A full description of them can be found at http://www.westbowpress.com/Packages/Default.aspx. WestBow also has color book packages at $1,599 (http://www.westbowpress.com/Packages/ColorBooks/PackageCompare.aspx) and "specialty" publishing packages ranging from $9,999 to $19,999 (http://www.westbowpress.com/Packages/SpecialtyPackages/PackageCompare.aspx). Only the standard packages are covered here.

Essential Access: This package costs $999 and includes:

- ISBN
- Template-based custom cover
- Book design and interior layout
- Distribution through Ingram's Lightning Source (which includes Amazon.com and BarnesandNoble.com)
- Ten complimentary copies
- Reps working to sell to Christian book buyers

Pro Format: For $1,799, this package includes everything in the Essential Access, plus:

- Twenty free paperback copies
- Ten free hardcover copies
- Ebook format and distribution

- Barnes & Noble See Inside, Amazon Search Inside! and Google Books submission
- Inclusion in WestBow Press Catalog

Bookstore Advantage: For $2,799, this package includes everything in the Pro Format, plus:

- Editorial review
- Forty free paperback copies
- Fifteen free hardcover copies
- Booksellers Return Program
- One hundred promotional materials (bookmarks, postcards and business cards)

Online Platform: For $4,999, this package includes everything in the Bookstore Advantage, plus:

- Sixty free paperback copies
- Twenty free hardcover copies
- Author website
- Social media set-up
- Three hundred promotional materials (bookmarks, postcards, and business cards)
- Windshield flier

Video Plus: For $6,499, this package includes everything in the Online Platform, plus:

- Eighty free paperback copies
- Twenty free hardcover copies
- Data entry service
- Indexing
- Book signing kit
- Book trailer (no voiceover)

OTHER SERVICES OF INTEREST:

Author Website: For $479 down and $29 per month, WestBow will set up and host your website, through AmericanAuthor

.com (http://www.westbowpress.com/Servicestore/ServiceDetail .aspx?Serviceld=BS-1105). WestBow has essentially the same deal as CrossBooks and cousins Trafford and AuthorHouse have with AmericanAuthor.com. Interestingly, the same package at Trafford is $399 plus $29 per month. My guess is that the additional amount is the cut taken by WestBow. The $29 monthly hosting fee is expensive. You can get hosting for $5–$10 per month.

Newsmaker Publicity Campaign: For $3,999, you get a publicist for six weeks. Not bad. But during that time, the publicist writes a press release and sends it out to one thousand media sources. There aren't a thousand media sources interested in even the biggest books, but hey—toss as much of it as you can against the wall, and some of it might stick. Then, you get one guaranteed interview on WestBow's internet radio show. This service costs a lot of money for what you get. A complete list of all additional services can be found at http://www.westbowpress.com/ServiceStore/ServiceHome.aspx.

RETURN OF DIGITAL COVER AND INTERIOR FILES: Like its cousins, iUniverse and CrossBooks, WestBow allows authors to purchase the interior and cover digital production files for $750 each, if the request by the author is eighteen months or less from the book's release date. If it is after eighteen months from the release date, it's $150 per file. It should be obvious that producing the files in the first eighteen months doesn't take any more time or effort on the publisher's part than providing them after eighteen months.

RETAIL PRICE OF AUTHOR'S BOOK: The publisher has final say over the retail price (which is a good thing). I took a random sampling of some of WestBow titles. I found:

- *Rajput* (6" x 9" / paperback / 212 pages / $17.95)
- *If You Can't Come In, Smile As You Go By* (5.5" x 8.5" / paperback / 108 pages / $11.95)
- *Heavenly Inspirations of Faith, Hope, and Love* (5" x 8" / paperback / 156 pages / $13.95)

PRICE AUTHOR PAYS FOR BOOKS: Authors receive a 50 percent discount off of their first order, provided it is more than 150 books. After this, as shown at http://www.westbowpress.com/FAQ/Pricing.aspx, the discounts vary based on volume ordered and are calculated at a discount off of the retail price. To get an example, I used *Rajput*, which is a 212-page paperback and retails for $17.95. Lightning Source charges $4.08 to print this book in very small quantities.

Quantity	Discount	Author Price	Markup
1–24	30%	$12.57	208%
25–49	35%	$11.67	186%
50–99	40%	$10.77	164%
100–249	45%	$9.34	142%
250–499	50%	$8.98	120%
500–999	55%	$8.08	98%
1,000–1,999	60%	$7.18	115%*
2,000+	65%	$6.28	225%*

For large print runs, I am assuming WestBow prints the books offset, which is much cheaper than print-on-demand—hence the asterisks. If you went to any online book printing company you could get one thousand copies of this example book for around $2.50 per copy. The cost for two thousand or more would be around $1.93 per copy. However, offset pricing can vary a lot; so again, the printing markups for the big runs are estimates only.

ROYALTIES PAID TO AUTHOR: This publisher pays a 50 percent royalty equal to what the publisher earns on each book sold after backing out print costs and trade discounts. Here is an example directly from the website at www.westbowpress.com/FAQ/Pricing.aspx. It was unclear to me what the COGS (cost of goods sold) was based on. It is the "cost" to print the book. The example on WestBow's site is EXACTLY, VERBATIM, the same example used on CrossBooks' site. Since both companies are operated by Author Solutions, I'm assuming that the answer I received from CrossBooks' sales rep (that it was based on a 200-page, paperback, 6" x 9" book) applies here as well.

$17.95 SRP (suggested retail price)
–$8.62 Retail discount (48%)
$9.33 Net retail discount
–$4.97 COGS (cost of goods sold)
$4.36 Net COGS
x 0.50 Royalty percentage
$2.18 Author royalty

The math for a web sale looks like this:

$17.95 SRP
–$4.97 COGS
$12.98 Net COGS
x 0.50 Royalty percentage
$6.49 Author royalty

There are few things of interest here. The COGS for this 200-page book is actually $3.90, not $4.97; thus, WestBow has marked up the printing by $1.97, or 27 percent (one of the lowest markups on record). In the "retail sale" example, the author doesn't truly make a 50 percent royalty because WestBow's $1.97 printing markup is hidden in the print costs. In that example, the author makes $2.18, and WestBow, with its printing markup, makes $4.15.

The same holds true for the "web sale" example (when the book is sold through the WestBow website). Here the author makes $6.49 per sale and WestBow makes $8.46.

When I look at these sales scenarios, another big question presents itself to me. Why is the cost to produce the book (in the royalty calculations) so much less than the production cost of the same book should the author want to buy a copy of it for his own use? In fact, there is no difference in actual production cost. So why does WestBow use one number for sales and one number if the author wants to buy copies?

NOTABLE PROVISIONS OF THE PUBLISHING AGREEMENT: The publishing agreement is only accessible after you start the publishing process. So, if you want to see one prior to actually paying WestBow any money, you'll need to select a package and begin the ordering process.

First, you will need to agree to the Editorial Standards Agreement (http://www.westbowpress.com/uploadedFiles/WestBow_Press/Packages/Order_Forms_and_Agreement/WestBow-Editorial-Standards_11-16-2009.pdf). Then you get to the contract (https://www.westbowpress.com/uploadedFiles/WestBow_Press/Packages/Order_Forms_and_Agreement/WestBow-Author-Agreement_1-31-2010.pdf). My favorite part about this contract is that it is almost identical to CrossBooks' contract (so it saved me a ton of researching time).

Section 6 states that the term is for three years from the date the publisher first sends the files to the printer for the initial print run. But, per Section 7, the author can terminate by giving thirty days written notice.

Section 11 gives WestBow up to 180 days to publish the work.

Section 12 gives WestBow control over the details of publication, including price, online presentation, whether or not to use DRM (digital rights management) on any ebook version, etc. These are generally good ideas. While it's important for authors to have control, so long as the publisher is doing things, in a way that helps the project (such as setting an appropriate retail price), this control is better left in the publisher's hands.

One portion of Section 12 worth noting is that the author is prohibited from utilizing "all, or portions of the WORK, the International Standard Book Number (ISBN), and identical or similar cover with any other PUBLISHER." I emailed CrossBooks and asked what this meant, and since both CrossBooks and WestBow are operated by Author Solutions and have the exact same contract, I'm assuming that CrossBooks' response to my question will also apply to WestBow. Here is the response (from CrossBooks): "The content remains always yours. You can reuse your own artwork as well. The only thing[sic] we do not release are the files we created with our process for the final design and formatting of your work. So…no problem, sir."

Now, that isn't exactly what the contract says. Clearly, another cover with the same image on it could be interpreted as being "similar." If I were you and I were considering this publisher, I'd get email confirmation about this clause.

Section 18 gives the publisher to the right to terminate and refund all fees less a $150 setup fee.

Section 24 allows the publisher to amend the agreement at any time with thirty days written notice. If the author doesn't object in writing and terminate the contract within thirty days, the terms are deemed accepted. The only thing that an author can do if she or he disputes the amendment is terminate the contract. So, the publisher could change the royalty structure, and if you don't like it, all you can do is terminate the contract.

Next is Schedule A.

Section 1 sets forth the royalties, as described previously. It also includes ebook royalties, which are 50 percent of the actual payments WestBow receives from ebook sales.

Section 4 sets forth that WestBow has final say over the retail price of the book and that all ebooks will have a default price of $9.99.

Section 5 sets forth a refund schedule, should an author back out during any part of the process. This is a nice touch that few companies include in their agreements.

Section 6 outlines the author discounts for purchase of their own books. These discounts are set forth within this review.

Section 8 stipulates that authors who terminate can purchase their production files for $750 each (interior and cover) if the termination is within eighteen months of the release date of the book. The files are $150 each if the termination is after eighteen months from the release date. This is contrary to the email I received from the sales rep about return of production files.

AUTHOR-FRIENDLY RATING: Thomas Nelson is a big name in publishing. Don't think that going with WestBow is like being signed by Thomas Nelson. It's not. In my opinion, WestBow is Thomas Nelson's name pasted onto Author Solutions' back end.

The packages cost more than some of the comparable ones at Author Solutions' other companies (like iUniverse, Trafford, Xlibris, and AuthorHouse). Interestingly, WestBow's packages are cheaper than very similar packages offered by CrossBooks. The packages are okay. They're priced a bit high for what you get, but I've seen worse. The printing markups are shameful, but not much different than Author Solutions' other companies.

If you review the royalty example, it appears that WestBow doesn't mark up the actual printing costs for the purpose of calculating royalties as much as the other Author Solutions companies do. That's a good thing. WestBow also has a fair refund schedule, also something the others don't. But, as with other Author Solutions companies, just when you think something is getting better, there's something to knock you back to reality. In WestBow's case, it's the $1,500 fee to get back the production files you already paid to have created.

If you are really interested in the services that WestBow offers, it's cheaper to use one of Author Solutions' other companies. If you really want a Christian publisher, there are some that aren't run by secular publishers. Since many of those who read this are probably also looking at CrossBooks, you should know that both CrossBooks and WestBow have the EXACT same address, 1663 Liberty Drive, Bloomington, IN 47403 (http://www.crossbooks.com/ContactUs/Default.aspx and http://www.westbowpress.com/ContactUs/Default.aspx), because they are both being operated by Author Solutions, also at 1663 Liberty Drive in Bloomington, IN.

XLIBRIS

http://www.xlibris.com

FORMAT OF BOOKS: Paperback, hardcover, and ebook

GENRES ACCEPTED: All

PUBLISHING FEES: Xlibris offers seven black-and-white publishing packages. The publisher also offers six color packages, which will not be covered here, but can be found at http://www2.xlibris.com/black_and_white.html, along with full descriptions of the packages below.

Advantage Package: This package (details at http://www2.xlibris.com/bw_advantage.html) is $449. It does not include distribution; books are sold on the Xlibris website only. It does include:

- Paperback version
- One author review copy of the book
- Choice of three cover templates for which the author supplies the image and author photo
- Choice of two interior templates
- Book and author webpages in Xlibris' online bookstore, which includes ordering and contact information, author biography, and an excerpt of the book
- Worldwide distribution

Basic Package: This package (http://www2.xlibris.com/bw_basic.html) is $649 and includes everything in the Advantage Package, plus:

- Five paperback copies of the book
- Choice of eight cover templates
- Choice of five interior templates
- Ebook
- Ability to track production progress online
- R.R. Bowker's Books In Print registration
- Bookmarks, business cards, and postcards (fifty each); five posters
- Book and author webpages on publisher's online bookstore
- Online sales and royalty accounting
- Author service representative to help you through the process

Professional Package: This package (http://www2.xlibris.com/bw_professional.html) is $1,099 and includes everything in the Basic Package, plus:

- Hardcover and paperback versions; you receive one review copy of each
- One hardcover copy
- Ten paperback copies
- Choice of eighteen cover templates, for which you can supply up to three images

- Choice of nine interior templates: This includes options for the head, foot, folio, and chapter heads, plus twenty-five interior tables and graphics.
- Registration with Google Book Search
- U.S. Copyright registration
- LCCN

Custom Package: This package (http://www2.xlibris.com/bw_custom.html) costs $1,699 and includes everything in the Professional Package, plus:

- Custom-designed cover: Includes consultation with cover and interior designers and, according to the Xlibris rep, as many comps as it takes to get the design right. But this is not in the contract or on the website. You must supply artwork or up to five images and your author photo.
- Consultation with interior and cover designer
- Forty graphs and tables
- Personal starter website with domain: Includes three pages, up to two images, an email account, and a choice of five templates. Xlibris owns the domain, but the site will remain live as long as you continue to pay the $89 annual fee. The à la carte cost is $349. This is outrageous. A domain costs $8–$10. And if you don't own the site, why should you pay the hosting fees?
- Twenty-five paperback copies
- Ten hardcover copies
- Google Book Search
- Barnes & Noble's See Inside; Amazon Search Inside!

Premium Package: This package (http://www2.xlibris.com/bw_premium.html) costs $3,299 and includes everything in the Custom Package, plus:

- Unlimited cover and interior photos/tables
- Author alterations service, which includes two rounds of changes

- Data entry service: Creates a digital file of your handwritten or typed manuscript. The à la carte cost is $2.50 per page.
- Copyediting service: Corrects grammar, spelling, and syntax. The à la carte cost is $0.01–$0.012 per word.
- Citations: Includes formatting for endnotes and footnotes.
- Indexing: This service does not include the actual indexing, but only the formatting of the index. The à la carte cost is $100.
- CD archive: Includes a PDF of the cover and an unformatted copy of your corrected manuscript. The à la carte cost is $99. (In terms of recordkeeping, you can scan the cover of your book yourself, and you'll get a PDF galley of the book during the proofing, not to mention your copy of the book. This archive will not be useful for printing a copy of the book because it is not formatted for a press. Although a rough text version of the book might save the author a little time if he or she ever wanted to print with another publisher, $99 is a lot to pay for what is essentially a Word document of your work.)
- Press release campaign: Includes one hundred media outlets. Xlibris publicists will write a press release, distribute it, send out requested review galleys (at no extra charge to you or the reviewer), and forward you any of the resulting interview requests. The à la carte cost is $349. (Note: If you were going to pay for an Xlibris additional service, this may be the best deal. This service costs the same amount as the book review campaign, yet your press release goes out to a targeted list, and the service description states no limit on the number of bound review galleys.)
- Forty paperbacks
- Twenty hardcover copies
- Opt-in email marketing campaign: Includes 200,000 recipients. This is simply an email with a picture of your book and click-through ordering that goes out to a massive, untargeted list. Even if the publisher insists it isn't sending out spam, you can rest assured that 200,000 people did not sign up for email alerts for books by unknown authors. The à la carte cost is $349.

Executive Package: This package (http://www2.xlibris.com/bw_executive.html) is $7,099 and includes everything in the Premium Package, plus:

- Basic cover design service
- Twenty-five hardcover copies
- Seventy-five paperback books
- One leather-bound hardcover edition
- Ability to set your own price: Allows you to raise or lower the retail price of your book. Under the terms of the service, you agree to take a $1 royalty—no matter where your book sells—and the price of your 200-page book goes down to $15.99; each additional $1 of royalty raises the price of the book by $2. The à la carte cost is $249. A company that charges you an extra $249 for the ability to set your own price is one that should make you wonder.
- Press release campaign: Includes outreach to five hundred media outlets. Again, Xlibris declined to reveal what tools it uses to compile this list, so it is unclear if there really are five hundred viable, interested media outlets out there or just five hundred spam receptacles.
- Opt-in email marketing campaign: Includes one million recipients. If this isn't spam, I don't know what it is. However, the Xlibris representative insisted that each of these one million people has individually contacted Xlibris asking to be notified when the publisher releases books. (If this is true and Xlibris can prove it, I'll fly to the publisher's offices and eat my book in front of all its employees.)
- Personalized regular website with domain, including six pages, five images, three email accounts, one animated image, and ten templates. The à la carte cost is $549.
- Newswire service
- Social media marketing service
- Three hundred business cards

Platinum Package: This package (http://www2.xlibris.com/bw_platinum.html) costs $14,999 and includes everything in the Executive Package, plus:

- Fifty hardcover copies
- 150 paperback books
- Advanced cover design service
- Ultimate customization: When asked how this level of customization differed from the Custom Package, the Xlibris representative had no specific answers except to sputter that this was "the Rolls Royce of publishing and, for what you're paying, you will get a lot more attention, if you know what I mean."
- Bookstore return status: Your book is listed as returnable, which may increase the chance of booksellers stocking it. The à la carte cost is $699 annually.
- Ad in the *New York Review of Books*: Includes a miniature picture of your book cover on a page with many, many other miniature book covers. This is not an effective form of advertisement. The à la carte cost is $250. Do not confuse this with the *New York Times Book Review*.
- Book trailer with voiceover
- 250-click Google Search Engine Marketing
- Book exhibit show
- Press release to one thousand media outlets
- Advanced personalized website
- Three hundred each of business cards, bookmarks, and postcards; thirty posters

Xlibris also offers a $449 ebook package. More details can be found at http://www2.xlibris.com/bw_eadvantage.html.

RETURN OF DIGITAL COVER AND INTERIOR FILES: Xlibris states in its contract that it retains the rights to digital property and ownership related to all completed production and data files. When I asked the Xlibris representative why the authors, who pay for this service, do not own the files, too, she said: "You retain the rights to the book, but the files remain ours because we created them."

The production files are not even available for a fee. So the author's only recourse, according to the representative, is to buy Xlibris' CD archive, which for $100 includes a PDF of the cover and an unformatted rich-text version of the manuscript, neither of which will be of any real use in printing. Whether you want to publish the book yourself or move to a new publishing house, you will simply have to reformat the book. What is the point of going with a company that you pay to create your book's production files, but then when you want them, you don't own them?

RETAIL PRICE OF AUTHOR'S BOOK: A detailed chart of Xlibris' book prices can be found at: http://www2.xlibris.com/bw_pricing_chart.html.

Page Count	**Retail Price**
<107	$15.99
108–399	$19.99
400+	$23.99

Ridiculously high printing markups and pathetically low author royalties are two reasons that a 200-page book that costs, at most, $3.90 to print is retailing for $20.00.

AUTHOR PRICE FOR BOOKS: Xlibris bases the price an author pays for copies of his or her own book on the page count and the number of books the author buys. For a 200-page, paperback book that retails for $19.99, the price per book the author pays is determined as follows:

Quantity	**Discount**	**Author Price**	**Markup**
1–9	30%	$13.99	259%
10–24	35%	$12.99	233%
25–49	40%	$11.99	207%
50–99	45%	$10.99	182%
100–249	50%	$10.00	156%
250–499	55%	$9.00	131%
500–1,499	60%	$8.00	105%

Marking up the cost the author pays for books at these levels is a formula for disaster, unless of course you're the one marking up the book. Do you get how impossible this makes it for an author to actually make money selling his or her books? The retail price is inflated to an unrealistic level in order to accommodate an excessive printing markup. Remember, you pay Xlibris between $400 and $14,000 to publish your book. Now every time you want to purchase a copy of the book they make another huge chunk? If you've ever seen the movie *Network*, this would be a good time to relive the famous scene: go to your window, open it, stick your head out, and scream as loud as you can, "I'm mad as hell, and I'm not going to take it anymore!"

ROYALTIES PAID TO AUTHOR: According to the Xlibris pricing chart (http://www2.xlibris.com/bw_pricing_chart.html), paperback and hardcover royalties are 10 percent of the retail price when the book is sold through a bookseller or online retailer, and 25 percent of the retail price when sold on the Xlibris website. Here's what that looks like on the 200-page book mentioned previously, sold on a website like Amazon:

$19.99	Retail price
x 0.10	Royalty percentage
$2.00	Author royalty

How much does Xlibris make on that same sale?

$19.99	Retail price
–$3.90	Printing cost
–$8.00	Amazon.com discount (40%)
–$2.00	Author royalty
$6.09	Xlibris profit

For a book sold through the Xlibris online bookstore:

$19.99	Retail price
x 0.25	Royalty percentage
$5.00	Author royalty

On direct sales, Xlibris' profit is even more outrageous:

$19.99	Retail price
–$3.90	Printing cost
–$5.00	Author royalty
$11.09	Xlibris profit

Repeat the scene in *Network*. This company makes 300 percent more profit on every sale through Amazon than its authors do, and about 225 percent more on direct sales.

NOTABLE PROVISIONS OF THE PUBLISHING AGREEMENT: The publishing agreement can be found at http://www2.xlibris.com/legal_agreement.html.

The section titled "Your Work...Your Rights" states that Xlibris acquires no rights to the work and only provides services such as printing and book sales. This section also states that Xlibris has no obligation to review or correct the work and that the book will be printed as submitted.

The section titled "Xlibris' Work...Xlibris' Rights" states that Xlibris retains all digital property and ownership related to all completed production data and files. However, the work itself is still the property of the author.

The section "Term and Exclusivity" states that the contract is nonexclusive, and the author can enter into other publishing agreements. If the author terminates the agreement before signing off on approval of work performed, all publishing fees will be refunded in full, which means that if you terminate *before* signing off on the final proof of your book, you're entitled to a refund. Otherwise, all bets are off. If Xlibris terminates at any time, all publishing fees will be returned or applied against outstanding balances in the author's account. Publishing fees are those fees directly associated with online, disk, and paper manuscript submission.

Under the section “Law and Venue,” the parties agree to arbitrate disputes. Should either party want equitable relief or need to enforce the arbitrator’s judgment, the remedy must take place in Bloomington, Indiana.

AUTHOR-FRIENDLY RATING: Xlibris is a bottomless well into which you will throw all of your publishing money. The publisher charges authors too much for books and takes a huge royalty on retail sales, leaving authors holding nothing more than an overpriced book for which they make a tawdry royalty. While Xlibris offers some cheaper packages, if you don’t pay to have a custom cover design, you are just wasting your money. (This applies to any company, not just Xlibris.) Taken at face value, the $1,699 Custom Package is decently priced, but the author website and the book’s production files, which you pay for but do not own, make that package not so great in the end.

And therein lies the rub: on their own, some of the packages aren’t so bad, but when you add in the huge printing markups and incredibly low royalties, the positives wash away. The inflated printing costs cause the retail pricing to be ridiculous. Xlibris sells its books at prices much higher than what is commercially viable. Couple that with the fact that Xlibris makes at least double what the author does in royalties, and it all looks pretty bad.

If 250 percent printing markups and the publisher making twice your royalties don’t bother you, just hang on—there’s much, much more. Rounding out the hellish trifecta is the price you’ll pay to purchase copies of your own book. The 200-page paperback can be purchased by the author for $13.99, a full $10.09 more than what it costs to print. At that price (plus postage, don’t forget!), you’d need to sell it for $20 to make any money, and your book would have trouble competing in the marketplace.

And last, yet hardly least—for all that money, if you leave Xlibris you can’t take your book’s digital production files with you. You’ll have to start all over with another publisher or pay a graphic artist another chunk of money to format the book and cover for you again.

On a customer service note, the publisher’s operator seemed annoyed to receive my call and suggested I look for the answers to my questions on the website. When further pressed, she forwarded me to a representative who would not answer any questions without taking down my address and phone number, seemed poorly versed in the company's offerings, and tried to strong-arm me into committing to a package. She even promised that, if I just went ahead and locked into the package at the sales price, I could cancel the purchase if I changed my mind.

If what you read here isn't enough to convince you to stay away, then P.T. Barnum was right—there really is a sucker born every minute.

CHAPTER 12

THE WORST OF THE WORST

The Lord really does work in mysterious ways. As this book was just about ready to go to press (literally, the day before), I received an email from an author who had just purchased the 2008 edition of my book. Here is what he said:

> *I've read your book…as a Christian I was especially interested in Pleasant Word because I was talking with them about pricing and very close to signing with them…When I asked about pricing, based on your book, they were evasive. When I said I needed answers to move forward, so I could resolve the issue of integrity with pricing, I received a twenty-point "e-missile" from an executive there……which told me that your book touched a real nerve. So I searched online for the results of the lawsuit they filed against you.*
>
> *I found that the judge dismissed all their complaints…and that they did not dispute your numbers…* ***By the way, they no longer have Pleasant Word****…they have brought everything under the banner of WinePress now, and raised their prices…*
>
> *I would like to see you include the webpage with their lawsuit being dismissed in your next edition. It would give people a* ***neutral source*** *to see the truth of what you are saying.*

So, here's the backstory. When the last edition of my book came out, Pleasant Word, a division of WinePress Publishing, didn't like my review of its company. It didn't like how I pointed out the huge printing markups and how I felt it made misleading statements on its website. The company had a lawyer send me a threatening letter, which mostly complained about how I rated Xulon Press (a competitor) better than Pleasant Word. I sent the lawyer back a note asking him to point out anything in my review that wasn't factually correct. Then I got an even more threatening letter, but without mention of one incorrect fact in the book. They couldn't find a single erroneous fact because all of the information that I put in the book came directly from their website.

I never heard from them again—until April 2009, when WinePress Publishing sued me for defamation. In November 2009, the case was thrown out, and a federal judge hammered these guys. You can read the court's entire opinion at http://www.bookpublisherscompared.com/winepress-publishing-gets-hammered-by-federal-court.

This company caused me to spend more than $20,000 in legal fees for a case they had no chance to win. At the time the company sued, they put a huge link on their homepage telling everyone how they sued me and that I lied about them. However, after they got defeated on every count and slammed by the court, they didn't put up a correct press release; they kept the (now very) false one up.

So, for all these months I've waited, patiently, to be able to share with everyone exactly who these people are. Is WinePress the worst self-publishing company? Yes. Is it because they forced me to waste $20,000 to defend myself against a frivolous lawsuit? No. It's because, on top of doing all of the things that bad companies already do, they put extremely misleading statements on their site about what services they do provide. I called them on it, and, instead of providing better services, they sued me.

The scariest part is that in early October 2010, WinePress Publishing made the entire Pleasant Word division go away, removed a lot of the specific information from the old site, changed the package names, and raised its prices. I guess getting called out by a federal court for your business practices leaves only one alternative—change everything to confuse those who start to discover the truth.

WINEPRESS

http://www.winepresspublishing.com

FORMAT OF BOOKS: Paperback or hardcover

GENRES ACCEPTED: WinePress has a description on its website indicating what it will and will not print (details at http://www.winepresspublishing.com/publishing/guide_quality). Specifically, the company will not print (a) anything that offends or denies the deity of Jesus Christ or the triune nature of God; (b) un-Biblical or "fad" theology, such as prosperity doctrine and hyped-up revivals; (c) any material that represents or promotes the confusion of Biblical gender roles or relationships, such as women in spiritual authority over men; (d) manuscripts that contain foul language or are crude, sexually explicit, or excessively violent in nature; and (e) libelous or slanderous content, or any other material that may be deemed illegal or immoral.

Considering that WinePress continued posting a press release calling me a liar after a federal court proved otherwise, I'm guessing that its standards about not printing libelous content are not too strict.

PUBLISHING FEES: Up until early October 2010, this publisher offered five main packages (other packages for color books). Complete details and a comparison of the packages are found at http://www.winepresspublishing.com/publishing/comparison. For purposes of this review, only the Starter and Advantage publishing packages are covered, since those are the only ones for which the company provides printing and distribution models on its website. Note that both of the packages described in this review require that the author purchase editing services. The cheapest package is now $1,499 (as opposed to the former White Ribbon Package, which was $999).

Starter Package: This package costs $1,499 and is almost identical to the former Pleasant Word Yellow Package (except that it's $200 more). It includes:

- ISBN
- Bar code
- Library of Congress Control Number (LCCN)
- Ten free copies of the book
- Standard interior formatting
- Standard cover design with two hours of design time
- Editing requirement: It appears that authors who choose this package are required to pay for their manuscripts to be edited for an additional fee. The company no longer lists the editing prices on its website. In the previous edition of this book, this package included the choice of a copyedit (grammar, spelling, syntax, and punctuation at $4.50 per page) or a pre-typeset read (spelling and typos at $0.50 per page). All Starter and Advantage authors must pay for proofreading in addition to copyediting after the manuscript is typeset, and the fee was $3.00 per page at the time that the previous edition of this book was published (it may have gone up since that time). If the author doesn't know his finished page count, WinePress calculates 250 words per page. Assuming that the editing costs are the same as they were when the last edition of this book was released, this means that the author is required to pay $4.00–$7.50 per page for editing. This means that, for example, copyediting and proofreading a 200-page manuscript would add between $800 and $1,500 to the cost of this package.
- Listing with online booksellers: Amazon.com and BarnesandNoble.com
- Espresso Book Machine availability: This is a print-on-demand machine, connected to Lightning Source, from which your book could be printed in a bookstore for purchase in a matter of minutes. (On paper, this sounds great, but currently there are only a handful of locations that house an EBM—the machine costs bookstores and libraries around $75,000.)
- Distribution through Ingram (via its Lightning Source printing service)
- R.R. Bowker's Books In Print listing

- Book return service
- Author discount of 58 percent off of the retail price (when author purchases copies of his book)

Advantage Package: This package is closest to the company's former Blue Ribbon Package, except it's $700 more and you now get less. The package costs $2,999 plus editing fees and includes every service in the Starter Package, plus:

- Premium cover design (five hours of design time)
- Distribution through ChristianBooks.com
- Thirty free copies of the book
- Toll-free number customers can call to order the book
- Author blog (for an example, see http://athenadean.authorweblog.com/)
- Authors can purchase books at 62 percent off of the retail price

OTHER SERVICES OF INTEREST: WinePress offers a variety of marketing and publicity packages, which can be found at http://www.winepresspublishing.com/services/overview. The company doesn't list the prices anywhere, so I can't add much. However, take the lack of transparency about the pricing for what it's worth. The service description pages are filled with buzzwords, but not specifics.

RETURN OF DIGITAL COVER AND INTERIOR FILES: WinePress, of course, does not provide information regarding the return of original production files. However, the contract that I was able to get in April of 2010 states that the "Publisher will maintain ownership of the specific printer-ready cover and typesetting files produced." I'm going to go out on a limb here and say that the "makeover" likely hasn't affected contract terms.

RETAIL PRICE OF AUTHOR'S BOOK: WinePress's retail prices are based on the page count, trim size, and cover of the book. A full discussion and examples of retail prices are available at http://www.winepresspublishing.com/publishing/guide_retail_prices. A 200-

page paperback will retail for $17.99 unless it is 8.25" x 11" (then it will retail for $19.99). Depending on the type of book, such a retail price may be too high. If the book is a 200-page novel and priced as WinePress requires, it is priced way outside of what the market will bear. If it's a business book or how-to book, this price might be a bit closer to where it should be.

PRICE AUTHOR PAYS FOR BOOKS: Author discounts are based on the retail price and vary from package to package. But guess what? WinePress only provides the author discount for the Starter and Advantage Packages. So, for the really expensive packages, you have no idea what type of discount is provided when you purchase copies of your own book. We know that with the Starter Package, and author can purchase copies if his own book for 58 percent off of the retail price (http://www.winepresspublishing.com/publishing/starter). For the Advantage Package, it's 62 percent off of the retail price.

If you publish a 200-page, 6" x 9" paperback under the Starter Package, your prices will look like this:

$17.99	Retail price
-$10.43	Author discount (58%)
$7.56	Author price per book
-$3.90	Printing cost
$3.66	WinePress profit

This is a 94 percent markup!

What's really egregious is the fact that the publisher gives the author the same discount for ordering one book as it does if the author orders one thousand, even though the publisher gets significant price breaks on printing as the quantities go up.

Because many of WinePress's books are printed at Lightning Source, instead of just merely using examples from the company's website, it's helpful to look at the actual prices WinePress authors pay for their books. Even under the most favorable scenario to WinePress, its printing markups are even more inflated than the examples used on its website. I took a random sample of three Pleasant Word (now called WinePress) authors. Giving WinePress the benefit of the doubt (which is hard to do), I assumed that each author was eligible for the highest printing discount available (62 percent). The following examples were used during the court case and were not disputed by Pleasant Word (WinePress).

Evelyn Geisler's book, *Sweet Talks with God*, has a retail price of $13.99. It has 112 pages. Assuming Geisler receives the 62 percent discount, she would pay $5.32 per copy. WinePress's actual print cost is $2.58 per copy, resulting in Ms. Geisler paying a 106 percent printing markup.

Virginia Garberding and Cecil Murphey's book, *Please Get to Know Me*, has a retail price of $13.99. It has ninety-two pages. Assuming the authors receive the highest discount possible, they would pay $5.32 per copy. With WinePress's actual print cost at $2.78 per copy, this would result in a 133 percent printing markup, which, in my opinion, is excessive and inflated.

W. Jay Pilgrim's book, *Lost and Found: A Love Story*, has a retail price of $18.99. It has 250 pages. Assuming Pilgrim receives the highest discount possible, he pays $9.12 per copy, while WinePress's actual print cost is $4.65 per copy. In my opinion, a 96 percent printing markup is also excessive and inflated.

If these authors order more than fifty books at one time, WinePress's printing costs decrease, but the author's purchase price stays the same. WinePress provides the same discount percentage whether the author orders one book or one thousand. If Garberding and Murphey purchase 250 copies of their book from WinePress, the publisher's print cost goes down by 20 percent, to $2.22 per copy, but none of this savings is passed to the authors. So, Garberding and Murphey pay a 139 percent printing markup on this larger order. The more copies of a book the author orders from the publisher, the more they pay for printing per book.

ROYALTIES PAID TO AUTHOR: For details on retail pricing, handling fees, and bookseller discounts, refer to http:// www.winepresspublishing .com/publishing/guide_royalties.

WinePress claims to pay the author 100 percent of the net profit. The publisher defines net profit as the retail sale price less the bookseller's discount, the author's discounted price (a.k.a., actual printing cost plus markup, disguised as actual print cost), and the handling fee of $1.95 per book sold on the WinePress website. However, visit http://www.winepresspublishing.com/publishing/comparison and you'll see that for the very expensive packages, instead of making "100 percent of net profit," authors make between 70 and 80 percent of all "net wholesale and retail sales." So which is it? Another head-shaker.

For the $17.99, 200-page paperback (Starter Package) sold on Amazon.com, the author earns the following:

$17.99	Retail price
-$7.56	Author price per book
-$9.89	Amazon.com discount (55%)
$0.54	Author royalty

That's a puny royalty, consider that WinePress is making $3.66 (the printing markup) on each sale—almost seven times what the author makes!

For the same book sold through WinePress's online bookstore, the author makes:

$17.99	Retail price
-$7.56	Author price per book
-$1.95	Handling fee
$8.48	Author royalty

The big problem with "net profits" is that if they aren't clearly defined, publishers like WinePress can add all sorts of markups, call them "publishing costs," and voilà—you have "net profits." Since "net profits" is defined however WinePress wants, the statements on its website aren't outright lies, but are certainly misleading. Take the first two bullet points at http://www.winepresspublishing.com/publishing/guide_royalties:

- WinePress royalties are based on the book price at point of sale, minus publishing costs.
- You receive 100 percent of the net profit on all sales of your book.

When you look at those, do you get the sense that "publishing costs" include a 94 percent printing markup? The author makes 100 percent of the profits after WinePress nearly doubles the printing price and adds a handling fee. The handling fee is acceptable. While I would never agree to a 100 percent printing markup, as long as the publisher discloses it and you can live with it, the royalty under this scenario is fine. Just keep in mind that for every book sold by an author, at least in our previous example, WinePress is making $5.61 after printing costs.

The most misleading part of the WinePress royalties page is bullet point number four, which states: "We charge a straightforward package premium instead of artificially inflating printing costs." Talk about insulting one's intelligence! The distinction between a "package premium" and "printing cost markup" is semantic only. It talks about not hiding printing costs, but on the very same page provides a sample of printing costs that are marked up between 75 and 93 percent. Publishers have a right to mark up printing as high as they want, but saying that you don't artificially inflate printing costs (when you actually do) is dishonest. It's even more insulting when you go to the company's "Our Team" page (http:// www.winepresspublishing.com/about/team) and the executive publisher states that the company doesn't use "flashy sales gimmicks."

On the same webpage where WinePress claims it doesn't inflate printing costs, it provides sample calculations of printing costs for a standard 200-page paperback. The more an author pays WinePress in up-front fees, the less the printing markup. So in their example, the author purchasing the Advantage Package pays a printing cost of $6.84 per book printed, while the Starter Package author pays $7.56 per book printed. The prospective author viewing this page would not know that these printing costs are marked up 73 to 93 percent.

Prior to the demise of the Pleasant Word website, "package premium" had a link embedded in it, which stated:

This means that Pleasant Word retains a percentage of each sale.

Why do we do this? *Pleasant Word provides continued customer service on your distribution and sales. And, as part of the WinePress Group, we actively engage in advertising and marketing initiatives that promote our brand, draw customers to our bookstore, and provide "across the board" benefits to all of our authors.*

The package premium helps us to help our authors sell books.

With other publishers, this is often hidden in the "printing cost" and authors receive far less benefits in return, so don't be fooled.

This section of the website was a big focus of the court case and now, conveniently, is gone.

WinePress allows authors to give readers a 27 percent discount on books sold through its website, which may result in higher sales, but will also decrease the author's royalty per book.

$17.99	Retail price
-$7.56	Author price per book
-$4.86	Reader's discount
-$1.95	Handling fee
$3.62	Author royalty

Note that WinePress makes $5.61 on this sale, too. The 27 percent discount is a great feature and helps a slightly overpriced book get to a better retail price, but only for sales on the publisher's website. The author can take the 200-page book that retails for $17.99 and sell it for as low as $13.09. But, even with that discount, the publisher is still making more than the author is for each sale.

To suggest that the author makes 100 percent of the net royalties is very misleading, because this definition includes excessive printing markups. The average author looks at that 100 percent and doesn't do the math. You can't inflate the "expenses" and at the same time pretend that the author is making all the money. But don't just take my word for it. Here is what United States District Court Judge Richard Jones said about Pleasant Word/WinePress's word games:

> *It* [Pleasant Word, now WinePress] *defines "net profit" in two inconsistent ways. First, it explains that "net profit" is the "actual sale price minus the printing cost," but if this is the case, then Pleasant Word does not merely charge authors the actual printing cost, but an additional markup as well.*[1]

NOTABLE PROVISIONS OF THE PUBLISHING AGREEMENT: The company does not post its publishing contract on its website. WinePress no longer permits people to sign up and pay for a package directly on its site. The only way to get any real information is to indicate your interest in WinePress and provide all of your contact information (via an online "Quote Request" form). I was on a live chat with customer service rep Adam Cothes, and I asked him, "So, is it your company's position that unless I provide you my personal information, I can't see a contract?" His response: "Yes, that's our position."

Any company that won't provide a contract for review without any requirement on your part is one that you should skip. (Should anyone want to see the entire online chat, just ask me—I had the entire chat emailed to me.)

I was able to get a copy of the Pleasant Word (now WinePress) contract as of 4/22/2010. I presume that nothing in the contract pertaining to important issues has changed, despite the makeover. Again, what follows is based on the contract as I last saw it.

"Author Right to Ownership" grants to the publisher a nonexclusive right to print and publish the work. The author can sell and distribute the book while the contract is in effect and can also terminate the contract at any time. While the author owns the book and the cover concept, the publisher owns the print-ready cover and interior files: "Author has the right to make copies of the cover (front and back) for

1 WinePress Publishing d/b/a/ Pleasant Word v. Mark Levine, Case C09-593RAJ, Order for Summary Judgement, November 9, 2009.

purposes including, but not limited to, advertising and promotional material. Author will be supplied, upon request, with PDF files of the final published version of the Work (including cover) within 90 days of publication. Author requests for files after 90 days will incur a fee for archive retrieval."

So while you're paying for these things to be created, you don't actually own any of them. If you decide to publish elsewhere at a later time, you will need to pay someone to recreate the interior and the cover.

"Copyright, ISBN/Library of Congress" states that the publisher will procure an ISBN, register the copyright in your name, and obtain an LCCN. These add-on services are a nice perk, because the services alone are worth around $100.

"Publisher Standards" outlines offensive materials that the publisher will not publish (see the genre section of this review). If an author submits offensive material, the publisher will allow the author to modify the material. If the author refuses to change the objectionable material, the agreement will effectively be cancelled, and the publishing fees will be refunded, with the exception of all fees and costs incurred up to that point and an administrative charge equal to 10 percent of the original payment.

The "Publication and Distribution" section makes it clear that the distribution is purely print-on-demand. This section also states that there is an annual maintenance fee to keep the files active, but the actual fee isn't spelled out in the contract.

The "Dispute Resolution" section is very interesting. If there is a dispute between you and the publisher, you must first attempt to resolve it using their "standard dispute resolution procedure" (which the contract states is online, but I couldn't find it). Then, if that doesn't work, you can submit the claim to arbitration—but any action you take must comply with the company's "No Gossip" policy (http:// www .winepresspublishing.com/about/no_gossip). While the "No Gossip" page doesn't expressly state the author's limitations, it alludes to them: "Therefore, our No Gossip policy guards the interactions, struggles, and joys between authors, printers, and WinePress staff."

Assuming that the contract has not substantially changed, it is a breach of contract for you to discuss your dispute "in any public forum and/or Internet service prior to the completion" of any dispute process. So if you have issues with the company, you are prevented from posting them online prior to resolution. If you don't comply, you could be sued by the publisher. Further, the dispute resolution clause requires you to physically attend any arbitration matter in King County, Washington.

AUTHOR-FRIENDLY RATING: Publishers who cloak their services around religion should be held to a higher standard, because many authors rely on such affiliations when deciding to trust a publisher—that fact alone may deter authors from questioning a publisher's fees. On http://www.winepresspublishing.com/about/team, Executive Publisher Timothy Williams says, "Above all else, the purpose of WinePress is to glorify God. You'll find this reflected in everything we do, and that is what really makes us different." He also says, "Scripture tells us that truth without action is dead, and at WinePress, we firmly believe that actions speak louder than words." I couldn't agree more. Actions do speak louder than words.

The words of this company say that they don't "artificially inflate" printing costs. The reality: they do. I'm not sure how marking up printing nearly 100 percent (or more) glorifies God, but I'm just a mortal.

I believe it's a compromise of Christian values (and just about every other moral value I can think of) when a publisher leads authors to believe that its printing costs are 100 percent higher than they actually are. The "author's discounted price" can easily lead an author to believe that somehow this is the actual printing cost, or close to it.

The author royalties on third-party sales, such as those on Amazon .com, are horrible. In the example discussed in this review, the author makes $0.53 per sale, while WinePress makes $3.66 through the extra padding it adds to the printing costs. The royalties for sales on the WinePress website are better, but only in comparison to the royalties paid on third-party sales.

Here is what Judge Jones had to say about the above paragraph (it's the same as it was in the last edition of this book):

> *Pleasant Word does not challenge Mr. Levine's numbers, it challenges his use of the term "extra padding." This is baffling. It is undisputed that Pleasant Word adds $3.66 to actual printing costs (for a 200-page book) to arrive at its "premium package."*[2]

On top of outrageous printing markups and tiny royalties, potential authors can only see a contract if they provide the company personal contact information. And, if you become an author with this company and have a dispute, you have to agree to not discuss the nature of the dispute online during the dispute process, under the guise of a "No Gossip" policy. Is it only me, or do you find this as ridiculous as it sounds?

It is undisputed that everything I said about Pleasant Word's pricing and markups in the last edition of my book was true. They knew it was true. In fact, they provided the numbers on their website. Telling the truth is a principle tenet of Christianity. So, how does one glorify God by suing someone who has told the truth? If you become an author and have a dispute with them, then have the gall to talk about it online, you could very well end up getting sued as well. Do you see a pattern here? Getting sued by this company cost me over $20,000. What could it cost you? Sometimes telling the truth and making people aware has a price. I was willing to take that risk. You should not put yourself in that peril.

When a publisher chooses to make religion a central focus of its service and writes copy that suggests that, due to strong Christian principles, authors "know they can trust us," the publisher has a duty to be over-the-top honest. Being less than forthright about the real printing costs—while quoting Scripture—instantly makes WinePress a publisher to avoid. Enough said. There are great Christian publishers. Find one.

---

2 Ibid

CONCLUSION

YOU FOUND A PUBLISHER— NOW WHAT?

Self-publishing is a lot like going to Las Vegas. There is a high probability that you will spend money and never see it again. For some, the roll of the publishing dice will lead to a rush that few authors ever get to experience. You'll sell a lot of books, have signings, get emails from fans, and so on. For others, you'll sell a few copies to family and friends and wonder why you didn't sell more.

When I go to Vegas, I bring a set amount of money for gambling. Once that money is gone, I'm done gambling for rest of the trip. I don't get cash advances on my credit card, drain my bank account, or pawn jewelry. Please view publishing the same way. Don't spend more than you can afford.

If you follow the advice in this book, you'll end up with a reputable, author-friendly publisher that doesn't gouge you by grossly inflating printing charges and taking steep royalties. That will put you in the best position to make a profit when you sell copies of your book. But, in order to make money selling copies of your book, you need people to learn about your book, find it, and want to buy it.

Marketing your book and making it sell, ultimately falls on you. The book publishing environment is not the "field of dreams"—there is no guarantee that if you publish it, someone will buy it. New, unknown authors face the same challenges, regardless of whether they were published by a traditional publishing house or by a self-publishing company. Both the first-time author fortunate enough to sign a contract with Random House and the first-time author who pays one of the publishers listed in this book launch off in the same boat. Sure, the other guy brags to his friends about his "publishing deal," but that's where the difference ends. Virtually all traditional publishers expect new authors to market and promote their own books with varying degrees of monetary assistance from the publisher. These authors face the same uphill marketing battle that a self-publishing author like you faces.

In February 2010, my company purchased ArmchairInterviews.com, a respected book review site. We are inundated with requests by major book publishers and publicists to review books written by their authors. We have 150 reviewers, so we can only take a small fraction of the books. That's how fierce it is out there—even the big guys are fighting for spots. So, for the new author, that means that you need to bring it. Your book cover, interior layout, and editing need to be flawless just to have a shot.

If you don't invest your own time and some money in the promotion of your book, don't expect it to sell. Yes, there are stories about the self-published author who sold copies out of the trunk of his car and hit it big. That's like betting everything on one number at the roulette table. Long odds. To sell a lot of books, you'll need some luck in there along the way. But, unless you run a PR firm or are an online marketing genius, you're going to need some outside help.

I'd forget all the bookmarks, posters, and other junk that ends up in the trash minutes after you hand it out. Some traditional marketing techniques (like hiring a publicist) still work. But today, if that publicist isn't well-versed in getting online media attention, the effort ultimately will not get you all that you may expect. When that publicist lands you a radio interview, the nexus between the interview and a listener actually buying your book is a chasm. Not everyone listening to that radio program is going to be interested in your book. If some are, you need to depend on them writing down and/or remembering your name or the title of your book, and then actually going to a bookstore or online retailer to look up the book and buy it. The longer the interval of time between the radio appearance and the potential reader taking any steps to buy your book, the more the chances diminish. TV ads, magazine ads, and articles in periodicals have the same problem—they rely on the person seeing them to get around to taking some action at some future point; plus, they aren't very targeted. For example, I don't advertise this book in *Writer's Digest* because, although the readership is almost all writers, only a fraction of them are thinking about self-publishing, and an even smaller percentage are actually considering self-publishing companies. Even though the magazine is targeted, it's not targeted enough for my advertising dollar.

Don't put your ego ahead of common sense. It might be "cool" to be interviewed on the radio, but I'd rather have a well-followed blogger write a review about my book. The internet has changed the advertising and promotion landscape. It's possible to create websites that rank high for specific search terms. For example, go to Google and type in "self publishing companies." In the natural results (not the ads) you will see the site for this book, www.book-publishers-compared.com, in the top few results. Why is that important? Because I know that most people who type that search term into a search engine are looking for information on self-publishing companies. Then, a description about my website (and book) appears. Once that searcher clicks on the link, they are on my website. Now, this already qualified prospect (based on the search query he typed into Google) is presented an offer to buy my book on a topic he's very interested in. That is the kind of lead I want for my book—laser-targeted, not just a tire-kicker. The same theory applies to purchasing online advertising. The difference between the natural results and the ads is that every time someone clicks on your ad, you pay a predetermined amount to the search engine, whereas there is no charge if the person clicks on the link to my site in the natural results.

I've built two companies solely on two factors: knowing how to create websites that rank well on search engines, and understanding how to effectively advertise online. Selling books online is no different than selling any other product or service. In order to be successful doing this, you need to spend your money wisely and put together an effective, laser-targeted online campaign. The learning curve is a big one. I suggest hiring someone to help you, especially with the creation of an optimized website and developing online advertising campaigns. I became successful at these by learning the hard way.

Not every web strategy works for all types of books. Online advertising isn't that effective for fiction, but promoting fiction within social networking sites is. The key to doing anything online is having a solid, well written, optimized website. When you market online, all roads leads back to your site, and you need a good one if you want potential buyers to take you and your writing seriously.

Twitter, Facebook, and other social media sites can provide amazing results for your book. There is a lot more to it than putting up a Facebook page and sending out friend requests. I employ several full-time staff whose sole job description revolves around handling social media for books. This stuff evolves so fast that, unless it's your job, I don't know how you can keep up.

The most effective book marketing techniques are the ones that combine traditional methods (e.g., sending out galley copies), a smart online strategy, and an author dedicated to hitting the pavement herself. If you can secure a real distributor for your book, that helps tremendously.

By no means should you take a few paragraphs about online marketing as anything other than a very broad overview. It's a book all on its own. The one thing I can tell you is that with so many books out there, you need to think far outside the box when it comes to marketing. Forget the rules. Be creative. In the last edition of my book, I decided to throw a sentence in this section that offered a free thirty-minute consultation if you emailed me and put "Hey, I actually read the conclusion" in the subject line of the email. I'd never heard of anyone doing anything like this before (although I'm sure it had been done). I just wanted to see if anyone would do it. What's two extra lines? Not only did it work, but there are weeks when I can barely keep up with the requests. But I love talking to authors about the process, and the authors seem to really appreciate it. So, if you've made it this far, email me at mark@hillcrestmedia.com and put "Hey, I actually read the conclusion" in the subject line. You'll get an email from me and we'll set up a time to chat on the phone. You can ask all the questions you want about the self-publishing process. See how some creative, free marketing can really work?

Also, check out www.Go-Publish-Yourself.com and www.Published.com. Our company owns these sites and both have some great information about marketing your books.

Whatever you choose to do with your book, it's an accomplishment to have completed it at all. How many people do you know who have a book inside of them, and yet never find the time or courage to write it?

I wish you success with your book. I hope I've helped make the process, especially your decision about publishing options, easier and less stressful. Good luck and good writing.

ACKNOWLEDGEMENTS

As it turns out, getting this book researched, updated, edited, and distributed takes a village. Luckily, for me, I have some great people in mine.

Sarah Kolb, my faithful researcher and editor, did an amazing job throughout this entire project. I couldn't have done it without her, nor would I have wanted to. Unless she agrees to help me do Edition #5, there may not be one.

Jenni Wheeler is the only designer I trust to touch the interior and cover of this book. Jenni has worked for our company since 2007 and knows her stuff. I'm one of those authors who follows her advice. If you ever get a chance to work with her, I hope you follow it, too.

Mark Pitzele and I have been friends for more than thirty years. Since 2007 he's been running our book printing division, BookPrintingRevolution.com. He got me pricing on these books that I could never get on my own.

Marly Cornell, thank you for your great editing.

I'd also like to thank Anna Schmeling. Anna put the final polish on this book and made it a better read for all of you. Plus, Anna is the first employee our publishing company ever had. Without her, my company would not be where it is today.

Lastly, thank you to everyone at Hillcrest Media Group. Your amazing work makes my life a lot easier and allows me to continue to put out new editions of this book.

INDEX